A New Life
Journal

A New Life
Journal

JANE CAFARELLA

PARTRIDGE
A Penguin Random House Company

To order additional copies of this book, contact
Toll Free 800 101 2657 (Singapore)
Toll Free 1 800 81 7340 (Malaysia)
orders.singapore@partridgepublishing.com

www.partridgepublishing.com/singapore

CONTENTS

The second year

The third year

DEDICATION

For Greta, who is 21 today, and Johannes, who is 29.
10 March 2014

ACKNOWLEDGEMENTS

I would like to thank former *Age* editor Alan Kohler, for inviting me to start *A New Life Journal*, Margaret Riddle, Director of Telling Words Co Pty Ltd, publishers of *Quality Time,* for keeping it going, and my loyal readers over the years for their support.

But above all I would like to thank my family—my husband, Rob Williams, my son Johannes Luebbers, and my daughter, Greta Williams—for providing the inspiration for these stories, and for their enduring love, support and tolerance.

PROLOGUE

In February 1993, I was working as a section editor at *The Age* newspaper in Melbourne, Australia, and preparing to go on maternity leave for the birth of my second child when I was approached by the editor, Alan Kohler, about writing a parenting diary.

Faced with the prospect of 12 months' unpaid maternity leave, the idea of a paid column about the first year of my child's life was instantly appealing, so I agreed.

I had no idea then that the first year would extend to the second, third, fourth and that the column would continue in one form or another until my full nest became an empty nest.

I guess that's one reason I used our real names.

At first I tried to think of aliases for my husband and children, intent on protecting their privacy. We were a blended family, which made life more complicated.

But as I tried to write the first few columns for Alan's approval, the aliases I had chosen jarred and I felt blocked.

In the end, I decided to just write the column using our real names and change it later.

But later never came. The words only flowed when I was writing about what really happened to us, not to some made-up family, so in my naivety I made our family life transparent.

In those days, reality TV hadn't been invented, but the reality of the columns had a similar effect to the TV reality shows of today.

People began to follow our lives and to write to me in response. Most often they wrote, "Your family life so often mirrors my own."

Over the years, the column took various forms. In *The Age*, it began in March 1993 as *A New Life Journal*, metamorphosing to *Family Postcard* from 1995 until July 1996.

By January 1997, it had been picked up by *Quality Time Magazine*, where it was published bi-monthly until December 2002. Since then, various selections have also been broadcast on the ABC Radio National program *Life Matters*.

With my daughter, Greta, approaching her 21st birthday this year, I sat down and began to read the columns with the idea of collating them in a book. I had done something similar for my son, Johannes, when he was 21, but e-books hadn't been invented then so I had just put them in a binder.

As I read, it occurred to me that a lot had changed about parenting. Many of the conveniences I wished for then are now the norm: special car seats, supermarket trolleys with baby carriers, state-of-the-art prams and public toilets that cater for mothers and children. Babies are big business now.

But some things never change—the joy and trepidation of bringing a new baby home, sibling rivalry, potty training, first words, searching for day care, juggling paid and unpaid work, starting school and eventually . . . letting go.

As I read, it occurred to me that this was not just our story: it was every family's story.

With this in mind, I humbly present *A New Life Journal*.

There are some topical references that are now dated, and some peculiarly Australian cultural references, but I hope that today's readers can overlook these and seek instead the universal themes.

There are many books today about *how to* be a parent. You can even buy pre-prepared diaries to fill in about your child's first year.

A New Life Journal is not one of these books. Instead, it offers a window to one family's experiences as they were lived, week by week, year by year.

Then, as now, I invite you to join us.

We are all grown up now, Rob, Johannes and Greta and me . . . . and this is how it happened.

Jane Cafarella
March 2014

1993

PREPARING A CHILD FOR THE NEW ARRIVAL

February 24 1993

AS HE stirred awake, I sat on the edge of the bed and stroked his soft brown hair, remembering how it had been damp and fair and sparse in babyhood.

He stretched one long, thin, white arm—the same arm that nearly eight years earlier had been a chubby mass of baby-fat bangles—and smiled, showing the new, big, white front teeth that looked outlandish in his small face.

"I've got something to tell you," I said. "By Easter, you'll probably have a baby brother or sister."

"How?" he asked in amazement. Although he knew the theory, just how this would be put into practice was a puzzle. I decided not to go into detail. Rob and I had made love and started a baby, I said.

He grinned and then reflected. "That means I won't be getting as much attention."

"That's right," I said. "But you won't need as much attention as a little baby. In fact, you can help me," I suggested. "Would you like to come and help choose some clothes for it later?"

"I'm just a kid. I wouldn't know what to buy," he said, overwhelmed by the responsibility already.

"No, but Rob and I will be there and you can help choose the colours."

Later, in the lounge room, as he was dressing, he said: "I'm thinking about that a lot now."

"So am I," I said. "But it's a long time to wait."

1

As I was combing his hair, he said: "Now I'll be able to see what I looked like as a baby." Apparently, he did not identify with the various photos around the house.

"But you and the baby have different daddies, so it might not look like you," I explained.

"But it's in you, so it's mostly you, and you're related to me, so it could look like me," he reasoned.

"Yes, it might look a bit like you," I agreed.

"Now I'll have something to say for Show and Tell," he said with satisfaction.

In the car on the way to school, he counted the difference in years between himself and his future sibling.

"If it was at the same school, I'd probably have to protect it from bullies bashing it up," he said.

He considered which toys he would let it play with and which videos it might like.

"I don't mind watching Mickey Mouse videos, because I still like them," he said magnanimously, then paused, "Can I tell Daddy (my ex)?"

"Yes."

"I thought you'd say it was none of his business," he said, grinning.

"It isn't, but you can't keep another member of the family a secret," I replied.

I waved as he ran into school, and wondered how things would change for us. With the happiness and excitement there was a tinge of remorse.

Like Christopher Robin farewelling Pooh, I had a sense that our time in the Enchanted Forest was ending.

I could explain the fact of a baby to him, but these other things were inexplicable.

I understood why Christopher Robin had tried to explain things to Pooh, and then left them unexplained.

"Still with his eyes on the world, Christopher Robin put out a hand and felt for Pooh's paw.

"Pooh," said Christopher Robin earnestly. "If . . . if I'm not quite . . ."

He stopped and tried again. "Pooh, whatever happens, you will understand, won't you?"

"Understand what?"

"Oh, nothing," he laughed and jumped to his feet. "Come on!"

"Where?" said Pooh.

"Anywhere," said Christopher Robin.
So they went off together.

Jane Cafarella, who is now eight months' pregnant, will write weekly about her experiences of pregnancy and parenting.

A NEW LIFE DAWNS AT DUSK

April 13 1993

IT WAS both an ordinary and extraordinary day. Ordinary because there was the ABC news bulletin as usual, the clatter of the trains, the roar of the traffic, the pop of the toaster—the ordinary sounds that slowly beat out the rhythm of the day—coupled with the extraordinary fact that this day our child was to be born.

Extraordinary also because it was the same day my son, Johannes, was born eight years ago. Medical complications meant the baby had to be induced two-and-a-half weeks early, which would have been the day after his birthday. Could it be the same day, he had pleaded?

So we rose in the fuzzy grey of the morning, when the dark still clings to the edges of familiar objects, making them seem unfamiliar, and prepared for another birthday of the child familiar to me from those soft nudges and undulations felt from within, yet a stranger still.

How would we greet each other, we strangers? This presence I could feel, yet not touch?

At 7.46, when the dawn had been replaced by dusk, she was born, but it was not her face that I will remember most: it is her fingers.

Long slender fingers waving searchingly like sea anemones, that is my first impression of my daughter as she lay on my breast in those precious moments immediately after birth.

That, and her nose. "She's got your nose!" I exclaimed to Rob as he cradled my shoulders and head, his face lit with joy. This was not merely an observation but a cry of victory, as the Cafarellas have never been known for their small noses.

I don't remember who told me it was girl, and I don't remember crying. But I remember tasting the salty tears as they poured down my face and repeating: "A girl! A girl!"

"You've no idea how hard it was not to tell you," Janet, my obstetrician, said. She had known since the results of the amniocentesis, but Rob and I had wanted it to be a surprise.

"Is she all right? Is she all right?" I asked, my joy turning to concern, as those long fingers remained tinged with blue.

"Blow on her," Janet said. "She needs some stimulation, that's all." So Rob and I gently blew, breathing life again into our daughter.

"What's her name?" asked Robyn, one of the two midwives.

"Her name is Greta," I said. "Greta Louise."

Robyn and Jenny smiled. "Thank goodness it's not Stephanie," said Jenny. "One day I think we had six Stephanies."

It had been a team effort. Like sailors who had successfully navigated a ship through turbulent waters, we were jubilant. Each contraction had been a wave that had brought our baby one step closer to shore, and here she was, in the safe harbor of my arms.

After we had cuddled, Rob went to ring Johannes. It was past 9 o'clock but we knew he would be waiting.

"Guess what! You've got a baby sister," Rob told him.

"How did you feel?" I asked him later.

"Funny and grown up," he said.

That night, Rob and Johannes cuddled up together at home in our bed, while Greta and I snuggled up together at the hospital.

"I feel so happy I could cry," Johannes told Rob that night.

And the next morning, as they were preparing to come to the hospital, he added: "You're my best pal ever."

Things in the Enchanted Forest had indeed changed.

Just as I had predicted, that special relationship that I had shared with Johannes as a mother and single parent had gone forever.

But in its place, he had not only gained a sister but found a friend.

Living proof of Darwin's theory

27 April 1993

BEAUTY is truly in the eye of the beholder, and so are family traits.

"She's just like you!" announced my mother when she first saw Greta.

"She's just like Rob!" announced Rob's mother, Judy, two hours later. It's amazing how they change so quickly, I thought.

Actually she's more like Buzandi, the little gorilla at the Melbourne Zoo. With her hairy arms and back and her miniature Bonds singlets, she puts Paul Mercurio* to shame. But it will be a long time before she can match him as a dancing partner. For one, the skin on her legs is so baggy she looks like she's got her big sister's stockings on. "Don't have wrinkles and baggy knees!" I chanted as I changed her nappy, reminded of that pantyhose advertisement from the '70s.

"She looks like a pharaoh," my husband, Rob, said, as she lay with her back straight and her little arms crossed over her chest.

"Fairy—not pharaoh!" I insisted.

"Queen Never-off-the-Titty!" he quipped.

He was right. But she has a powerful thirst rather than a thirst for power. Still, she has definite leadership qualities—no neck, a double chin and a tendency to dominate.

"Why do all babies look like world leaders?" I mused one morning as I noted her resemblance to former Soviet leader Mikhail Gorbachev. Perhaps it is because they are all losing it—their hair that is.

"There's a touch of the Uncle Leo's about her," Rob said, as he fondled her furry ears.

"There is not!" I defended. Charming as he may be, Uncle Leo is more Buddha than bud-like.

But it was true. The fruit of my womb looked like it had fallen straight from Rob's family tree.

---

* *Paul Mercurio, Australian actor, dancer and TV presenter, best known as the star of the Baz Luhrmann film 'Strictly Ballroom'.*

"They change as they grow," consoled a friend. How true. After 16 days, her complexion had changed from peaches and cream to peaches and pimples. One eye was half closed, oozing green goo from a blocked tear duct. Her tongue was white with thrush and her bottom was red. And already she had a charge account at the local chemist.

"Who does she look like?" inquired a friend who telephoned one day.

"Quasi Modo," I said.

"She's gorgeous!" lied the tellers at the local bank, as they crowded around the pram, only to be rewarded by the sound of non-too-gentle breaking wind.

"Pardon me, er, I mean her," I said as I made a hasty retreat. Perhaps she is more like her great grandmother on Rob's side, I thought—famous for her knitting and her farting—although Nana was a lady, and so always pretended it was someone else.

Though Johannes's baby photos show that Greta is also quite like him, it seems obvious to all that she is like Rob's side of the family, particularly his father, Cec.

"Gee, she's like Cec!" proclaimed Rob's mother one day as she cuddled her.

Later at home, as Greta lay drunk in my arms, a dribble of milk escaping from her cupid's bow mouth, I could not deny it. The receding hairline, the furrowed brow, the chubby chops and putty nose . . .

"You just look like Grandpa Cec!" I exclaimed, and then paused. "I never realised how beautiful Cec was!"

Touched by family ties and magic

4 May 1993

ONCE upon a time, all children, not just princesses, had fairy godmothers.

Now they have videos, Reeboks, Nintendo and other things that even fairy godmothers would have trouble conjuring up.

Indeed, many have everything they could ever wish for, except that special person, a guardian or mentor, who may offer wise counsel, hope and encouragement with a wave of a wand, and who somehow magically appears when you most need them.

But not my daughter. Apart from the normal quota of grandmothers, like the little princesses of long ago, Greta has an official fairy godmother in the form of a dear friend, and a few unofficial ones to boot.

Before she was born, her official fairy godmother (FGM for short) told me I would give birth to a daughter. She had not seen the results of any tests, but she had seen my aura. It was pink and silver, she said, and gave me a pink and silver wand from the fairy shop, just to prove the point.

Now, I don't believe in God, or Krishna, or economic rationalism, but I do believe in magic—that special magic that is made possible with love, encouragement, humor and faith in the human spirit. So when Greta's FGM gave me that wand I put it in a special place and vowed to use it only for good, like the magic fishbone.

"We could use it to wish for a million dollars," suggested Johannes, one morning.

"No," I said. "It doesn't work like that. It only works if you use it to help someone."

He was disappointed but he knew enough about magic to understand that it must not be abused.

When Greta was born and her FGM had been proven correct, she gave her a card in the shape of a pink heart, confessing that she had bought it before the birth, such was her faith in my pink and silver aura.

My husband, Rob, hung it respectfully from Greta's cradle, like a talisman, as FGMs have a knack of knowing what is going on, and what is to be done about it.

At least this one has. Over the years, when I have been in trouble, she has somehow known it and turned up in one form or another. "You beamed me up," she would say if she telephoned and found me in need.

But it is not just official FGMs who have magical powers. When Greta was born, my aunt, Tess, brought a special gift—a gift that linked new life with old and the present with past. It was a beautifully knitted white matinee jacket, a little yellow with age.

"You know who knitted that?" she said, her eyes shining as she handed it to me.

"No?" I said, puzzled.

"Nanna," she said.

Nanna? But Nanna, my Italian grandmother, had been dead for some years. How could it be?

"She knitted it for me," Tess explained.

Nanna was always knitting and she must have knitted hundreds of similar jackets for her own children, grandchildren and friends. But Tess had no children.

One day, a while before Nanna died, Tess had seen her knitting a jacket for a friend's child. "Would you knit one for me, just to keep?" she had asked. It was for the child she never had.

As she handed the jacket to me, it seemed to hold the memory of those old and capable hands, as well as Nanna's familiar and triumphant cry of "You like, I make!" and the unfulfilled hopes and dreams for a child never born.

New Pecking Order Ruffles a Few Feathers

11 May 1993

WE ARE curled up together in bed, my new lover and I—soft downy hair and sweet warm breath against my cheek, little body resting trustingly against my shoulder.

A face appears at the door. A large face with huge eyes and eye lashes as thick as brooms. An anxious face.

I open the covers like a door and let in my son, Johannes, feeling the hard bones of his long legs against mine, feeling a hardness in myself, resenting this intrusion.

I cuddle up to him with a pang of guilt, like a spouse who has taken a mistress.

Why, with the joy of my new baby daughter, do I feel so impatient with my older son?

"I felt like that towards the older one," a friend consoled me. "It's like your instinct is to kick the older one out of the nest."

Perhaps it is also because an eight-year-old looks so competent, so capable and independent, and that faced with the utter helplessness of a baby, it is easy to feel impatient towards the older child.

But he is still a child, I remind myself. Guiltily and jokingly, I tell Johannes how big he looks to me in the morning after having focused on his sister's tiny face in those silent meditative hours of night feeding.

He roars with laughter, rolling around on the bed, at the idea of himself as a giant. But it is no joke. He is a clumsy giant invading our territory and making us both feel vulnerable.

But he is also a child, my first child, the one who first awakened in me these strong maternal feelings.

I weep with fatigue, frustration and remorse as when we say good night he kisses me too much and tells me he loves me too often, then adds: "Why don't you ever read to me anymore?"

I tell him that I love him and try to explain that, at the moment, Greta's needs must take precedence as her survival depends on it. I try to point out that what I am doing for her, I also did for him, and show him

10

pictures of himself, lying content on my shoulder as a baby, just as she is now.

"You're doing fine. Just try to be consistent," comforts my husband, Rob, who himself is treading a tightrope between his role as friend and step-parent.

Consistent! I am about as consistent as Melbourne's weather. One minute I am all sunshine, the next minute storms and rain.

I rely on Rob, who now does the night reading while I am doing the night feeding, and who plays games with him and takes him to the movies and, when all else fails, comforts him.

But the centre of the universe has shifted, as Johannes well understands.

"I'm the boss and I don't take crap from no one," he wrote on a tiny paper cut-out of a baby's jumper which he had pegged on the clothesline over the bath, along with the Greta's singlets and fluffy pants.

I wondered if he would resent this new "boss". Perhaps eight years was too large a gap and my children would remain competitors rather than companions, I thought ruefully, as Johannes went off to play at a friend's house one afternoon.

But I had underestimated him. One morning, as I was showering, he came into the bathroom to clean his teeth. As the minutes passed and I could not hear the sound of brushing, I stuck my head out of the shower, frowning with impatience, a scold ready to spill hot and angry from my tongue.

Written in the steam on the bathroom mirror in an innocent and childish hand were three little words: "I love Greta!"

THE UPS AND DOWNS OF BEING A MUM

18 May 1993

IT'S 10am: At last! Greta is asleep. After an hour of rocking her in her bouncer and poking the dummy into her mouth every five minutes, I can sit down and write this column.

The bed is still unmade, last night's dishes are on the sink and I am still in my nightie, but mothers can't be choosers.

It's amazing what you can achieve on five hours' sleep. It was 9.30pm before we could get Greta to sleep. I sank into bed half an hour later and congratulated myself when I was not woken again until 2.30am. Five hours! A miracle!

By 3am, after only half a feed, she was sound asleep again, and I was left lopsided. I decided to express. Things were going marvellously well—60ml in five minutes!

But my hand was falling off. So I swapped hands. Big mistake. I lost the rhythm and 30ml of me landed on the kitchen floor and all over my nightie. By 3.30am I had cleaned up and changed and was back in bed, exhausted.

Half an hour later Greta was awake, frantically looking for the other half of her feed. When she is in that mood, there is nothing dainty about her table manners. Slurp, guzzle, gasp! You can practically hear it splashing down—like a coin hitting the bottom of a well.

An hour later, the result was something akin to World Championship Wrestling: Guzzling Greta, bug-eyed, writhing and grunting, versus Manic Mother. Every time I thought I had her down, she was up before the count of three.

By about 6am, she'd thrown in the towel and thrown up the feed, before falling asleep in her favorite position, face down on Rob's belly.

At 7.30am I got up to have breakfast, but just when I had started mine, she demanded hers.

Uh, oh! Speak of the devil! Now she's demanding morning tea! Where's the dummy? Quick! 11am: Phew! Where was I? Oh, yes, welcome to my nightmare!

It's been a tough few weeks as we are selling our home and must therefore achieve what is entirely impossible when you have a young baby—a tidy house.

Oh no! Greta is purple in the face and pop-eyed. Here comes another nappy change!

11.40am: Back again. The bouncer is next to the desk and I am bouncing furiously with my left foot as I write. Do bouncinettes cause brain damage? Only if used as catapults, I suppose. I've stopped worrying about harelips and birthmarks now, and have progressed to brain damage and cot death. Hang on! There's the phone! Back in a minute.

11.50am: It was the real estate agent. He's bringing someone through at 2pm. I have just over two hours to finish this, shower and clean up. Help! The agent prefers it if we are not here for the inspection. So do I, especially if the potential buyer is inspecting unmade beds and unwashed dishes.

Ouch! My left foot is dropping off from bouncing and so is Greta, dropping off to sleep that is.

Hooray! Quick! What shall I do first? Finish this? Shower? Or clean up? The question is, do I have two minutes or two hours?

11.52am: Two minutes. Greta is awake again. Perhaps she is dirty again, or wet, or in pain, or hungry? After all, it has been two hours since her last feed, and mine.

The sun is streaming in the lounge room window, the petunias and impatiens on the balcony are nodding their heads in the soft autumn breeze and Ivan Hutchinson* is just about to introduce the midday movie.

I think I'll finish this later.

---

* *Television presenter, 1928-1995. Australia's 'Mr Movies'.*

WHY CAN'T I CRAVE A GREEN SALAD?

25 May 1993

EVERYONE talks about cravings during pregnancy, but nobody tells you about the cravings afterwards. While I craved pickled onions and cream when I was pregnant, I now crave sleep, and in lieu of that, carbohydrates and sugar—anything to keep me going through the day and night.

We are trying to stick to a budget when it comes to food, only buying essentials—such as lamington cake and Tiny Teddies.

"Where did these come from?" demanded my husband, Rob, as he found yet another packet of Tim Tams hidden at the back of the fridge.

It is not where they come from that is the problem, but where they go. While the waif-look may be in, I prefer a wafer—especially if it's covered in maple syrup and cream. I'd rather do sit downs than sit-ups and as for touching my toes, I consider it a breakthrough just to see them.

"There are two types of people when it comes to breastfeeding," my friend Liz said. "Those who get really thin and those who get really plump." (Pause). "I got really thin."

Bully for you, Liz, I thought as I hoed into another hot cross bun. No more buns in the oven, but plenty in the microwave. While others were lamenting the sacrilege of Easter Buns being available four weeks before Easter, I was praying that by some miracle, the dozen I had eaten, would not rise again on the third day.

My post-pregnancy bible, *What to Expect the First Year*, advises that I should stick to a daily dozen nominated vitamins and minerals.

Instead, I stuck to a daily dozen Easter buns, as I couldn't stop at one, or two, and three looked greedy. Better to destroy the evidence completely.

I have become an expert on the energy value of junk food. Chocolate biscuits also rate highly, but since the caffeine in chocolate gives my daughter, Greta, wind, I am looking out for decaffeinated varieties.

But shopping these days has become a hit-and-miss activity. Like that television game show where contestants have to grab the correct items

14

from the supermarket shelf before the bell rings, I try and grab what I can before I have to grab Greta.

That's if I manage to get to the supermarket at all. "What's for tea?" asked Rob during Easter.

"Twenty-eight Easter eggs," I replied. "We can have Easter eggs on toast, or Easter-egg casserole or Easter-egg stir fry."

Johannes had won the Easter egg raffle at school and had come home with a basketful, and Easter Bunny had been unusually generous this year.

At the end of the day, I always vow to turn over a new leaf, but my promise is nearly always sabotaged when I turn over another leaf of *The Hobbit*, which we are reading to Johannes at night.

After all, the hero, Bilbo Baggins, may be far from home, but his thoughts never stray far from his "beautiful pantries" in his Hobbit hole.

"He was deep in thoughts of bacon and eggs and toast and butter, when he felt something touch him," wrote Tolkien.

I felt something touch me too. It was my stomach touching my back bone. `

"How about a midnight snack," I suggested to Rob.

"Yes?" he said hopefully. "What of?"

"Bacon and eggs!"

Rash plans come to a sticky end

1 June 1993

> *A hungry feeling came o'er me stealing,*
> *As the mice were squealing in my prison cell*
> *And the old triangle, went jingle jangle,*
> *All along the banks of the Royal Canal.*
> —***The Old Triangle,*** **by Brendan Behan**.

SO WENT the song as with Greta on my shoulder, I paced the floor of my little prison cell and contemplated my own hungry state.

There was nothing to eat except some stale fruitcake as my little prison warden would not give me leave to go shopping. While other people go to *42nd Street*, I'm lucky if I get to Puckle Street.

It seems the only place I have been for the past 11 weeks is to the doctor. Last week, we thought it was her ears. She kept shaking her head and crying. But we'd been looking at the wrong end. It was her rear not her ear that needed attention.

The only other trip I managed—to buy Johannes some jeans—was planned with military precision: "Meet me at the school gate at 1530 hours sharp," I told him, as I armed myself with six nappies and three changes of clothes for Greta.

But while I was expecting an attack from the rear, there was trouble at the front. My front. She had had her main course at home, but was insisting on dessert, so while Johannes tried on jeans in one cubicle, I breastfed in the one next door.

"How are they for size?" inquired an attendant, sticking her head in through the closed curtain.

"Fine," I replied, smiling, as Greta turned my D cups into C cups.

So it was with similar military precision that I planned my escape this week. When Greta's eyes finally closed, my prison door opened.

But life on the Outside was never meant to be easy. I was waiting in the queue at the bank when I heard a familiar grunting from the pusher, followed by a miniature explosion. Oh no!

I headed back to the car, where I had left the nappy bag, my pace accelerating with her screams.

By the time I'd finished changing her, she was drowning out the V8 revving up in the next parking spot and attracting the attention of other shoppers.

"Nappy rash," I explained. Rash indeed! Rash of me to even consider surviving half an hour on the Outside, let alone half a day. I made a mental note to change the "Baby on Board" sign on the car to "Screaming Baby on Board" as I backed out of the car park.

At home, things were no better. Greta was inconsolable. Finally, in desperation, I dialled the doctor and put Greta on. We got an immediate appointment. Half an hour later we were at the chemist clocking up $33 on my credit card for four different creams for nappy rash.

She screamed all the way home and by the time I had undressed her and put the fourth layer of cream on her bottom, I was screaming too.

There was only one thing to do: ring Rob. "Come home! Quick!" I pleaded.

Half an hour later he arrived to find the washing, dishes, nappies and me all over the place. Poor man! He cleaned up, ordered a pizza, went out to get some money to pay for it, returned to serve it then went out at 9pm to do our weekly shopping.

I didn't complain when I noticed he had bought four different types of dry biscuit. It was an improvement. Last week, when I sent Johannes into the supermarket for toothpaste and cereal while I waited in the car with Greta, he came back with bubble-gum flavoured toothpaste and Coco Pops.

"Yuk!" I said the next evening, as Rob gave me a bubble-gum kiss. "Go and clean your teeth."

"I have," he said indignantly.

"Well, go and eat something to get the smell out of your mouth," I said.

He got up, opened the pantry door, and came back to bed munching something.

"What's that?" I asked, thinking he had discovered some long-forgotten delicacy at the back of the pantry.

"Coco Pops!" he replied.

THE HAPPY DAYS OF OUR NEW LIFE

8 June 1993

IT'S BEEN an emotionally exhausting day. First there was Fran, who confessed tearfully that she hates her face. Poor girl! It looked quite a pleasant face to me, but Fran says she was persecuted at school because she had no chin.

Now she has two and she's still not satisfied. Fran has started a Self-Esteem School for Chinless Girls and is making heaps of money, which has helped her own self-esteem no end.

Then there was Ted, who cheated on his wife at his buck's turn (with a stripper) and videotaped it. Poor Ted. He made it to the altar but quickly had to go to confession and has been in purgatory ever since.

Then there was Sid and Alice, apple-cheeked oldies from down home on the farm. Thanks to a therapist, their youngest daughter has remembered that she was sexually abused as a child and Sid and Alice are actually leaders of a satanic cult. Sid and Alice are trying to get to see the same therapist to see if they can remember, too.

Phew! With all that, it was nice to see Jenny and Gloria popping in every now and again to remind me that I can take all the time I need to lose 46 kilograms.

What with Mr Antenna offering to give me a great reception, and various other offers for not one, not two but three super bargains, I'm afraid it all got too much for me, and I just switched off.

Grounded by Greta planted firmly on my breast, and with strict instructions from my doctor to get my feet up, I lie on the couch with the remote control and steer my way through a galaxy of bizarre stars.

Bert, Ernie, Denise, Jessie, Ivan, Ray, Phil and Oprah, all make brief appearances in an array of Salvador Dali images. Like the disconnected but vivid dreams I had during epileptic seizures as a child, they appear real and surreal.

I am a day-dream believer, turning up and down the volume of life at my whim, making my visitors brighter and more colorful, or, sweetest of all, striking them mute if they offend me.

I doze and wake when Greta stirs, to find super-bitch Barbies fighting over their Ken dolls as soap Oprah is exchanged for soap opera.

I doze again and find Granny, Jethro and Elly-May, Chip and Ernie, and the Fonze, Richie, Potsy and Ralph Malph, childhood friends, replaying the episodes of their lives . . . my life.

I am the child again and Greta, asleep on my tummy, is as undemanding as a doll. My little doll. What will she make of this little window into a world of bizarre pantomime? A family feud, a wheel of fortune, wonder years, happy days, dreamy days, lost days . . .

"What did you do today?" asked my husband, Rob, when he got home and Jessie, Phil, Oprah and Ivan and the problems of cheats and chinless wonders had made way for Real Life and the problems of Bosnia, Africa, Ireland and Indonesia.

"Oh nothing," I said. "Just watched a bit of telly."

Making waves for the right to change

29 June 1993

IT'S AMAZING what you can get for babies these days. In the eight years between the birth of Johannes and the birth of Greta there has been a baby-product boom.

When Johannes learned to crawl, calloused knees were considered a proper rite of passage—a necessary stage before standing, after which bumps on the head were another necessary stage. Then came walking and skinned knees. Then came Band-Aids.

These days Band-Aids are in danger of becoming obsolete. The modern baby has terry-towelling knee pads. What next? Crash helmets?

The modern baby also has glow-in-the-dark dummies, microwave steam-sterilising units, and personalised birth certificates. Even the humble nappy pin has been replaced by something snappier.

Yes, in eight years a lot has changed. Yet, as the saying goes, the more things change, the more they stay the same. I still can't get the pusher through the doors at the local bank, and the local post office is still doing battle with the National Trust over the installation of a pram ramp.

History, of course, must repeat itself: if it was inconvenient for women with prams 100 years ago, then it must stay inconvenient for them today. Since this post office was built, man has walked on the moon, but women still have to cross the post office's threshold with their babes in arms.

While local retailers are anxious to compete for the parental dollar, it seems few are interested in providing parental services. Even those that attempt to are often way off the mark, as I found on a recent trip to one regional shopping centre.

The baby-change room was barely big enough for Greta and me, let alone the pusher. There was one plastic chair and a toddler toilet, but no nappy-change table—just a stretch of bench near the basin. When another woman arrived she was forced to sit on the toilet to feed her baby.

Whoever designed this room must be a misogynist with a diploma in child abuse.

Strip-shopping areas are even worse. Most don't even have a clean toilet, let alone a baby-change room. The moans from traders in these areas about the exodus of consumers do not move me one inch.

What moves me, right into the big retail stores, is the large comfortable lounge chairs, proper change tables, easy access to a phone and anything else that makes shopping with a baby easier for parents. Yes, mothers *and* fathers. Only the big retail stores seem to acknowledge that these days Dad often has to change a nappy as well as a tyre.

It is about time retailers and local councils realised that service means much more than insisting that staff repeat endlessly: "Have a nice day!"

In a ring-around of local councils in my area, none provided baby-change facilities open to both mothers and fathers and only the City of Melbourne had any plans for such a service.

The city council has received a grant of $70,000 from the Federal Government's One Nation package to transform the ladies' toilet in Collins Street, between Swanston Street and the Athenaeum Theatre, into a baby-care room, to be completed by spring or early summer.

They say the hand that rocks the cradle rules the world, but if I ruled the world there would be facilities like this in every shopping centre, as well as priority parking for parents with babies and young children, priority service in shops for nursing mothers with screaming babies, ramps everywhere, special areas in cafes for parents with pushers and more . . .

But to achieve all this, parents will have to stop rocking the cradle and start rocking the boat.

MAKING A PITCH FOR REALITY

13 July 1993

"OH WHAT a feeling!" said Johannes, mimicking the Toyota advertisement for the millionth time that day as for the millionth time that day, Greta filled her nappy.

OK, I'm exaggerating, but when you live with a television that can never be switched off, it is no turn-on.

Johannes has a photographic memory—for television programs and advertisements. Not only does he remember the jingles, he re-enacts them, once, twice, three times a day. With feeling.

Once, when he complained about Greta crying, I tried to explain that this was her only way of communicating with us. "It's natural," I said.

"Sugar—it's a natural part of life," he chanted back.

He doesn't just watch TV. He watches TV, TV and more TV.

Of course I feel guilty about it, but the days of our lives are so busy with packing, moving and being married with children that I can only do things step by step. Yet I fear he's in jeopardy as he watches far too much, whether he's home or away.

Hang on! As you can see, I'm just as bad. The difference is that while I turn it down for the advertisements, he turns it up.

"I like this ad," he says, grinning, as he fiddles with the remote control until Magda Szubanski is screeching "Wheeeeeee!!!" at the top of her voice as she sails through the air on a flying fox after having made a flying visit to the smallest room in the camping ground.

"Mum, can we have Chicken Tonight tomorrow?" he says, as I serve up yet another bowl of spaghetti Bolognese.

In the shower, apart from singing as many verses of the *Purple People Eater* as he can remember, he sings of his friend Maggie, who makes his day.

"Whose Maggie?" I said.

"You know—Maggie, the two-minute noodles," he said.

"That's Maggi," I corrected.

"Well, it's spelt Maggie," he said.

Advertisers aren't too bright, I explained. Why else would they spell Mrs Bright, Mrs Brite?

I decided we needed to have a little talk about reality and virtual reality, truth, justice and the American/Australian way of advertising. Yes, he knew advertisers exaggerated, he assured me. He wasn't impressed with what they advertised, just the way they advertised it.

But his scepticism did not stretch to the programs themselves. A few weeks ago, as we passed our Chinese neighbor's house on the way home from school, he asked: "Do Chinese people really eat dogs?"

"Of course not! What makes you think that?" I said, horrified.

"Well, on *Neighbors* the other night . . ." he began and went into that breathless word-for-word "he goes/she goes" recounting at which primary school-aged children seem to excel.

Apparently the TV *Neighbors* had some new Chinese neighbors who had been accused of turning a bow-wow into wow chow.

Dogs may have gone wokkies rather than walkies in China once and, perhaps they still do in some parts, but, no, Chinese people did not eat dogs, I assured him. That scene in *Neighbors* was trying to show that the Australian neighbor was racist. She hadn't bothered finding out the truth about her neighbor but was motivated by fear and misinformation, I told him.

Everyone knew that like us, Chinese people ate Kentucky Fried Chicken, Red Rooster and Hungry Jacks—at least they do on the ads.

THE SHADOW OF A JOB LOST

20 July 1993

DEAR FAIRY Godmother, we need you. Last night, for the first time, I opened the package that contained the wand you gave us, and gingerly, hopefully, waved it over Rob.

You see he has lost his job, and is in danger of losing his way. The path that seemed so clear and welcoming now seems fraught with danger and we are not sure which way to turn.

Due to the state-funding cutbacks to legal aid and consumer affairs, he has been made redundant.

It was not entirely unexpected. What was unexpected was the pathetic redundancy package offered. It was eventually reviewed and improved slightly, but the process added insult to injury.

Of course, we had a contingency plan. I would return to work and Rob would look after Greta. But that was before I knew Greta; before I knew how hard it would be to leave her—even for a day. Before I knew the joy so exquisite it almost hurts, of holding her little body close to mine; the sweet satisfaction of comforting her when she cries, and the excitement of hearing her chuckle for the first time.

Still, at least I had a job to return to and we were optimistic that Rob would eventually get another one. So, after the initial shock we set about making plans.

Johannes, busy cutting out a cardboard top hat from his latest magic pack, was sent to his room while we conferred.

Greta, lying on the bed between us, refused to acknowledge the seriousness of the situation and kept grinning. Rob, ashen faced with shock, looking strangely formal still in his jacket and tie, was saying over and over, "I'm sorry, Jane. I'm sorry."

I tried to reassure him. This would give him the chance to catch up on all those things he wanted to do, but had never had time for: playing music, golf, cooking . . .

"What would you really like to do if you didn't have to work—your ultimate fantasy?" I said.

"Sleep," he said, looking accusingly at Greta.

We hugged a little and wept a little. I looked at Greta and wondered how she would cope. How I would cope?

"I don't want to go back yet," I whispered. Rob put his arms around me. "You'll be the worker bee and I'll look after you," he said, stroking my hair as the tears fell.

"I don't want to be the worker bee. I want to be the queen bee," I said.

"You'll still be my queen," he said.

"We'll have to tell Johannes," I said.

But we didn't need to. "Rob's lost his job, hasn't he?" Johannes said as I walked into his room.

"Yes," I replied. I led him to our bedroom and the four of us sat on the bed as I explained that I would have to return to work.

"Poor Greta!" Johannes said. "She's not going to be happy about that."

"It'll be all right. I'll feed her in the morning and at night and we'll have to try to get her used to the bottle in between," I explained.

There was a pause, and I waited for him to speak, wondering how this latest crisis would affect him.

He looked up. "You know this magic pack has some really good tricks."

"That's good," I laughed.

I hope it can pull a job out of a hat for Rob. We need a little magic right now. Dear Fairy Godmother, if your magic wand doesn't work, I suppose there is always Johannes's.

Playing spot the silver lining

27 July 1993

LIKE Pollyanna, I have a "glad game".

I am trying to be glad that I only have to leave Greta and go into work one day each week; glad that I enjoy my job; glad that Rob will have precious time with his daughter; glad that we are able to hang on to the house we just bought; glad that Greta has accepted the bottle on the one day I can't be there; glad that I haven't got cancer . . .

Being glad helps stop me being mad—mad that I must perform once again, when I had mentally bowed out from centre stage.

Being mad stops me from being sad. Sad that the joy of moving into our new home has been spoilt; sad to see Rob feeling helpless, vulnerable and guilty, undervalued and lost.

I must be his rock now, even though I feel as lost and vulnerable myself as a pebble on the beach. I call on my innermost resources and find myself using the same little feel-good tricks I developed as a child when despair overtook me.

Then, each morning as I woke, I thought of all the good things that would happen to me that day. And every evening, as I snuggled down for the night, I thought of all the good things that had happened.

Now as Rob and I snuggle down together, I find myself saying: "The good thing is that" . . . or "It's good that . . ." or "At least . . ." I feel like Sarah Bernhart, whose favorite consolation was the phrase "Even though . . ."

I find, too, that my shower repertoire has changed. "If you don't mind having to do without things, it's a fine life," I sing, like Nancy in *Oliver* or "When you walk through a storm, hold your head up high, and don't be afraid of the dark, at the end of the storm is a golden sky and the sweet silver song of a lark."

Or simply "Whenever, I feel afraid, I hold my head erect and whistle a happy tune, so no one will suspect I'm afraid."

What am I afraid of? Failing, of course. Failing to support our little family; failing to be able to write to standard when my home is being dismantled around my ears and when Greta is crying for me and when Johannes needs me to help settle into a new school and when, like refugees, we are camping out at Rob's parents' home.

They are wonderful: providing meals, washing, ironing, love, support and encouragement. But it is a life in chaos and limbo still. Our lives have been boxed and are waiting to be unpacked.

Meanwhile, I must find and unpack prematurely that little box that represents my professional working life—the one that I had tucked away for 12 months while I worked at being "just a mum".

I am trying to be strong, for Rob's sake, but when I am talking to my own mother I am no longer a wife and mother myself, but a child: her child. "I don't know if I can do it!" I cry.

Poor Mum! Across the kilometres on the phone from country Victoria, I feel her muster her own resources and nudge me on my feet again. "Yes you can," she says. "Things will get better. Nothing stays the same.

"Being angry was good, it helped in the beginning, but it's not helping now," she says. "Now, you've got to stop being angry and use your intelligence."

It is a familiar pep talk. If I have ever dropped my bundle, she has never picked it up for me but has always encouraged me to do so myself.

And she has been right.

The golden sky at the end of the storm seems very far away, but I'll walk on.

Happy to spread our wings at last

3 August 1993

IT WAS raining as we moved into our new home, and a pair of kookaburras was laughing at us as we scurried in and out with our boxes full of ticky-tacky.

But for me, it was the sunniest of days.

Suddenly, I could breathe. Outside, the air was crisp and clear, inside was warm and spacious. For Rob, Johannes, Greta and me, the barometer had moved from "Change" and "Stormy" to "Fair".

I didn't mind returning to work if this is what I would return to at the end of the day.

Even Greta, who normally only catnapped, had relaxed completely when we walked in the door and fallen into a deep sleep.

"She's been a little angel," declared her Nana, Judy, who cared for her while Rob and I unpacked.

For two days we mostly stayed inside, playing house and admiring the view of the backyard as one might admire a painting: beautiful to look at but unreal and inaccessible.

On day four, we had still barely ventured out. Like laboratory rats, we had adapted perfectly to our former environment: a two-bedroom flat. Now, finally uncaged, we remained huddled around the coffee table, our noses twitching with eager anticipation, but too cautious to venture further.

It was the rosellas that finally tempted us. On the back veranda, nailed to a post covered in budding jasmine, was a tray left by the previous owners. We put some parrot seed there, only half believing that any bird would visit.

But within half an hour, there was a flurry of green wings and a green parrot arrived, looked around and walked confidently on to the tray. He, or she, was joined by a friend, then there was a flash of red, and a crimson rosella arrived, and another, and another, until there were four or five jostling for position on the little tray, glaring at the gang of pigeons that were waiting in the queue.

"Look! Look!" we cried, as sitting in our lounge room, we watched the green parrot puff out his chest and claim native title over the little cache of food.

"Can I go outside and put some more seed in the tray?" asked Johannes.

Poor little fellow. At the flat, he had been unable to go exploring downstairs alone as some other residents were liable to use the driveway as a drag strip or a drug strip.

"You don't have to ask me if can you go outside here," I said. "You can go where ever you like."

A few nights later, he called out: "Mama! There's a possum outside!"

Sure enough, outside the kitchen window there was a fat brush-tail possum, its eyes blinking and bleary in the bright veranda light.

"Don't feed it!" warned Rob from the next room. His experience as a bush boy had taught him that if they found you neighbourly, possums tended to move in.

"All right!" I said, as I rummaged through the fruit bowl for an apple, cut it in half and dashed outside with Johannes.

We approached slowly. Gingerly, I held the apple out, half expecting the possum to flee. Instead, she leaned forward and took it politely. I'm sure, if she could, she would have said, "Thank you".

"You didn't feed it, did you?" wailed Rob, when he saw the cut apple. But by the end of the week, the possum not only had more apple but a name.

"Let's call him Percy," said Rob.

Needless to say, Percy has since brought a friend.

There goes the neighbourhood.

UNCOVERING THE TRUTH ABOUT BEDTIME

10 August 1993

THERE were three in the bed and the little one said: "Roll over! Roll over!" So they all rolled over and Daddy fell out. Thump! Poor Daddy!

Yes, it is remarkable just how much room one small baby takes up in a queen-sized bed—especially a baby that likes to sleep crucifix-style.

Greta Louise (and Les Poohs, as she is fondly known these days) is now sleeping through the night, and so are we: as long as we all sleep together.

Of course, I know it's against those unspoken rules dictated by most of the baby books and everyone else who thinks they are experts on your baby.

But after nine cosy months in a womb-of-their-own, few babies want a room of their own.

"Is she sleeping through?" well-meaning strangers ask.

"Yes," I lie.

Actually, she is sleeping between, not through. Between Rob and me.

I wake to find her rooting around like a little pink, fat piglet looking for the breast. We find each other somehow like lovers in the night, and thus embracing, fall blissfully asleep undisturbed until 5.30am when she invariably wakes and grizzles for a nappy change.

Then it's more breakfast in bed until about 8am, followed by a workout of smiles and stretches before getting up.

"She smiles like someone who's got no teeth," said Johannes one morning, making it four in the bed.

"She is someone who's got no teeth," I laughed.

"She's got you over a barrel. She's smart. She's figured you out," warned my father-in-law, Cec.

"You can't talk," I said. Greg, their eldest son, had had his own cot, but it was Cec who had slept in it.

Of course, my education has suffered. Gone is my budding interest in statistics, French and whatever else was offering on the Open Learning Program on TV.

Gone, too, is the knot in my stomach that tightened as I lay trying to go to sleep while waiting to be woken up.

And gone, you may say, is Greta's chance of ever having a sibling.

"I like sleeping with her, don't you?" I confessed to Rob one morning, and begged him to rub my aching back.

"No," he frowned.

"Why not?"

"It's like sleeping with a dozen eggs!"

True. And it was this that made me finally crack. While Greta was at the front all night, war was being declared on my back, which was in need of a chiropractor.

As we set up the new cot in the Noffice (nursery-cum-office) of the new house, I introduced her to her new sleeping companions, Annie May, a large rag doll her grandma had given her, and Teddy.

But they have not hit it off. For a start, Annie May is as flat as a tack and unable to provide midnight feasts.

Still, we are persevering, and so is Greta. She and Annie May and Teddy begin the evening together in the cot but by about 2am, there are three in the bed and the little one says: "Ha!"

GETTING INTO THE FLOW OF THINGS AT THE OFFICE

17 August 1993

THE EDITOR'S secretary looked at me in horror. "I can't go in there," she said, "He's in a meeting with the managing director."

"But I'll miss my train, and I need my milk," I pleaded, beginning to panic. It had taken me all lunchtime to express 100 millilitres and I was not going home without it.

I had left it in the editor's refrigerator on the advice of a colleague who was also expressing milk for her baby while she worked part-time. Of course, there is a fridge in the staff tearoom, but it doubles as a toxic waste dump, as people bring their leftovers from home and leave them indefinitely.

So we of the breastfeeding brigade favor the editor's fridge, obviously at our peril. But it's hard to argue with a mother on a mission. After a few moments hesitation, the editor was interrupted and I had my milk.

Being a portable dairy has its ups and downs, particularly let-downs. Every time someone asks me how my baby daughter is, I swell with pride, literally, as my milk begins to drip.

At least I had remembered the pump that day. A week or so later, sitting on the train on the way into work, I had just begun to appreciate being able to read the paper uninterrupted when I remembered that I had forgotten the breast pump.

I had an interview for a story early in the morning and had planned to review my questions beforehand. Instead, I leapt off the train and began dashing around the streets of Melbourne looking for a chemist that sold wide-necked baby bottles. But at 8.30am in the west end of Melbourne on a weekday the only bottles for sale came already filled with something a lot more potent than mother's milk.

Finally, I found a chemist open. "Have you any wide-necked baby bottles and some sterilising tablets?" I panted. An old man, hunched and frail, pottered out from behind the counter, and took a dusty, skinny bottle off the shelf. "We don't have much demand for things like this round here," he explained.

I dashed back to the office medical centre to stick the bottle in their steriliser, then, with bottle and tape recorder, dashed off again to the interview. By the time it was over, I was beginning to feel like the Incredible Hulk, in danger of exploding the buttons on my shirt.

Whereas others were stopping off for espresso, I needed to expresso.

Where better than at the Victorian Women's Trust, where I had my next appointment? "Relax! Relax!" I told myself as, sitting at the trust's empty boardroom table upstairs, I extracted five miserly millilitres.

I was just starting to get into the flow of things when I glanced up at the darkened windows in the building opposite and realised that while I couldn't see in, they could probably see out. Should I wave, or keep pumping? I did both.

Back at the office I put my milk in the staff fridge, alongside the mouldy mandarins and cartons of curdled milk, and hoped I'd remember to retrieve it for Greta's tea before it ended up in somebody else's.

Four hours later, sitting on the train home, my cup was again overflowing—my D cup that is. As I walked in the door, Greta already had a tell-tale trickle of milk oozing down her chin.

"She couldn't wait," my husband said, brandishing the bottle.

Neither could I. I sat down for dinner and Greta, otherwise known as the girl who can't say no, sat down for dessert.

CONTRADICTIONS OF A WOMAN'S WORLD

31 August 1993

PINK HAS always been my favorite color, much to the disgust of other feminists, but my penchant for pink was immediately justified when I gave birth to a daughter.

In fact, Greta has been pretty much in the pink since the day she was born: pink jumpsuits, pink booties, pink dresses.

"Where are your feminist values now?" sniggered one male cynic.

"Pink will be the new feminist color for the '90s," I retorted, "When she is an old woman, she can wear purple, but for now . . ."

But having a daughter has meant much more than a licence to indulge in pink. "A daughter is such a wonderful gift," wrote one well-wisher after Greta was born. "Sons are wonderful too—just different."

How true. But what is different about having a daughter? Well, one day she will be a woman like me and, therefore, her experience of life will have some parallels with mine. Rightly or wrongly, I identify with her. For the first time, I understand the importance a man may place on having a son. There is an understanding of how she may experience life; the knowledge that in some ways she will be travelling a path familiar to me.

Suddenly I want to point out the pitfalls and the pleasures, to tell her when to run the other way and when to stop and smell the roses.

Suddenly, I want her to have my grandmother's pearls, my wedding dress . . . things whose only real value is the stories attached to them. My stories. I want her to know my stories and to keep them for her own children, if she has them. If she doesn't, then perhaps she will hand them like an unexpected gift to some other child of the future; the custodian of my past?

Johannes, too, will have custody of my past, but Greta will know more of me, whether she acknowledges it or not, because she, too, will be a woman in a man's world.

Fortunately, she inherits more freedoms than I have known and many more than her grandmother knew, some of which my generation fought for. I hope she guards them well.

But even today it is rare for women to be heads of state, judges, top executives or wealthy in their own right. It is rare for women to be winners. Such women make headlines, and so, too, do the losers—like Debbie Fream, the mother of a newborn son, a woman who had so much to live for but who was senselessly murdered this week.

Dear Greta, today a woman may be free to choose a career, but not to drive to the local milk bar alone; free to buy a house, but not to live alone. I rejoice for you and fear for you. How can I encourage you to be a risk-taker, to say yes to life, when I fear I must always be saying no?

How can I preach courage and caution? I can give you wings, but I must warn you not to fly too high or too far.

But perhaps things will be different for you? Perhaps by the time you are grown, the word feminist, like the word suffragette, will be out-dated, not because it is a rejected label but because it will be obsolete?

Like universal suffrage, perhaps by then the rights of women to equal participation, equal access to resources, equal justice, and equal freedom of movement, will be universally accepted?

Perhaps by the time you have a daughter of your own, you will be able to give her wings and tell her that the sky's the limit? That would indeed be a wonderful gift.

OFFICE POLITICS

7 September 1993

WORK IS no longer a place that I go: it's just something I do—or should I say something else I do. That is the beauty and the beastliness of working from home. It sounds ideal: no fares, no lunch expenses, no travel time, no over-active telephones and no boss looking over your shoulder . . . just Greta looking accusingly over Rob's shoulder.

For the past 17 years, I've worked in the same room as many other reporters, with phones ringing and people chatting, and have seldom been distracted. But trying to work with a baby in the next room is trying indeed.

"Hello, I'm working from home today. May I please have a Canberra number," I ask *The Age* switchboard after having fed Greta yet again to keep her quiet. Mary Bloggs in Canberra is busy, so I leave a message.

Then it's back to the switchboard. "Hello. It's me again. May I please have another Canberra number?" I repeat.

And so it goes, as I cast my research net into a sea of information, oceans and eons away from the domesticity of home.

Outside my office window a willy-wag-tail is hopping through the undergrowth and cockatoos are screeching noisily above. The sun is shining and Rob is taking Greta for a walk in the sling to help her get to sleep. I am going to sleep too, as I plough through a 35-page fax of Canberra-speak.

The phone rings. I have caught a fish. I start my interview but in the middle of it Rob bursts in with Greta who is half squealing and half screaming. "I think she's hungry," he says. Again? I try and wave them both away while I continue to take notes.

My interview subject pauses for breath. Now is the time to ask an intelligent question, but I've forgotten who I'm speaking to so I revert to the old standby: "And how do your spell your name?"

"B-L-O-G-G-S," says my fish in surprise.

I finish the interview and hurry to the lounge room bare-breasted. We all have lunch then it's back to work answering all those messages from people I left messages for. I write my byline at the top of the page and pray for inspiration.

There is a timid knock on the door.

"Sorry," says Rob apologetically. "Just need a nappy."

Inspiration comes. I start writing and like a child running downhill, find I can't stop, until I glance at my watch—3.30pm!

"Can you pick up Johannes?" I yell to Rob, who charges off, leaving me with Greta.

What's that smell? Not those rotten possums again. I look at Greta who is grunting, and head for the nappy table. Yuk! It's all over her singlet. I ease the singlet carefully over her head, but she moves and cops it in the ear.

The phone rings but I can't reach it without leaving Greta, so I let the machine answer. It's my boss. "I need the story tomorrow," she says. I start to panic.

Rob returns with Johannes. Good—another babysitter. Johannes plays with Greta while Rob does the breakfast dishes and thinks about tea. I try not to think about tea as my stomach rumbles.

Greta starts squealing and whingeing, so I scoop her up and balance her on one hip while I survey the debris in the fridge.

The phone rings. "Yes?" I yell above the squeals. It's the minister's right-hand man, ringing from his mobile phone on the way to an urgent meeting. What is he doing ringing me at home at this hour, I think crossly, as Greta chews on the phone cord.

"Do you have everything you need?? he asks obligingly.

"Oh, yes," I reply.

Everything except something for tea.

GIVING BROTHERLY LOVE THE RASPBERRY

14 September 1993

YOU'VE heard of sibling rivalry but what about sibling ribaldry?

"Thrrrrrghhhh," says Greta, lying on the floor blowing raspberries.

"Thrrrrrghhhhh," replies Johannes, as he buries his face in her belly, blowing even bigger raspberries.

"Ahhhhhhh!" squeals Greta, at the top of her voice.

"Ahhhhhh!" replies Johannes, making Greta chuckle. `

"Who's a chuckleberry baby?" he asks, mimicking us. And so it goes on.

"Don't stimulate her!" I beg later, as I bounce her gently in the bouncinette. "She was almost asleep."

"No, she wasn't," he says, grinning at her. She was, but she isn't now. Now she's grinning back. Perhaps it is because they share the same birthday that they also seem to share the same sense of humor, despite their eight years difference.

"Hello, Knobby-Nose!" he says, as he comes in from school. Defiantly sober for Rob and me, she lights up the minute Johannes enters the room, her knobby nose screwing up in delight. Who cares if he calls her Knobby-Nose, Spike or Greta Grub? She knows that's Big-Brother Talk for "Hello, Greta! I'm so pleased to see you!"

There are times, of course, when he's not so pleased. "Greta gets A1 attention and I get B2," he said under his breath one day.

"Is that what you think?" I asked.

"Yes."

"Why do you think she gets A1 attention?"

"Because if she doesn't, she screams."

"Yes," I explained, "But also because she needs it."

Half of me felt guilty, the other half felt outraged. After all, hadn't he had eight years of A1 attention? And hadn't I provided him with a big brother as well as a little sister?

Officially, Rob is his stepfather, but in reality, he is more like a big brother. At least that's what it feels like when they alternately collude or collide.

While the cubby house is still at the planning stage in that we have a site and a plan, the swing has been fully operational for several weeks, and so have my two Tarzans.

It's just a thick rope with a stick on the end to sit on, hanging from a medium-sized branch of a wattle tree, which is why I don't want Rob to keep using it.

"Get off that swing!" I yelled at him, as he "tried it out" just one more time in the first few days. Of course, he was really only trying to encourage Johannes, who after half a dozen tries was complaining of sore hands.

But there's a fine line between being encouraging and being incorrigible.

It wasn't long before Johannes came up the stairs with blistered hands and a tear-stained face. "Rob pushed me," he sniffed.

A few moments later Rob came up. "I did not," he said in exasperation. "His hand got caught on my braces."

"Yes, but then you pushed me," Johannes retorted.

"They're silly boys, aren't they?" I said to Greta, as she grinned at both of them.

"Can I hold her now?" Johannes asked, his big blisters forgotten as he turned to his little "skin-and-blister", as Rob calls her.

"Yes," I said, handing her over as she leaned forward and tried to suck his face.

He may well get B1 attention from me these days, but from Greta he gets A1.

It's back to our traditional grinds

28 September 1993

ROB HAS found a job. It is strange, the range of emotions that this news has brought—from elation to relief to nostalgia for the three months we spent working together at home.

Unemployment makes time hang heavy. Unlike holidays, which are time for relaxing and spending, there is nothing to spend and no way to relax. Every day without a job feels like a day without a future. You are perpetually on the starting blocks, but the gun never goes off.

Now, at last, the gun has gone off, and Rob is in the race again.

We are delighted and grateful, but cautious, too. These months have taught us that there is no security in employment any more. These days, people must save for a flood, not just a rainy day.

Although it was only a short period and we had the security of my job to turn to, it gave us some idea of what it must be like to be out of the race for months and months, even years. To feel, even for a short time, that your time and skills are not valued erodes your confidence.

What must it do to people and families who have been unemployed in the long term? For men in particular, whom society still judges by their status as breadwinners or losers, it is difficult to adjust to not having paid work.

Women who choose to stay home and care for children find it difficult enough to be constantly confronted with the question, "And what do you do?" only to be dismissed because they "don't work". But women at least get some kudos for the sacrifice of staying at home with little children.

For men, such sacrifice is seen as little more than a short-term novelty. It is certainly not seen as a long-term option, which is why men caring for young children at home face even more isolation than women.

Daddy may be a big hit at the supermarket when he takes the baby shopping, but where does Daddy go apart from to the shops?

Women have worked hard to develop and maintain community networks to support each other when they are at home with young children. The Nursing Mothers' Association, new mother's groups, neighborhood houses and playgroups all help women cope with the isolation of caring for young children at home.

But men, who traditionally have sought the public domain rather than the private, can find being in the private domestic world of mothers and children is like being lost in alien territory without a map or compass.

Of course, playgroups and neighborhood houses welcome men, too, but few feel confident or comfortable in such situations, just as women are not confident or comfortable in male-dominated areas. For Rob, this situation was made worse by the fact that Greta was still so dependent on me. He dared not venture far in case she needed a feed.

Still, the experience taught him a lot. Before, he had sympathy for those alone at home caring for young children. Now he has empathy. He also has a closer relationship with Greta.

As for me, I am returning to the job I left unfinished—caring for Greta and completing my maternity leave. The hours are long and there's no money in it but, for now, there is nothing I would rather do.

GRETA WON'T TAKE IT LYING DOWN

5 October 1993

THERE IT was in black and white: "Where sleep is a problem after six months of age you have the power to change things, and now you must decide whether to be or not to be tough." So wrote Dr Christopher Green, in his book *Babies!*

It was time for Baby Obedience School.

No more sleeping in the bouncinette until 10pm or midnight for Greta, and then bingeing in our bed until dawn when the mobile milk bar was conveniently immobile. The cure for milkaholics who liked to party all night, Dr Green advised, was the "controlled crying technique".

"When I first started this technique, I didn't try it on any child under the age of 18 months . . . I now find success right down to the age of six months," he advised.

The technique, he said, allows babies to cry for a short period, but not long enough for them to get upset or hysterical. The parent waits a few minutes before giving some reassurance. If the crying starts again, the parent waits a minute or two longer before offering further reassurances. "Eventually, the message will get through that Mum and Dad will always come when he cries, but is it really worth it?" Dr Green said.

That night, when Greta nodded off after a feed, I put her gently and gingerly in the cot. But as her head touched the sheepskin, she opened one eye, looked at me accusingly and began to howl.

I patted her reassuringly and resolutely left the room.

She screamed.

After one minute, I was pleading with Rob: "Can I go in now?"

"Yes," he said, not looking at his watch.

I dashed in, shaking, desperate to offer reassurance. But Greta refused to be reassured. She looked at me frantically and screamed harder. Dr Green's words rang in my ears: "You may lift, cuddle and comfort him if you wish, but it is preferable just to pat and soothe him where he lies."

Preferable for whom? I scooped her up, held her close and waited until her screams ebbed to sobs before putting her down again.

But before her head even touched the mattress, she began to scream again. Should I stay and comfort her again, or go out?

"You must be firm and go, even though the crying will start again with gusto," I heard Dr Green say. So I went.

Two minutes later, I was begging: "Can I go in?" And so it went on for 15 minutes—or was it 15 hours? Greta, purple in the face, with tears streaming down her cheeks, was inconsolable—and so was I.

"What should we do?" I shouted, consulting Dr Green's treatise again, while Greta's screams rose to a crescendo.

"Don't give an inch, whatever you do," Dr Green advised.

"Go and get her—quick!" Rob said.

I ran in, snatched Greta from the cot, and clutched her to me, chanting "It's all right, Mummy's here!"

"Are you all right?" called Rob as he came up the stairs and found that all the Controlled Crying Techniques had achieved was half an hour of uncontrolled crying from both Greta and me.

For us, six-and-a-half months was obviously too early for controlled crying. But having just taught Greta that her cot was an instrument of torture, what should we do now?

We consulted Dr Green again. "If after half-an-hour of being awake and using this method, all else fails, sedation may be used."

Thank goodness! Gratefully, we squeezed the last few drops of chardonnay out of the cask, had a drink and went to bed: me, Rob and Greta.

At last, a feather in mum's cap

12 October 1993

There was a little girl who had a little curl, right in the middle of her forehead.

And when she was good, she was very, very good, and when she was bad she was horrid.

Greta Louise does not have a little curl in the middle of her forehead but she does have two spikes of hair that Rob is fond of curling into miniature devil's horns.

You see, she has inherited his widow's peak, or should I say half of it. For the first few centimetres her hair grows back from her forehead, but for the rest it grows forward, meeting in one dark line and then growing straight up.

"She's been licked by two cows," said my mother when she first saw it.

"That's a beauty!" said the local hairdresser when she saw it. "As her hair grows, the weight of it might cover the cow-licks," she said optimistically.

I'm hoping that it will eventually be curly, like Rob's. She has inherited his face shape, and, of course, his knobby nose. But, unfortunately, she does not have his personality. Like me, she's, er . . . assertive.

"Agghhh!" she says, when she sees something she wants.

"Aaaghhhhh!" she says, if she doesn't get it.

"Aaaaaaggghhhhhh!" she says, if I put her down on the floor to play while I try to do the dishes, make the bed or write this column. Then, if I pick her up, she squeals with delight and pats my arm approvingly.

In the past few months she has learnt to sit up, roll both ways and manipulate small objects—and big objects, like her mother, father and brother.

To encourage her to sleep in her cot, we have embarked on a positive reinforcement project. "Where's your clown light? "I ask, as I stand her on the nappy table, supporting her under the arms. She looks obligingly at her night light, a clown sitting on a sickle moon holding a star.

Sometimes I try to obstruct her view with my face, and she cranes her neck this way and that until, realising it is a game, she breaks into a big grin.

"Where's Annie May?" I ask then, and she turns to look at her big rag doll sitting in the cot and shrieks with delight when I hand it to her.

"Where's squirrel?" I ask, and she drops poor Annie May on her head and seizes the furry brown squirrel.

Then I put her in her cot.

"Aaaaaaaaghhhhhhhhh," she screams, almost as if she has been plunged into boiling water instead of into a nice warm bed.

She has similar objections to sleeping in her pusher. I had tired of carrying her while shopping the other day and had put her in her pusher. I was immune to her yells, but the other shoppers weren't.

"Oh you poor little thing!" declared one kind woman.

"She's having a tantrum," I said sternly.

"At that age?" the woman said.

Yes, at that age. Babies know more than we think. Greta knows a cocky when she sees it now, and a parrot—and what a galah her mother is for coming running every time her little fledgling squawks.

But there are times when this old bird gets the worm, or, in this case, the Greta grub.

"Do you want some carrots?" I asked her one day as I sat her in the high chair for lunch, forgetting carrots rhymes with parrots.

Greta, not too fond of carrots but very fond of parrots, peered around the back of the chair to look out the window, her neck craned and mouth wide open.

And this mother bird, brandishing a spoonful of pureed carrots, quickly popped it into that little sticky beak.

MANY ADVENTURES ON THE HOME FRONT

26 October 1993

STORY time in our house always begins with a warning: "I'm very tired tonight, so I'm only going to read a few pages and then you can read to yourself," I invariably tell Johannes.

And invariably, when the chapter ends and we are stranded like two adventurers on a broken bridge, I say: "Shall I read on?"

"Yes!" he commands, and we leap over the chasm to the next chapter.

Adventuring into unknown literary lands while cuddled up securely in bed is one of the joys of childhood and parenthood. In the past eight years, I have introduced Johannes to some old friends, such as Pooh and Piglet, Moonface and Silky, Alice and the White Rabbit, and The Famous Five.

We have also discovered some delightful new ones, like the Witch, from *Simon and the Witch*, by Margaret Stuart Barry.

Surely, Ms Barry, an English writer, based her character of the witch on the poem *Warning* written in 1962 by Jenny Joseph, which begins: "When I am an old woman I shall wear purple, with a red hat that doesn't go and doesn't suit me"? The poem warns of nonconformity, of the pleasures (so often denied women) of simply pleasing oneself.

The Witch doesn't wear purple but she does wear a chicken around her neck, instead of the standard fox fur. And she seldom makes more than a half-hearted attempt to wipe the soup stains from the front of her dress.

She catches spiders in her hairnet and has them on toast for breakfast and at school (she's a mature-age student), fed up with "adding up", she changes all the children's work into "takeaways" of fish and chips.

Simon and the Witch has been dramatised for television, but the series, although enjoyable, is not a patch on the books. But then dramatisations seldom are. It is the dramatisation in a person's head that brings the most vivid images.

These days, our shared reading time is more sporadic and Johannes has often gone adventuring without me. His latest joy is comics such as *Tin Tin* and *Asterix*, which are another form of dramatisation.

Still, as a cartoonist myself, and one whose inspiration came from Disney comics, I am pleased rather than perturbed at his new interest. Not only have they encouraged his interest in art, they have added greatly to his general knowledge.

"What's an orgy?" he asked at the dinner table last Sunday, having just come home from a weekend at his father's. "Some kind of party?"

"Where did you hear that word?" I demanded, dropping my fork and my jaw at the same time.

"In *Asterix* all the women are always going off and having orgies. Well, not just the women—the men, too," he said. "All the important men say their wives are going off to orgies."

"It's a party where everybody has sex with each other," I said frankly, while Rob tried to hide his grin behind his glass.

Johannes was horrified. "Why would anyone want to do that? They must be weird!"

He paused. "Do they have orgies these days?"

These days? I thought back to the last party I had attended. I must admit the guest of honor was rolling around the floor semi-naked, but you'd hardly call it an orgy—more like a nappy change.

TOO LONG IN THE TOOTH TO FIGHT IT

3 November 1993

In the past week, Greta has cut her first tooth, and mine have been ground down to the gums in the process.

There is only one thing worse than staying home with a teething baby and that is going out with her, especially if the outing is to the local Department of Social Security to give your shoe size and your mother's maiden name yet again to prove eligibility for Family Payment.

"I'm afraid we need more information," said the lone officer dealing with a queue of harassed mothers and irritable children.

I was about to offer my father's mother's maiden name but Greta, no longer amused at Johannes doing wheelies with the pusher, was screaming.

"Look, let's just forget it," I said impatiently. "For a lousy $10 a week, it's not worth it."

"Now Jane! Jane!" the officer chided, reading my name on the form and presuming instant intimacy. I was a name, not a number, after all.

"Is there anywhere here I can change a nappy, er, Mary?" I asked, joining in the game of tag.

"I'll ask if you can use a back room," Mary replied sympathetically.

The toilets were, of course, downstairs and across the road in another building. I hurried to the car to get the nappy bag, leaving Johannes in charge of Greta who was now gnawing frantically on the strap on the pusher.

I dashed back and, in my haste, pressed "Alarm" on the lift, instead of "2". I waited but could hear no alarm, only a miniature siren in the form of Greta, wailing in the distance.

The manager, thinking I had abandoned my children, was waiting for me.

"The officer said I could change a nappy here," I explained.

"I'll just see what I can do," she said, then kindly led me to a tiny room and stood waiting with her clipboard.

"Are you staying?" I said in surprise.

"Yes," she said apologetically. "For security reasons."

I took Greta's nappy off and Johannes immediately began to gag and choke. "Ooh, yuck!" he complained as he tried to stop her from rolling off the table after the plastic bag.

I turned to explain to the department officer that teething was a pain in the bum as well as a pain in the gum, but she had mysteriously disappeared.

We headed for the lift, which, strangely, was now out of order. A nice man offered to carry the pusher down the stairs, while I carried Greta. Down we went and emerged in what appeared to be unfamiliar territory.

While we were wandering around looking for the car, it began to rain. Finally, we found it. I buckled up Greta who had fallen asleep, despite the rain. I was just about to shut the driver's door when I saw it on the bitumen: a huge pile of fresh, recently squashed, dog pooh.

"Get out and check your feet!" I shrieked to Johannes.

Miraculously, nobody had put their foot in it, no one except the department, that is. A week later, they sent me another letter, asking for the same information.

We are still sorting it out and Greta now has two teeth. I know they will get it right soon before I'm toothless, balding, cranky and incontinent.

The Apple of My Eye Blossoms

10 November 1993

I DON'T know when it happened exactly, somewhere in the space of two weeks, or was it two months? But suddenly Grumpy Greta has changed into Glowing Greta, Gurgling Greta, Gregarious Greta.

Perhaps it is because her teeth have stopped hurting. Perhaps it is because of her new-found passion for avocado followed by peach yoghurt dessert. Perhaps it is because she can sit up. Or is it just because she has quietly turned some corner and changed from a tiny baby into a bouncing baby.

There are some babies who just don't like the helpless stage, and I'm convinced that Greta is one of them. A little independence has gone a long way.

"She's a good baby," said the local doctor recently, when I left her briefly, sitting on his desk, examining his stethoscope.

A good baby? I remembered all the times I had reprimanded her with "Oooh, you're a bad baby!" and punctuated it with a kiss, just to reassure her. Good babies are undemanding, so it is understandable and desirable that there are very few good babies, at least in the early stages.

But now she is a good baby, and by that I mean a (mostly) contented baby. Now, at seven-and-a-half months, she is no longer as easily startled. She no longer winces in anticipation just before I shut the car door and she no longer cries when Rob sneezes. Life has become a little more predictable, and so has she. Now, she enjoys sitting up in her pusher observing the world and I enjoy the world observing her.

I remember my mother telling me how she used to dress up my sister and me and proudly push us down the street in our double stroller, enjoying the smiles and comments of passers-by. Now, I think of her as I proudly push Greta in her stroller, and I understand the love and pride she must have felt for us.

As I look at Greta, I am touched by her innocence, her wonder and her alert and fearless interest in the world around her. The dissatisfaction and ennui with the world and self that plagues adults is so refreshingly absent. The world is her oyster and she is my little pearl.

As she sits in her pusher, her little fluffy dark head bowed in concentration as she examines, with all the dedication of a scientist peering through a microscope, a speck she has noticed on the sheepskin, I think of the restless teenage girls I see in the local subway, hiding their breasts and hips under oversized windcheaters, and tugging furiously on cigarettes.

Do their mothers remember these moments of innocence when they see their daughters, like insects struggling to shed an old skin; trying so hard to shed their childhoods and become "adult"?

I think, too, of Johannes as a baby, and how I urged him so eagerly on to each new stage, forgetting or not realising that there is no going back and that babyhood, toddlerhood and childhood are precious moments too soon past.

As I watch the young girls sitting on the steps outside the shops, I wonder what my girl will be like when she is a teenager and what sort of woman she will be. I am looking forward to the woman she will become, whoever she may be. But for now, I am rejoicing in the baby and the little girl.

CAMOUFLAGE AND **57** WAYS TO SWITCH TO SOLIDS

17 November 1993

SHE'S HUNGRY. At least, she was. She opened her mouth eagerly when she saw the spoon, but just when it reached its destination, she slammed it shut and turned her head, and copped another earful.

"Don't distract her!" I ordered Johannes, as he sat at the dinner table playing with his food and pulling faces at Greta.

He was hungry too, but not for lamb shank broth, or fat weevil soup, as the ABC cook Ian Parmentier calls it. He does not mind the weevils, otherwise known as pearl barley: it is the carrots he objects to, arranging them like a row of jaunty buttons around the edge of the plate.

I persevere with Greta, offering one spoonful of mashed avocado, for which she opens her mouth eagerly, followed by one spoonful of "chicken supreme" (chicken and vegies steamed with a little apple juice).

She frowns and begins blowing raspberries, spraying chicken supreme all over my clean shirt.

I give up and decide to offer it to a more appreciative and discerning diner.

"Hmmm! What's this?" says Rob hungrily, as he comes in from work.

"Dip," I say.

"Yum! What's in it?"

"Chicken."

He is impressed. "You don't have to go to all that trouble," he says gratefully hoeing in.

What trouble? I am into recycling—egg cartons, newspapers, bottles, and baby food. Baby food! Why does most of it end up *on* the baby rather than in the baby? And why is all baby food somewhat orange? Carrots, pumpkin, apricots, peaches . . . From now on, I vow to buy clothes with orange splotches on them as a form of camouflage or, better still, dress for dinner—in wetsuits and straightjackets.

I vow, too, not to get offended when Greta rejects my home-cooked offerings, preferring Mr Gerber's carrots, and Mr Heinz's peaches and apple and fruit yoghurt desserts.

Like me, she has a sweet tooth, opening her mouth and grunting with pleasure at fruit and yoghurt and pretending to examine the pattern on the high-chair when anything more savory is offered.

But what do you do when your sweetie doesn't even want a sweetie?

"She hasn't eaten a thing today!" I complain to Rob, forgetting about the four litres of breast milk she has drained from me.

On days like that, the logical me realises she is just not hungry. The illogical me says she is teething, or sick, or both, and I whip up another five varieties of pulverised vegetables to tempt her palate. The result is a stunning array of party dips and less stunning-looking me, trying to squeeze into last season's summer dresses.

But the worst thing about starting solids is that what goes in is not much different to what comes out.

"Yuck! Now I know why they call them solids," Rob said, as he changed yet another nappy. "Mega-disgusting!"

"Don't say that," I said. "You'll give her a complex! She'll end up anal retentive."

Rob looked hopeful. "Really?"

It is amazing how when you have a baby, you really get to the bottom of things, and rarely rise above that level.

But starting solids has at least made her meal times more predictable as well as her nappy changes: she always needs one just after she has been dressed up to go out.

A WONDER DRUG BUT STILL FEELING GUILTY

24 November 1993

THE PHARMACIST looked at me accusingly. "That's not usually recommended for babies under 12 months of age."

It had taken all my nerve to ask, and now I could feel my face reddening. Across my forehead in huge letters, I was sure, were the words: CHILD ABUSER.

All we wanted was a night off. One night without Greta spread-eagled in the middle of the bed while Rob and I clung to the sides like two shipwrecked sailors clutching the wreckage of a boat.

We had been to see the paediatrician that day for advice about sleeping problems. It was bad timing, he said. From seven months to about 11 months, babies began to realise that their mothers were not just extensions of themselves and were wont to panic about it. So it was not the time to introduce controlled crying. All we could really do was keep presenting her with the cot, and occasionally, when everyone was strung out and overtired, resort to sedation.

So here I was, like a 16-year-old buying his first condom, fidgeting with embarrassment as the local chemist viewed me with increasing suspicion.

"What was the recommended dose?" he asked, consulting his book.

"10 millilitres," I said, blushing.

The pharmacist looked shocked and his two female staff members began to close ranks around me. "The recommended dose for babies 12 months and over is only 3.5mls," he said. "Are you sure he said 10mls?"

"Yes," I replied, beginning to feel hot, as I rested Greta on one hip and then the other.

The drug I wanted had been implicated in cot death, he explained.

I explained that the paediatrician had recommended the dose and had assured me of its safety. Why not ring him and discuss it right now?

With one eye on me and one on the phone, the pharmacist rang: but of course, the doctor was out. Perhaps this was a delaying tactic, I thought. Perhaps he was ringing the child protection authority and they would be around any minute to collect me?

But no, the cashier handed me the bottle and I slunk out, embarrassed and furious.

Later at home, I rang the paediatrician who reassured me. The dosage recommended by the pharmacist would be an effective decongestant, but would not induce sedation, he said.

We were relieved, but too traumatised by the event to open the bottle that night. But the next night, feeling like Snow White's stepmother, I administered the Wonder Drug, while we plotted what we would do with our precious night off.

The verdict, of course, was that we would do what Greta was doing—sleep. But somehow I couldn't. It was so quiet. "Is she breathing?" I asked Rob. She was more than breathing, he assured me. She was snoring.

I turned over and the bed, which on other nights had seemed crowded, now seemed vacuous. I was relieved when she woke at her usual time in the night, despite the Wonder Drug, and took her place between us. I heard the kookaburras greet the morning as I watched the grey dawn turn to lemon and then gold.

I was angry at the pharmacist. He was right to question people about the drug, but wrong not to listen to their answers.

"Next time, get the paediatrician to write a prescription," said my friend Carolyn. The point is, she said, where do these conflicting opinions leave the tired, confused and ever-guilty mother? Tired, confused and guiltier than ever, of course.

The paediatrician rang the next day to offer further reassurance and the next week I confronted the chemist. I would appreciate it, I said, if he would ring the paediatrician and discuss this issue because I did not like feeling like a criminal when I came into his shop.

It would make no difference, he said. He was still obliged to go by the book.

We mothers like to go by the book too, but which book? The pharmacist's or the paediatrician's?

As for the next time, no prescription will be necessary. The bottle of Wonder Drug is still almost full as the conflicting views left us wondering too much.

SPLASHING OUT FOR CHRISTMAS

1 December 1993

I THOUGHT it would be nice. After all, for the past eight years I had had the fun of choosing a Christmas present for Johannes. Perhaps Rob would like to choose Greta's first Christmas gift?

Yes, he said, that would be good, not acknowledging, or perhaps not realising, that this would be yet another act of paternal sacrifice.

Like most men, Rob hates shopping. No, hate is not the right word . . . he is uncomfortable about it: about as uncomfortable as a wild rabbit who wanders out of the bush and finds himself in a cosmetic testing laboratory.

You see Rob is a country lad and in the country, you do business differently. For one, you talk to the proprietor. You begin with the weather and end up discovering that you are related and then you invite each other around for a beer. If anyone else happens to be shopping at the same time, it is a good chance that you will be related to them too.

But in the city, they say "have a nice day" without looking into your eyes, and then they check the number of your credit card under the desk against a secret list to make sure you are merely shopping and not committing a criminal offence.

He had really wanted to finish building the cubby, but I had wanted to get organised. I know there are at least another 20 shopping days until Christmas, but why waste one? Besides, it was best to go now before the crowds got even worse, I rationalised.

So, there we were in the Mega Toy Store, arguing, not about the toys but about Rob's attitude. "Stop looking like that," I said.

"Like what?" he asked, breaking out in a sweat.

"Like you're not enjoying yourself."

"I can't help it," he said. "These places affect me like this. They make my heart race." (They make mine race too, but for a different reason.) "Perhaps I'm agoraphobic," he said.

"Agoraphobia is fear of wide-open spaces. You love wide-open spaces. It's crowds you hate," I told him. After all, didn't I know him almost better than he knew himself?

"Oh," he said, knowing me well enough not to argue.

He tried to look enthusiastic. A bath toy might be nice, he suggested.

"For whom?" I thought. Although we took it in turns to bath with Greta, it was nearly always his turn.

He decided Greta would like a water wheel, but, after gazing at the shelves for several minutes, he glazed over and began to look faint.

We staggered farther down the aisle, taking it in turns to hold Greta, who also appeared to hate crowds.

"What about this?" he said, picking up a packet of three plastic floating toys for $6.95 and looking for the exit.

"It's a bit mean," I said.

"Oh, I didn't know how much you wanted to spend."

As much as possible, of course.

About 20 minutes later we emerged with a water wheel, some stacking barrels and some floating balls. Back at the car, Rob's oxygen and enthusiasm returned. They were nice gifts and good choices, he said.

Yes, I agreed, making a mental note to buy him some Winnie the Pooh bubble bath. I don't know how Greta will feel about her first Christmas, but I'm sure Rob will make a big splash.

Invalids and Cockies—A Bad Combination

15 December 1993

WE WERE having friends stay for the weekend, so naturally I wanted everything to be perfect. Especially Greta. They had not seen her for months, so I dressed her up, sat her on the floor with her toys and ran around shoving flowers in all the vases while I waited for them to arrive.

I should have known better. She cried every time they looked at her, and, of course, they brought enough flowers for a funeral.

That night we discovered that she wasn't unsociable, just unwell. She had a fever, which seemed to get worse the next day, so on Sunday morning we went to a local emergency clinic. But the doctor could find no cause for her illness. Come back tomorrow if she doesn't improve, he said.

That afternoon she had diarrhoea, so on Monday morning, I headed for our local doctor. We were just leaving when I received the phone call every mother dreads. It was Johannes's teacher. He had hurt his ankle, she said, and couldn't walk home.

I picked him up on the way to the doctor and we got a double diagnosis: gastro for Greta and a sprained ankle for Johannes.

Great. Last week he had a swollen head, the result of a schoolyard collision. This week he had a swollen foot.

The next day, I planned to play Florence Nightingale to my two invalids, but I had forgotten about my other charges: the local cockatoos.

These days, they have taken to pacing up and down outside the kitchen window if I fail to put seed out in the morning. Now, with breakfast long past, they were getting impatient. When pacing didn't produce results, they started chewing the veranda post.

I was desperate. I couldn't take or leave the children, but if I didn't buy seed, the cockies would have my veranda for breakfast.

I opened the pantry door. Lentils? No. Barley? No. Nutrigrain? Anything that ate veranda posts for breakfast would appreciate Ironman food. I rushed out and poured half the pack into the feeding tray and before I had a chance to retreat an army of cockies had advanced.

The boss cocky surveyed the tray, raked the Nutrigrain with his beak, sending most of it flying, and flew over to the veranda post.

"Bad cocky! Naughty cocky!" I said, running out every time I saw him take a piece out of the post. He was unfazed, merely flying to a nearby tree and returning later.

I gave up. I sat feeding Greta, watching the cockies eat me out of house and home, while Johannes watched telly. But while I was stroking Greta's fevered brow, I noticed something even more disturbing. Spots. They started on her forehead, went behind her ears and were all over her body.

Half an hour later, the three of us struggled into the local hospital, Johannes limping and leaning on me, while I carried spotty Greta. It was a non-specific viral infection, the doctor announced, commenting on Greta's unusual hairstyle and consoling me with the advice that it was personality that counted. I hoped that what Greta had was not contagious.

We limped home, but not before getting four kilograms of parrot food.

Now, bird seed is at the top of my shopping list, along with a couple of kilos of gravy beef for the latest avarian visitors—three kookaburras.

They arrived unexpectedly the other day, but all I had was corned beef. They hated that, but loved the leftover roast lamb I put out the next day. I just wish they'd stop trying to "kill" it by bashing it on the veranda post.

A MERRY, MERRY INNOCENCE

22 December 1993

"OH WHAT a tangled web we weave when first we practice to deceive," my mother used to chant whenever I even contemplated getting out of line. How true, especially at Christmas.

Up until now, Johannes has been well and truly deceived. Until now, he has believed in the Tooth Fairy, the Easter Bunny, and Santa Claus with all the faith of a religious zealot. But now reality, that robber of childhood dreams, has reared its ugly head. After all, it is difficult to ignore the reality of plastic bags from the Mega Toy Store being used to line the kitchen tidy.

"What did you buy at the toy shop?" he asked nonchalantly one night.

I didn't miss a beat. "Oh, just something for Sian, Gareth and David (Rob's niece and nephews)."

A few days later, I was colluding with his father over his Christmas gift. "I can't work out whether he still believes in Father Christmas," his father chuckled.

Such faith, we decided, was too expensive to be encouraged any longer. After all, it meant presents from Santa and presents from Mum and Dad—which is probably why Johannes, after years of being deceived, is now anxious to be the deceiver.

After all, for years I have warned that if you don't believe, you don't receive. But now I am both curious and guilty. Will he be the only VCE student still leaving beer and cake out for Santa?

"Have you talked to the kids at school about Christmas?" I hinted one day.

"No, not really," he said, putting *The Simpsons* on pause.

"What do they think of Santa?"

"Some of them think he's a superstition and others believe in him."

"What do you think?" I asked.

"I don't know," he said, grinning.

But this week, he was confronted with a dilemma. His classmates had been discussing God and declaring himself agnostic, Johannes was greeted with the disapproval of the faithful. One classmate, anxious to convert him, said a prayer for him during art class and asked God to speak to him that night.

As he lolled on the floor in front of the telly after school, he was sceptical.

"Ahhh," said Rob. "But if you don't believe in God, where does that leave Santa?"

Johannes blushed and laughed. "Well, nobody has seen God."

"No one has seen Santa either, or at least the real Santa," I said, although I had to admit, his regular Miracle of the Presents was evidence of some Presence.

He giggled.

"And if Santa doesn't bring the presents, then who does?" continued Rob.

"Yes, who do you think brings them?" I asked, hoping he wouldn't answer.

"You?" asked Johannes.

I should have said yes, but I couldn't. If I let go of such dreams, wasn't I letting go of his childhood? "Santa brings them—at least I believe he does, "I said staunchly.

Rob shook his head in exasperation and he and Johannes both laughed.

The game is up, I know, but I refuse to stop playing. He can grow out of his clothes, his shoes and his comics but I want him to keep his innocence.

It's wrong, I know. Innocence can be a liability in an adult. But, dear Santa, just let him keep it for Christmas.

Tired of always coming last

29 December 1993

THE NAPPY bag was packed, the baby fed and changed and the car and my friend were both revved up ready for the weekly visit to the local maternal and child health centre. She had been planning this visit for a week. Her son was not gaining much weight and she was concerned.

Today's tally would determine whether or not she sought help from the paediatrician or a lactation expert.

She arrived early. Although the session did not open until 1pm, she needed to get away by 2pm to pick up her daughter from kindergarten. A few other mothers were also early and by 1.15pm there were 15 mothers waiting. Waiting. Waiting. Waiting.

Forty minutes after the session opened, when no nurse had appeared, she began to make inquiries.

Someone at the council casually replied: "The nurse called in sick this morning but no one thought to post a notice on the door." My friend came home and wept with anger and frustration.

Sound familiar? It is not just at these sessions that mothers and children are kept waiting. It is everywhere.

Visit any supermarket during the day when it is mostly mothers and children shopping, and you will find two, maybe three checkouts open and mothers queuing and juggling tired babies on their hips or trying to prevent exuberant toddlers from helping themselves to sweets, while other staff pack and label goods, seemingly unaware and unconcerned.

Recently at the Mega Toy Store, I did something very unmotherly. I complained. Loudly.

The store was packed with many women and children waiting to be served, yet only three or four of the 14 or so checkouts were open and each of these was six deep.

I hailed a uniformed staff member. "This is outrageous," I said. "I'd like to see the manager."

The manager was young and fresh-faced and eager to please.

"Look at all these women and children waiting," I said. "Why aren't all the checkouts open? If you spent half the money on service that you spend on advertising . . ."

The young man tried to calm me as several other women nodded in agreement. Perhaps he feared a revolt?

"I agree. I agree," he said. "At this time of year we should have all the checkouts open."

I've forgotten what excuse he gave for this lapse in service but within minutes another checkout was open and Greta and I were being processed and placated. I strode out, no longer a victim.

Having cut my teeth on the Mega Toy Store, I was ready to bite the waitress's head off at the local coffee shop when Greta and I stopped for lunch.

The place was deserted, as it was way past the lunchtime rush hour. I sat down at a table to feed Greta and the waitress plonked my sandwich on top of the counter. When I asked her to pass it to me, she rolled her eyes in exasperation. Naturally—at least it was beginning to feel natural—I complained.

I felt like a bitch (aren't all complaining women made to feel that way?) but I am tired. Tired of shops where it is women and children last. Tired of trying to navigate the pusher through crowds of people who walk resolutely ahead, as if I and my cargo, did not exist. Tired of people who want sales but don't provide service.

What we need is a mother's club: not the sort that provides service to others, but the sort that demands quality service and respect for parents, particularly mothers, as it is they who still largely do most of the "gathering" while the men are at the office "hunting".

Standing up for ourselves alone will bring only temporary apologies.

We need to stand up together.

1994

PULLING SOMEONE'S LEG, BUT NOT MINE

5 January 1994

THE CHRISTMAS tree has come down just as Greta has got up.

"She'll be crawling by Christmas," I had said to Rob, as Greta, who could only manage to get up on all threes, instead of all fours, cried with frustration at our feet.

Within days, she was trying to pull herself up on our trouser legs, on the couch and anything else that was handy.

Then, about a week before Christmas, when we were visiting her Nana, it happened. I was sorting old records while Nana held a toy just out of Greta's reach.

"C'mon," she coaxed, while Greta, used to instant gratification, whinged and cried in frustration as she dragged herself forward. It seems it was worth it because she has now perfected the technique.

That week, I had been jauntily singing *All I Want for Christmas is My Two Front Teeth* to Greta as I spooned mashed cereal into her when I noticed that her top gum seemed to be bleeding.

The next time she opened her mouth, I had a good look and, lo and behold, there were her two front teeth. I had a sudden desire to ring my mother and crow about yet another milestone, mingled with a tinge of nostalgia for that gummy grin.

But while Greta got her two front teeth for Christmas, Rob and I received something even better. The same week, she began sleeping in her cot: not all night, but it's a start.

It was my friend Carolyn who helped break the impasse. "You're trying to do two things at once," she said, when I told her how controlled crying hadn't worked.

"You're trying to get her to sleep in a new place and do controlled crying. Why not just stay in the room with her until she's asleep?"

The next morning, I took Greta and a book into her room and nursed her to sleep on a chair in front of the cot. As I lay her down, her eyes fluttered open and shut, then she breathed a long sigh and went to sleep.

Twenty minutes and three chapters of my book later, I crept out. She slept for a further 30 minutes that morning and another 40 minutes that afternoon, but the real test was the evening. She went down all right, but woke an hour later, whimpering.

For once, I decided not to pick her up. "Listen to the music," I cooed at her, and she stopped, listening momentarily before crying again.

"Pick her up!" pleaded Rob from our bedroom. I ignored him, and kept cooing and stroking her chest. She was more tired than upset, rubbing her eyes and fighting sleep while trying to keep up the momentum of crying. Eventually she gave up.

It had taken 15 to 20 minutes. Too long for Rob. "Poor little thing," he said. Indeed! It wasn't him that she gnawed on all night when she slept in our bed. My heart was getting as tough as my nipples.

Besides, she wasn't as innocent as she looked. A few days earlier, I was braving the Christmas rush and browsing through CDs at a local store. Greta, who had been enjoying the view from the backpack, suddenly got bored and started to pull my hair.

"Yow!" I yelled. "Stop it!"

Obediently, she stopped, but I was distracted suddenly by a succession of "Yows!" from shoppers behind me.

She can't pull my leg any more, but that doesn't stop her from pulling my hair, and anybody else's.

IT'S A FAMILY COZ THE CEREALS SAY SO

12 January 1994

WHAT IS a family? To most people it can be any number and variation of people, generally related, most commonly adults and children, who live together.

But to many of those who are touting for the family dollar, a family is just two adults and two children. Any parent who has had the temerity to have more than two children pays for it—through the nose.

Such discrimination starts at the family breakfast table. Any family with three or more children that wants a free trip to Disneyland or any other exotic place will tell you that, according to breakfast cereal manufacturers, a family is two adults and two children. Your family may be winners, but if you have more than two children, there will be at least one born loser, as anyone extra has to pay.

A friend whose three children are avid applicants for such competitions was complaining recently about this inconvenient and expensive definition. And it doesn't end there. Family rooms in hotels are often restricted to two children. The family of three children or more must pay for an extra bed or cot or room.

Fortunately, many promoters of holiday attractions are now broadening their definitions of the "family".

A quick ring around to several popular attractions showed that while two adults and two children is still the basic definition, many promoters do offer a variation on this. For some, a family ticket can also mean one adult and three children, or even one adult and four children. For others, any number of children from the same family may be included.

For families of three children or more this can mean the difference between going out or not.

While statistics show that the average Australian family now has 2.3 children, the statistics do not show that many families that have two children most of the year, may have more or less at holiday times.

These are the blended families, where children spend time with the non-custodial parent. As some family numbers ebb, others swell.

Perhaps in this Year of the Family, organisers and promoters could be mindful of these family variations and stick to the broader definitions?

As for our family, it has ebbed for the first part of the holidays. We had our little Christmas celebration early as Johannes had Christmas with his father this year. It was sad for us, and for Greta, this being her first Christmas. But for Johannes it was a chance to regain that lost status of the "only child" and to have undivided attention for about the third time in nine months.

We had a happy "pre-Christmas Day", with presents for Johannes and Greta from Rob and me, and presents from Santa for Johannes (he came to Greta on Christmas Day). But it is now obvious that I am the only true believer.

After opening a present from Santa, Johannes looked at me and said, "Gee, thanks!"

As for Greta, she was more interested in the wrappings than the presents.

Until Johannes comes back, we dare not mention his name for Greta looks around eagerly, and then when he doesn't appear, is confused.

This is the downside of the blended family: they are not only blended, but must be regularly torn apart, and then mended.

GROOVY GRETA ROCKS AROUND THE CLOCK

19 January 1994

IT STANDS to reason really, that Greta would be a groover. Before she even had ears she was listening to music, although how a tiny fetus interprets rock and roll I don't know.

During the long months before her birth she heard our regular Wednesday night sing-alongs with our good friend Bevan. So it is not surprising that now she sits transfixed when anyone plays guitar, rocking gently back and forth on her bottom.

And it's not just the guitar that gets her going. When the Australian Ballet danced *The Merry Widow* on television recently, Greta danced too, rocking back and forth, mesmerised by the color and movement. The following night it was the beloved folk-singing group, *The Seekers*, for whom she flapped her arms with delight.

"Aaahh!" she says, when she sees something she wants or likes. She recently learnt to clap hands, so now she can truly show her appreciation.

While she enjoys ballet and opera and folk music, her real love is rock and roll—the louder and faster the better. And Rob and Bevan are happy to oblige.

"Look at her!" they crow, as she shakes her head back and forth furiously, flaps her arms and rocks back and forth.

The trouble is when the guitar is around, especially if it is around Bevan, Groovy Greta wants to rock around the clock.

I had been feeding her in her room and then transferring her, asleep, into her cot. But this night she wouldn't have a bar of it. "Aahhh," she kept saying, as she craned her neck to look at her clown light, then tried to sit up.

We tried a lavender bath but this merely refreshed her. Eventually, we decided to fight fire with fire. Johannes had given Rob the Baby Animals' latest EP, for Christmas, plus Tony O'Connor's *Bushland Dreaming*.

While the Baby Animals' loud and rhythmic song *At the End of the Day* would have delighted this baby animal, if this day was to ever end for Greta we thought she had better start *Dreaming*.

More of a relaxation tape, really, *Bushland Dreaming* combines bush sounds with soaring and soothing orchestral backing, just the thing for a busy baby who insists on being nocturnal.

We closed the door, leaving Rob and Bevan and the amplifiers in the kitchen and turned the bush music up full blast. Then I lay on the bed with her and fed her.

Slowly, gradually, her eyes grew heavy.

Half-an-hour later, I transferred her to the cot and sneaked out to join the others.

It was a late night. The next morning, Rob and Bevan had to drive into work early, but Greta and I slept in until nine. I would have a quiet day, I thought, as I held Greta in my arms while I opened the lounge room curtains.

Suddenly, her eyes lit up. "Aahhh!" she said, pointing and struggling to get down, having spied a guitar in the corner.

I put her down and she immediately began rocking on her bottom and shaking her head.

I had planned to put her in the cot to watch *Playschool* while I had a shower, but who wants to listen to "The babies on the bus go waaa! waaa! waaa!" when you can listen to the Baby Animals going "Waaa! Waaa! Waaaa!" at the beginning, as well as the end of the day?

Good enough for
Dr Spock is good enough for me

26 January 1994

I'M HAVING one of those days. Everything is going fine on the outside, but on the inside things are a mess. You see it's one of those days when you realise what a bad parent you are.

At the moment of birth, it is difficult to imagine that you could ever be unkind, unfair or even cruel to this tiny, vulnerable perfect being. But they don't stay that tiny and vulnerable for long and soon the daily frustrations of life are competing with their demands and you find yourself saying and doing all the things you judged others for and vowed you wouldn't do.

These days, imperfect parenting is allowed, at least. All a child needs is a "good enough" parent, it is said. But even a parent who is good enough can see the cracks in the paintwork of their child's personality, inflicted by shoddy workmanship.

The point is I have a bad temper, a short fuse, a hair trigger.

Sometimes when I feel like a car getting out of control, I manage to slam on the brakes, and get back in the right direction. But other times I go over the edge. It is a kind of madness: like a youth who drinks and then drives recklessly, knowing he is on the path to self-destruction, yet driven by something that seems beyond his control.

The truth is it is never really beyond his control—or mine. It is just easier, and less courageous to scapegoat something or someone rather than confront the source of your fear and frustration.

You may forgive me, just because I have the courage to confess. But confessing does not lessen it. Nor does it repair damaged egos, or cancel out the little hurts, like poison darts, inflicted by snide remarks and outrageous impatience. What is needed is the courage to change.

"Perhaps I need a shrink!" I wailed to Rob one night.

"You don't need a shrink," he consoled. "It's been a hard year."

What I needed, what we both needed, was a rest, a break, a vast expanse of time when there were no life crises, he said.

But it is more than that. I hate to quote him, as it seems like such a cliché, but in his book *Parenting,* Dr Benjamin Spock, confessed: "Parenting is such a strange mixture of stress and joys. I realised when my sons were young that I was always slightly tense when I was with them, watching, worrying and correcting, much more than was necessary. But when I was away from them, on a speaking trip, for instance, I would be overcome by feelings of pride and love. I would feel ashamed that I couldn't show my approval and enjoyment of them while I was with them—for my sake and theirs."

The book is more a confessional than a "how to". Despite his theories, Dr Spock was just a "good enough" parent, and quite a rotten step-parent.

I don't swear by him, or any of the parenting gurus, but in him I recognise a fellow traveller because he was in some ways also prey to that crippling perfectionism that can create impossibly high standards for everyone. The "good enough" parents must learn to accept "good enough" children, and above all, themselves.

A TIRED, VAGUE COUPLE BUMBLE THROUGH SUMMER

2 February 1994

IT WAS raining, as it seemed to have done all throughout the summer holiday, and Greta and I were returning in the late afternoon from the shops.

As I drove up the hill, I saw a short, rather stout man struggling against the torrent, his face shielded by a newspaper, which was all he had to protect himself.

Poor bugger, I thought. Perhaps I should give him a lift? It was an idea I never would have considered in the city, but here in the hills on the outskirts of Melbourne, it felt different—safer.

Still, I thought: Rob wouldn't like it. Although he was country born, he was city cautious. So I drove on.

Ten minutes later as I was unpacking the shopping, the short stout man appeared at the door dripping with water and spluttering with rage.

"Didn't you see me?" he exclaimed, jumping up and down with exasperation.

"Dada!" said Greta. Indeed it was.

Poor Rob. He had left work early hoping to surprise me, but not that much.

"Paula, (our neighbor) recognised me, and she's only known me three months!" he cried.

"I'm sorry," I said, trying not to laugh.

I blamed Greta. After all, it was her fault that I was so tired. Although she was sleeping part of the night in her cot now, the other part she spent kicking me in the bladder in our bed.

"I'm tired and vague," I admitted.

"Me too," he said, and proved it a few weeks later.

He was going to Tyers by train after work one Friday night to help his brother, Greg, to cut a load of wood. In exchange, Greg would drive back here and spend a day digging in our garden.

I was going to drive Rob to our local station early in the morning. But at 7am, when he had to leave, Greta and I were curled up together like two mice in a nest and Johannes had buried himself under his doona.

"Just put them in the car and put your dressing gown on and drive me down," Rob urged, tugging at the covers. He did not have time to walk and besides it was pouring again.

I snatched the covers back. "No way!" I hissed, trying not to wake Greta. A friend's mother had once done that and, of course, the car had broken down. She was forced to catch the bus home in her dressing gown.

Rob finally gave up. We would revert to Plan B, he said. He would drive my car (with the baby seat) to the station, and Johannes and I would put Greta in the pusher and walk down to pick up the car later.

I bade Rob farewell and drifted back to sleep, waking at 9am, glad I hadn't acquiesced to plan A. Glad, that is, until I went into the carport and realised that Rob had driven off with the pusher, the backpack and the umbrella still in the boot.

"Plan B failed," I said, when he rang an hour later. He had realised it as soon as he had hopped on the train, but it was too late. He was profuse in his apologies. After all, he was vague and tired.

As Johannes and I trudged up our road, famous for its steep inclines, taking it in turns to carry Greta the 1.5 kilometres to the station, I thought of that short, stout man with the newspaper covering his face on that rainy day, and wished I had picked him up.

TIME TO EMERGE FROM THE COCOON

9 February 1994

TIME TO get ready for work. The alarm is set for late February, Greta is enrolled in the local creche, Johannes will go to family day care and I am busy preparing myself for the "real world": the world of clean shirts, dress shoes, of uninterrupted thoughts, finished sentences, and in-depth discussions about what was in the paper this morning, rather than what was in the nappy.

And how am I doing this? Am I reading a wide range of newspapers and periodicals? Am I taking notes during the morning and evening news programs?

No, I am eating—low-fat yoghurt, low-fat crispbreads, low-fat jam, and low-fat cheese.

After a year of being cocooned at home, I must emerge and put on my finery once more and spread my wings beyond home and hearth. Trouble is, the finery doesn't fit.

What goes up must come down, they say, but while my weight went up during the year, the only thing that has come down is my bustline.

Don't get me wrong. I have had some success. Several of my old dresses do fit me. It's just that the waists need to be let out to accommodate my breasts. Still I must persevere as our budget does not permit a new wardrobe and with the choice between an extension for me or an extension for the house, we chose the latter.

How else am I preparing for work? Well, I am nursing Greta when she sleeps instead of putting her in her cot, as I should. I'll put her down in five minutes, I think, and then find myself watching the end of the movie.

When I finally, guiltily, place her in the cot, she wakes and cries or only lasts a few minutes. "She only slept for five minutes!" I complain to Rob, forgetting that the five minutes in the cot was preceded by 45 on my lap.

I should be training her for crèche, I know. "She is still very attached to me," I explained to the mothercraft nurse at the crèche where Greta is enrolled. By attached, I mean literally. She is still breastfeeding, and although she drinks juice and water from a bottle, when it comes to milk, she prefers the designer kind, designed just for her.

"Here comes the old nose-bag!" my father-in-law, Cec, had said when Greta was small. Nearly 11 months later, the old nose-bag is battered and lopsided (as Greta favors one side), but still going strong.

The designer milk will still be on tap four days a week as I will only be working three, but they will be three long days—11 hours—for both Greta and me, as the trip into town takes more than an hour each way.

She is ready for it, I am sure. She is crawling properly now, saying Dada, Nan, Mum, Bub and is curious and eager to reach out to others.

I am ready, too, despite my sadness at leaving her. I may not be ready to fit into all my old dresses, but I am ready to wear the other item I discarded for a year—my watch. The metal clasp pinched Greta's neck when I nursed her, so I took it off and never found the need to put it on again.

But now it is time, time for both of us to emerge from the cocoon, just a little.

READY TO TAKE HER PLACE IN THE WORLD

16 February 1994

THEY BARELY had one good set of teeth between them as they sat like 12 miniature geriatrics at their miniature tables in miniature chairs with arm rests and pommels to keep them from falling into their plates.

But what they lacked in teeth, they made up for in enthusiasm.

"It's a real social occasion," said one of the caregivers, smiling, as the toddlers and babies at the local crèche sat down to lunch.

How true. Babies who were particular about sharing toys had no qualms about sharing spaghetti. It was the spoons they were territorial about. It wasn't a matter of where you put your spaghetti as long as you put it there yourself.

"Do you want some help?" inquired one caregiver, taking the spoon from young Thomas. Talk about spoiling a man's appetite. Poor Thomas sobbed uncontrollably until his spoon, independence and honor were restored.

And where was Greta during this Lilliput luncheon? Asleep. Yes, the girl who wakes if I plonk a coffee cup on a table at home was sleeping soundly through the chatter, the banging spoons, the occasional wail and the distant hum of the clothes dryer.

Perhaps I'd better book an afternoon session and an extra cot for me, too, I thought, as I wandered around with a cup of coffee, wondering what to do.

It was her first day of assimilation at crèche, but after a few hours she had not only been assimilated but obliterated.

"It's important to make a good impression," I had told her before we left home, as I placed her pink headband carefully over her weird hairline. I was nervous, of course. What if she wouldn't let me go? I remembered how it was decided that my sister could forgo kindergarten rather than be surgically removed from my mother.

But Greta, who gets free taxi rides all around our house because she won't let me put her down, was struggling to get off my knee within five minutes of arriving at crèche.

Within half an hour, her headband had popped off and was resting like a crown on her dark head as she sat, like a gnome queen on a miniature throne, grinning and rocking back and forth to yet another chorus of *Little Peter Rabbit Had a Fly Upon His Nose*.

After choir, it was time for morning tea, and time for me to go for an hour, just to see how she, er . . . I, would cope.

As I shut the door behind me, with ne'er a second look from Greta, I felt a mixture of relief, regret and liberation. I spent the hour on the phone, uninterrupted, and managed to drink a whole cup of coffee while it was still hot.

When I returned, Greta came crawling up to me, glad to see the old nose-bag after all.

"She wouldn't go down," the caregiver said.

Now she wouldn't sit up. She flung herself in feeding position, latched on and immediately began to snore. I placed her gently in a cot and waited for her to protest. But she snored all through lunch and woke after an hour and 20 minutes, just as our assimilation morning finished.

As we left, I had to sign her out. It was strange to see her full name written in the official book. She was no longer just "Greta", my baby, but a little person, ready to take her place at crèche and in the world, even if she took it lying down.

JUST WAITING TO WALK AND TALK

23 February 1994

"NO, NO, NO!" says Greta, shaking her chubby fist at me. It is 8am and this is her first utterance for the day. Along with her new mobility has come a new vocabulary.

I know, the Baby Book of Guilt says that it is better to childproof your home before baby starts crawling, thus avoiding the constant need to say "No!" But one minute she was dragging herself around on her arms and the next she was up on all fours and heading for trouble.

"No! No! No!" she chides, as she pulls herself up on the dressing table drawer handles and, peering over the edge, waves one chubby arm around like a miniature mine-sweeper, collecting my perfume, trinket box and several hair brushes.

To keep her away from the kitchen cupboards, I decided to provide something more tempting, so I moved all my plastic ware to an open, bottom shelf. But what could be more tempting than the kitchen tidy parked nearby? She is not interested in her toast in the morning, until it goes into the bin and is flavored with used teabags and orange peel.

"This is blackmail," Rob said, when we went to the Mega Baby Store to buy a ridiculously expensive childproof gate to keep Greta out of the kitchen. He was right. How safe your home is depends on the distance between your arms and your pockets.

Luckily, we no longer have to buy toys as Greta is not interested in them. What she wants is contraband, illegal substances, stolen goods: Rob's wallet, my keys, pens, tissues, plastic bags, the beads from the vertical blinds, Johannes's Sega Master System, library books, my glasses, dead blowflies, possum pooh . . .

"Di, do, di, do," she says to herself, meaning "tick, tock", as she looks admiringly at the kitchen clock. She's right. It's only a matter of time.

Already she has her eye on the top shelf in Johannes's room, where all toys with small moving parts have now been banished. Poor Johannes, he is blissfully ignorant of what lies ahead.

"I can't wait for another five months," he said one night. He always "can't wait" for something, but I was puzzled. It was only one month until his birthday, two months until Easter and another 10 until Christmas.

"Why? What happens in five months?" I asked.

"Greta will be walking," he replied.

"She'll be walking in two months," I said, watching her stand up and try to demolish the new gate separating the kitchen from the lounge room.

It is not just brotherly love that makes him impatient. It's boredom.

He felt similarly about our friend's daughter, Hannah, when she was a baby, but quickly tired of her idolatry when she could walk and talk enough to follow him around grovelling for attention.

"H-e-l-l-o, H-a-n-n-a-h," he would say robotically, when she bounced into the room.

These days he is grateful for any companion who can play with toys with small parts without tasting them first.

"Hannah's coming over tomorrow," I told him one day recently.

His face lit up and all day he was in a jaunty mood. "I can't wait for Hannah to come," he confided. "I can't wait to play with someone who can walk and talk."

BILLS THAT GROW FASTER THAN WEEDS

2 March 1994

WHAT IS more responsibility than a dozen children, grows four times as fast, is twice as difficult to tame, devours all your money and ties you down forever?

You guessed it—a garden. I expect Johannes and Greta to be able to take very good care of themselves by the time they are 18 or so, but poor old Rob and I will be nurturing our garden until we are ready for the compost heap ourselves.

The garden at the flat was much more manageable. Admittedly, it was only a coffin-sized balcony, but it faced north, and as it was on the second floor, it only attracted the occasional cabbage moth or aphid. There wasn't room for any more. There, my imagination and ambition was only limited by the television antennae, which took up one-third of the space.

Here, our ambition is limited by the appetite of the local possums and cockies, who have thoroughly enjoyed our early gardening efforts and are now lining up for seconds.

So we have given up feeding the natives and are going to plant them instead. So far, we have dug a huge hole out the front, which we are filling with money, or at least it seems that way. Don Burke* forgot to mention that the bills grow faster than the weeds.

For budget-style inspiration, I bought a recent copy of gardening and alternative lifestyle magazine, *Grassroots*.

"Why don't we get a worm farm?" I suggested, browsing through the ads one night.

"No," Rob said dismissively. "You don't want one of those smelly things."

Yes I did. "It sounds good," I persisted. "You put the scraps in the top, then the worms and this compost liquid comes out."

Rob, who was keen to build his own compost heap down the back yard, was as resistant as I was persistent. "Do you want the worms to go fishing?" he said.

"I don't care what they do," I replied.

Why waste worms on fish when you could get them to recycle your garbage?

But for real inspiration, we only need to glance across the road. There, Crystal, our neighbor—30-something, blonde and Amazon-like—has recently built a mortarless stone retaining wall with her bare hands. She has lugged huge rocks. She has carted hundreds of loads of mulch and soil in a hessian sack slung over her back. She has planted scores of tree ferns and native plants, and a tiny seed of envy in the heart of every man in the street.

"She's an inspiration!" said my father-in-law, Cec, a veteran gardener himself.

Morris, our next-door neighbor, was less impressed. "It's depressing," he said, watching Crystal lugging logs up the hill in the rain.

He had given up long ago, he admitted. Unless you're out there every moment of the day, he confided, the weeds just grow back. Indeed they do. Which is why Crystal is out there every moment of the day.

When Rob was lamenting the rotten gardening weather over Christmas, Crystal was waving cheerily from her front yard, her Japara coat dripping and beads of perspiration gleaming through the white splotch of sunscreen on her nose.

Perhaps this is why when Rob's brother, Greg, came up to help in the garden recently, no one mentioned the weather. It rained all day and Rob and Greg barely stopped for lunch. Of course, Crystal was out there too, her slim blonde ponytail dripping wet.

But for once, I saw her stop, march over the road and begin to chat to Rob. Perhaps she was trying to encourage a fellow gardener, I thought.

"What did Crystal want?" I asked eagerly at lunch.

"Oh, she just came over to borrow the wheelbarrow," Rob said.

HANGING ON TO OPERATION WORK

9 March 1994

I HAD NEVER been so ready. A week's worth of cut lunches and casseroles were stacked in the freezer, all my clothes had been washed and ironed, my shoes were cleaned, my briefcase packed, my brag-book filled, and I had memorised the weekday train timetable.

Operation Desert Storm was nothing compared with Operation Work. So I was not surprised when, on the Sunday night, I began to feel sick. I was more surprised when Rob was sick, too. Such empathy! I thought.

By Monday morning we were going all right, but not to work, as we each wrestled with our own version of gastric flu.

I felt embarrassed and disappointed when I rang to say I wouldn't be in. "It's Jane Cafarella, ringing in sick," I groaned.

"Who?" said a strange voice on the phone. A lot had changed in a year.

Two days later, when I finally made it, I was dotting the last "I" on a story before leaving to pick up the children, when the computer system "went down", taking my story with it. "Help!" I wailed to Rob, who then left early while I stayed late.

The next night I noticed Greta's brown eyes were slowly turning green.

"It's conjunctivitis—highly contagious," the doctor said, and promptly banned her from crèche.

"Help!" I wailed to Greta's Fairy Godmother. But it seems Fairy Godmothers were in big demand that week as she was already booked.

"Help!" I begged Greta's Nana and Pa. But Nana and Pa had their hands full, literally, caring for Greta's little cousin, David—three months her junior and three times her size.

In the end, David's Daddy stayed home to care for him and Nana and Pa minded Greta so that I could go to work.

I felt guilty and relieved as I hopped on the train that night. It wasn't so bad, I consoled myself. At least the hour-long trip allowed me to read and relax.

"The next train will stop all stations and passengers are reminded that there will be no train services tomorrow as there will be a 24-hour stoppage," a muffled voice announced as we pulled out of the station. So much for relaxing.

So much, too, for conjunctivitis cures. When I returned that night, Greta had a green nose as well as green eyes—and croup. "We even bulk bill in special circumstances," boasted the booklet handed to me by the doctor's receptionist at the emergency clinic.

I was broke, so I told the doctor about my special circumstances. "Oh, we don't bulk bill," she said firmly. I was too tired to tell her where to shove her stethoscope.

It had cost us as much in medical fees as it had in child-care for the week, and Operation Work was beginning to look like Operation Won't Work.

So why bother? Admittedly, I am doing it for me, but I am doing it for Greta and Johannes, too. I am lucky enough to have a job I enjoy, unlucky enough to need the money and the security, and experienced enough to realise that motherhood is a relationship, not a career.

Greta still needs me, but she needs other people, too. She and Johannes also need an education and a secure future, which we cannot provide on one income. And they need to know that just as they will survive when they choose to become independent, so will I.

"Always have something of your own," warned my mother. And she was right. All parents need something to hang on to while they are letting go.

So far, as Greta's immune system strengthens, I am hanging on by the skin of my teeth. But I also know from experience that, eventually, the only thing we will catch is the train.

A CELEBRATION OF SURVIVAL

16 March 1994

TOMORROW is Greta's first birthday, and Johannes's ninth, and here I am at work—remembering. It has been a big year—birth, job losses and gains, moving house and now returning to work part-time

Greta's first birthday is as much a celebration of our survival as hers. Now, 12 months later, I am remembering the uncertainty and anticipation of that early morning when Rob and I left Johannes at Carolyn's and went to the hospital, and how, together with the doctor and midwives, we worked to ensure Greta's safe arrival.

Now the sea anemone-like fingers that waved searchingly at the moment of birth, are still long, but dimpled. Her hair, black and damp at birth, is still black and is still growing like Camberwell Junction—in five different directions.

She had her Daddy's face then and now she has his smile too—a cheeky grin that makes her knobby nose screw up. She is almost walking and as far as she's concerned she's talking, with a repertoire of sounds that I, as her official interpreter, willingly translate. She clearly says Mamma, Dadda, Nana, teddy and sometimes duck, she can tick like a clock, bark like a dog, she eagerly puts her hand up when anyone mentions the word ``school" and has quickly established herself as the boss of the family—which brings me to Johannes.

The past year has been a mixed bag of gains and losses for him. There is no doubt that his little sister has brought him joy that even I could not have anticipated and hoped for. He is tender and loving towards her, but also great fun. He is both her hero and her slave.

But while she was his gain, I was his loss. For the past year we have lost each other, Johannes and I. Totally immersed in Greta's and Rob's needs, I have struggled with Johannes's. I am only just emerging from that now, to find that he has grown so much—without me. I notice it now like someone who has been away.

Never a very demanding child, for the past year he has learned to keep his small needs small indeed: clinging to me at night for ``just one more hug", but accepting his role as chief babysitter and helper rather than a child with childish needs of his own.

His ninth birthday marks the end of a difficult, if rewarding, year.

This year, I hope I can give him what he wants most: time together. As for Rob and me, this has been our most joyous and demanding time. The birth was a team effort and this is how it has continued. I don't know how we would have fared had we been pushing against each other instead of pulling together.

For Rob, too, Greta's birthday is a celebration of his first year of parenthood. Tomorrow night we will have a small family party, blowing out the candles and making a wish. And what will we wish for? For such happiness to continue, of course. Who could ask for anything more?

A PARTY THAT IS GOOD FOR EVERYONE

23 March 1994

A BALLOON is an innocent toy—until you give one each to six nine-year-old boys. Then it is a fart machine. A straw is an innocent tool, too, until you give it to the boys with the balloons. Then it is a hose. Add some soft drink and some slightly chewed hamburger and you have enough ammunition to fight any battle.

"Thank goodness we didn't have this at home," I said to Rob, as we watched Johannes turn from a mild-mannered boy into a full-blown gremlin as, with five of his mates, he celebrated his ninth birthday at McDonald's.

Greta, sitting in a high chair eating her first chip, was fascinated. To have Johannes around was a party on its own. To have five of his friends, too, meant she was having a ball.

It didn't matter that everyone ignored her—everyone except Rhys, who, being familiar with her party tricks, was anxious to show her off.

"Hey! Look at Greta," he called to the others several times over the din. "What do you do when you go to school?" he prompted, waiting for her to put her hand up.

But she was not interested. Neither were the boys, who were too busy watching Steven sit on his balloon to see if it would burst.

"Steven is a little bit wild," Johannes had warned me when he wrote the invitations. I could see what he meant. And I could see why Johannes liked him, too. He was a real party animal. So was Greta, who was struggling to reach for a balloon of her own.

Afterwards, Rob and I agreed that the party had been good for Johannes, but good for us, too. "It helped me remember that he is only nine years old after all," Rob said.

Yes, but nine had seemed so old. Nearly double figures, as my mother had said. Almost half the time he was likely to spend with me was gone already, I mused.

So old, yet so young. One minute he is commenting on a report on the Greek-Macedonian row which he saw on the ABC children's current affairs show *Behind the News*, the next he and his friends are inspecting the contents of their ears with the torch someone gave him for his birthday. "Johannes had the most cauliflowers," his friend Kym told me pointedly.

As they all hoed into the ice-cream cake, adding blobs of ice-cream and sugar to their drinks to make "spiders", Rob and I sat back and surveyed the debris with unusual magnanimity. With no responsibility for catering and clearing up, we were feeling relaxed and mellow.

"You boys should come round and play in our back yard some time," offered Rob.

"Yes, you could all come," I added, sipping coffee and imagining the gum trees in our back yard dripping with boys and rain.

"Now?" said Steven, his wild brown eyes matching his wild brown curly hair and his Peter Pan looks.

I faltered. "Well, not now," I said. "Maybe another time."

GRETA'S FIRST STEPS
ON THE PATH TO INDEPENDENCE

29 March 1994

SOMETIMES a girl can be too assertive. Take last Friday, when Grandma and Grandpa came down from the country for a belated birthday celebration for Greta and Johannes.

Johannes was sitting on the couch, using his arm to shield his new stamp album from Greta, when we heard a howl of pain.

The clink of wine glasses and the buzz of adult chatter stopped abruptly. "What's the matter?" I asked in alarm.

"Greta bit me!" he sobbed.

There was a moment's stunned silence while we all looked at Greta who, having made her point, was cruising around the couch bub, bub, bubbing to herself.

"Bad baby!" I said lamely as I tried to comfort Johannes. She grinned up at me, showing all of her eight, very sharp teeth. Having missed the actual moment of attack, the connection between her action and my displeasure was somewhat lost on her.

"What are we going to do about her temper?" Rob asked me later, when she had thrown her bottle on the floor in disgust after having been refused the wine glass.

"Ignore it," I said. "Don't reward it, and above all, don't laugh."

I should know. After all, didn't she take after me? At least that is according to family lore. Johannes has never been a rebel: so he is innocent. Rob is about as aggressive as a teddy bear, and just as cuddly: so he is innocent. That leaves me. Like Greta, I want things to go my way, and I want it now. But seeing your own faults magnified in your children is disconcerting.

While I am mindful of the sin of labelling, there is no doubt she is more intense than Johannes. Right from the start she was easily excited and easily frustrated. She exclaims loudly over things that delight her— as she did over the oil painting of two golliwogs that Grandma painted especially for her birthday—and protests equally loudly over things that frustrate her.

While Johannes would sit in the pusher gazing placidly around, Greta insists on standing up, clutching the hood and rocking back and forth, urging me to go faster. Johannes went through the normal tantrums if I forgot that he could actually dress himself, feed himself, or wash himself. But he was about two years old then, and this was expected. I had not expected it to start so early with Greta.

Already she wants to put her shoes on herself, and if she can't, nobody can. But putting your own shoes on is a bit premature if you can't even walk. So far her first few steps towards independence have been taken from behind the safety of her little push cart which she leans on as she pushes it up and down the lounge room, like an old lady with a walking frame.

"Clever girl!" we chorus in that soupy sentimental voice that parents are only entitled to use in the privacy of their own home. Then we clap furiously.

Chuffed, Greta takes her hands off the cart and gives herself a resounding round of applause, standing briefly unsupported. Realising this, she quickly drops to the safety of the floor.

Johannes did not walk until he was 16 months old, so I am not surprised that Greta is not game to try it yet without support. And frankly I'd rather she had trouble standing up by herself, than for herself.

Learning to walk takes most people only a year to 18 months at the most. Learning to stand up for yourself may take a lifetime.

TA TA, IT'S TIME TO CLOSE THE DOOR

5 April 1994

FOR the past year it has been open house with us. Anyone has been welcome to glance in the window, or to come in and quietly observe our family life, with all its ups and downs.

But now it is time to draw the blinds and close the door.

Yes, this is my last entry for this *New Life Journal*. Now that we have journeyed together from pregnancy to birth and through that first exciting and challenging year, it seems to me that we have reached our destination.

I could, I suppose, continue writing about the journey through toddlerhood to school to university etc until this new life begat another new life and the whole thing became an old-life journal. But in doing so, you would risk boredom and I would risk my family's privacy and my children's mental health.

Johannes is already suffering from an inflated ego. After meeting a fan in the street recently, he cheekily offered his autograph.

"Goodbye, fan!" he yelled after the poor woman as he sauntered off.

As I gave him a quick lesson in the meaning of the word "humility", it occurred to me that it may be time for us to say goodbye not just to one fan, but to all.

So now, after more than 12 months, it's goodbye from us. And thank you. Thank you for reading and writing.

Throughout the year, we have received many letters of goodwill, advice and concern from readers. This was gratifying, touching, but most of all encouraging. It meant we were not alone in our joys and struggles.

It also meant that writing this column became like writing a letter to a dear friend, or in this case, many dear friends.

To those I did not manage to reply to, I apologise. Most who wrote were busy mothers, so I am doubly grateful they chose to devote some time to writing to me.

Your letters also showed us that the family in its many forms is alive and well in Victoria. Like us, some who wrote were "blended", others were traditional "nuclear" families, some were single-parent families, some were grandparents writing about the parallels between our life and the lives of their children and grandchildren. Almost all commented that "Your family life so often mirrors my own."

This was heartening, personally and generally. Despite persistent reports of the breakdown of the family, child abuse, violence against women, and all the other ills of family life so often paraded in the media, the mirror we held up to our own life has reflected back much more positive images of family life—of men and women striving to bring up children in the best and most loving way they can.

In this Year of the Family, I hope that politicians of all persuasions make the family the subject of action rather than rhetoric and, above all, do not pit families against each other in the scramble for resources.

Whatever their differences in style, all families share a common goal: to raise children in a secure and loving environment. The goal of politicians should be to encourage and facilitate that.

As for our family, you may catch a last glimpse of us as we quietly close the door. There is Rob, writing a list of "things to do" on his Easter mission to try to resurrect the garden. There is Johannes, packing his bag for his holiday at his father's, and there is Greta busily trying to unpack it.

She is an expert at waving goodbye now, so I will let her do so now. But saying goodbye seems too blunt and saying farewell seems too formal, so perhaps I will let her say it in her own, newly acquired words and simply bid you "ta ta".

Post script: Well, the door didn't remain closed for long. I returned to work three days a week, but found the travel to the hills and back each night too arduous. News being a fickle thing, I'd stay back late, convinced I had the scoop of the century, only to find that something more important had bumped my story off the front page and that Greta and Johannes had missed out on having their mother home again, seemingly for nothing.

The following story heralded the beginning of a new resurrected column in The Age called **Family Postcard.**

1995

SOMETIMES I IMAGINE—BUT NOT FOR LONG

8 February 1995

MONDAY morning at the station, breathless and late for work, with the echo of my daughter's plea in my ears: "No see Sarah! My holiday!"

I sink into the seat, guilty at first, then grateful: a chance to read, a chance to think. I think of leaving work. How unthinkable! I have a career, not just a job.

I close my eyes and dream of writing again, rather than reporting. I dream, too, of being a super cartoonist instead of a super woman, devoting myself to my small cartoon business instead of dabbling in it. What did Gary Larson do for child care?

What a joke! Any one serious about a career draws the line at having children. Any serious woman that is. But I can't imagine not having my children. Perhaps I should just buy another Tattslotto ticket?

"Sometimes, I imagine . . ." I sing softly to myself, like Ernie from *Sesame Street*. I imagine saying something to my children apart from "Hurry!" I imagine leaving work. How unimaginable! I imagine I am just tired. Other women do it all: mothering and working outside the home. I should not give in. Besides, I have been warned: women who don't "go" to work, go mad.

But what if going to work meant staying home? I pick up my magazine, a new publication called *HomeBiz*. It says that around 300,000 Australians now have a home office. By the year 2004, 25 per cent of all workers may be working from home, the magazine says. And women are leading the way.

I imagine working from home. I imagine going broke. But I also imagine not having to pay 75 per cent of my part-time wage for childcare, fares, home help and clothes.

My magazine has a drawing of a woman working from home. She has not really left work; just changed work. She sits at a computer, while a child plays happily at her feet. Impossible! No one would imagine that a male office worker could get the job done with a toddler at his feet. Why do they presume women can?

The train arrives at Richmond. It is city-bound, but here one can get off and take a train to almost anywhere. Perhaps I should too? I need a new direction. I vow to talk to the boss. The Year of the Family is over, and I no longer want to be the family reporter.

Then I remember it is now the Year of Tolerance. Perhaps I won't talk to the boss after all: tolerance is not my forte.

Flagstaff Station. I scramble out on my way to the office. I have to leave early for crèche today so there will be no time for lunch.

I think of changing my work. After all, everything else has changed. I now have two children, not one. My husband has a new job that requires longer hours in the city. I have an established career where I can work any hours, anywhere.

I bump into the boss. He is fresh from holidays, smiling. "Come and see me at three," he says amiably.

I make my plea at three. He gives me a new job, working from home writing about family issues.

And this is it.

MAKING A CLEAN BREAST OF IT

15 February 1995

THEY say once bitten, twice shy, but it seems no matter how many times I am bitten, I cannot wean my 22-month-old daughter.

I vowed that this time would be different, but Greta is just as firmly attached to me, literally, as my son, Johannes, (now nearly 10) was at that age.

"No milk today, my love has gone away," she chants as I drop her at crèche in the morning. But the minute I walk in the door, she says hopefully: "Milk bar?" Then pleadingly, holding up one small finger: "Just one minute?"

I am not alone. Throughout history and across cultures it seems that weaning has required a little more than gentle persuasion.

Mamatoto, A Celebration of Birth, published by Virago for The Body Shop in 1991, says: "Many people encourage their babies to stop breastfeeding by stuffing their mouths with special delicacies; fish eyes among the Utku of Canada and Tchambuli children of New Guinea are given lotus stems, lily stems and pieces of sugar cane."

"Would you like something special?" I asked Greta, as she lay in my arms, firmly attached, one chubby arm toying with my earrings.

"Yoyyies?" she said, meaning lollies.

Perhaps I should just buy a dozen doughnuts, and wean Czechoslovakian style. According to Mamatoto, Czech babies were once weaned with a touch of humor. "The mother would bake a cake with a hole in the centre and put it on her breast, so that her nipple protruded through the hole. The child, laughing so much that it couldn't suck, would take the cake instead, and so the weaning process began."

All very well for Czech babies, but after every doughnut, Greta insists on having something to wash it down.

Of course, the Nursing Mothers Association of Australia sees this as a triumph, not a tragedy. At its 30th birthday bash last year, in the hope of some sound advice on letting go, I broached the topic of weaning. "Oh yes, speak to Cate. She's just weaned," advised Sue Byrne, the association's Victorian spokeswoman.

I asked Cate, "How old is the baby you've just weaned?"

"Three and a half," she said.

Their advice is similar to that given to women who insist on walking alone at night: don't wear suggestive, accessible clothing; arm yourself with various distractions, and if necessary, call on friends and relatives for help.

Or you could wait until a full moon as women in East Prussia were once advised. Weaning must not take place with a waning moon, and should only be undertaken when the migratory birds are settled, according to an extract from a German historical, gynaecological and anthropological compendium, sent to me by lactation consultant Maureen Minchin.

I fear I will have to wait until menopause, when everything dries up. But even then, the German compendium warns that in some cultures, menopause is just a minor pause in a woman's lactating career. "One woman had fed her last child at least 15 years before, but she applied her grandchild to her breast and was able to give it quite sufficient milk," it says.

For those who want to wean before they wane, the Nursing Mothers Association of Australia has special meetings. "Our meetings on weaning the older child are always very well attended," says national spokeswoman, Karen Commisso. Very well intended, too, I'm sure.

Perhaps the best solution is to go cold turkey, as White Russian mothers used to do. "She sews up the opening in the breast of her chemise, cooks some groats for the child, makes the sign of the cross over it and says: 'Now thou hast salt and bread; eat what we eat; thy time is up!'"

But perhaps this tussle between a mother and her older child is natural. On TV recently, a mother monkey was trying to push away her 12-month old baby as it tried to nuzzle in for a feed.

In the end, just like Greta, the little monkey won.

THE PRICE WE'LL PAY TO BE NORMAL

22 February 1995

"MICHAEL'S had his ears pinned back," my 10-year-old son said matter-of-factly one day after school.

"How do you know?" I asked. "He's got a bandage around his head. He says he didn't have his ears fixed, but that's what everyone thinks. Some kids are saying he's had his brain removed."

Other kids, my son shamefacedly admitted, were saying that he couldn't have had his brain removed because he didn't have one to start with.

Poor Michael. He couldn't win. Having big ears made him the subject of ridicule and having them fixed made him the subject of further ridicule.

Michael's sticking-out ears had probably contributed to his sticking-out personality. Now that he looked more "normal", perhaps he might behave more normally? But "normal" covers a lot of ground when it comes to looks and behavior.

To most parents, "normal" means having the right number of things in the right proportions, all in good working order. But what if everything works, yet is not quite in the right proportion? Does a child's fate and happiness in life really depend on a perfectly proportioned body, and is correcting nature worth the risk?

A recent report in *The Guardian* showed that sometimes the price of perfection is too high. One London teenager, Janine Connor, who had begged her parents for years to let her have her ears surgically pinned back, died when her lungs collapsed under the general anaesthetic. Tragically, she was not the first. A 12-year-old boy also died during a similar operation in 1988 after an adverse reaction to the anaesthetic, *The Guardian* said.

No parent would knowingly risk the life of their child, but most believe the risk of a miserable life must be weighed against the relatively small risk of an operation. If the emotional scars from teasing would

96

harm a child's development, then perhaps it is better to submit to a few physical scars at the hands of a skilled surgeon?

The Guardian report reassured parents that the medical risks for cosmetic surgery are, in fact, extremely small.

However, it failed to say that the real risk with cosmetic surgery is that it will not necessarily bring happiness. Perhaps the first doctor that anyone seeking cosmetic surgery should see is a doctor of psychology.

Either way, it is a difficult decision: what may be character building for one, may be soul destroying for another.

"Children can be unbelievably cruel to anyone who looks different," English cosmetic surgeon, Edward Latimer-Sayer, said in the article.

I should know. I was born with congenital lymphoedema in my right leg, making it twice the size of the left. I had cosmetic surgery when I was 18, but when I was a child, little was known about it, and it was considered that nothing could be done.

Strangely, although I was sometimes teased in early primary school, other "normal" children were teased more.

Why? In my opinion, Mr Edward Latimer-Sayer is only half right. The truth is that children can be unbelievably cruel to anyone. It is not imperfections that draw children's barbs, but how one feels about them and copes with them. Children sense vulnerabilities and insecurities with the same acute sense that dogs can sniff out rabbits, and it is these they target.

Still, parents have their vulnerabilities, too, and one is the fervent desire to protect our children from life's hardships. When my 22-month-old daughter, Greta, developed a small mole on her right cheek, I consulted the doctor immediately about whether it was dangerous, and what could be done if it grew unsightly.

And when I am alone with her at bath time, I admit that I sometimes make her stand up in the bath, while I carefully measure her bare, chubby, perfect, legs.

When going green won't wash

1 March 1995

"THAT'LL be $24, please," the shop assistant said, as she lined up the four 250-millilitre recyclable bottles of environmentally friendly shampoo.

How come everything good for the environment is bad for the hip pocket?

It's not easy for families to be green, particularly when it puts them in the red. I considered $24 for 1000 millilitres of shampoo exorbitant. Then I considered the cost to the environment of buying another set of shampoos, in another set of plastic containers every three or four weeks.

"Thank you," I gulped, wondering how $24 worth of shampoo would wash with my husband, Rob.

With one-quarter of the food budget blown on politically correct shampoo and conditioner, I considered how else I could save the environment and spend a fortune. Going green is all very well, but who wants to turn thoroughly green when they see the bill?

It was not always so. Once, buying in bulk meant buying cheaply. Once, you could go to the local bulk health-food store and buy everything from cornflour to crackers in bulk. But these days, the bulk of my shopping ends up in the bin and has little messages printed on it, like "Keep Australia Beautiful" and "Please dispose of thoughtfully."

Disposing of all this in our overflowing bin made me very thoughtful indeed. I wanted to buy biscuits without the little plastic trays, yoghurt in refillable pots, toothpaste without the box, cheese without the plastic wrap. I wanted a clear conscience as well as a clear bin.

"Why don't you join the food co-op?" suggested the man at the local environment store. So what if it cost the earth to save the earth? I was thinking of my children's future. I called the co-op and asked the woman who runs it how much it cost to join.

Saving the earth would take time, she explained—my personal, precious, limited time. It seems you can't join unless you join the local barter scheme, swapping your personal skills and services for other people's skills and services, or in exchange for "auras", units that you can save in order to buy other goods and services later.

How kind to pay in kind, but the kind of payment they were asking was beyond my means. The only personal time I have is usually spent on urgent business in the smallest room in the house. To amass enough auras for $100 worth of food would take me a few eras.

But I was prepared to consider it if I could do a one-stop green shop and still stay in the black. "And can you get things like biscuits and shampoo?" I asked eagerly.

There was a pause. "We only sell whole foods," the co-op woman said. It seemed you could buy a whole lot of ingredients for biscuits, but then you had to bake your own.

Still, I was determined to make a difference, even if it meant mortgaging my future as well as my future earnings. Determined that is, until I saw the local paper. It seems our green belt is about to become a brown belt, as the Planning Minister, Mr Maclellan, has karate-chopped resident protests and rezoned the bush and farm area to residential.

What is the point of saving shampoo bottles when concerned residents cannot even save a stretch of bush and farmland as a buffer zone between forests and suburbia?

I am still determined to make a difference, of course, but it will not be by recycling the cereal box. It will be at the ballot box.

HAIR TODAY, GONE TOMORROW

15 March 1995

LONG HAIR has always been fashionable for women, even in Biblical times. "If a woman have long hair, it is a glory to her," it says in Corinthians.

But these days, it depends where that long hair is. Hair that you can sit on is fashionable only if it starts on your head.

It is one of the cruel ironies of middle age that as men lose it, women gain it. And once they gain it, women are duty-bound to lose it.

There are only two places women are allowed to have hair these days and, even there, the protagonists of political correctness draw the bikini line.

After 15 years of remaining determinedly hirsute, a friend announced last week she was thinking of joining the razor gang.

"I think I might have to start shaving my legs," she said, idly plaiting the curling tendrils on her calf-muscle.

Shaving your legs is one thing, but what happens when the curling tendrils are creeping from under your chin?

It is common knowledge that giving birth ruins your figure. But few books tell you that it also ruins your face. It starts with one long stray hair that is furtively and frequently plucked and ends with a job in the circus.

Unless, of course, you visit Madam Zap. You may tweeze with ease and wax to the max, but nothing works as well as waving that magic wand, otherwise known as electrolysis.

My first visit was furtive and fearful. But these days, I find myself actually looking forward to it, as it's the only chance I get to lie down without a baby attached to me. I can even prattle between prods.

"It's very common," assured Madam Zap, when I asked her how many women were turning into men. "A lot of women do have The Problem."

The Problem, she said, is that everyone thinks they are the only ones with The Problem.

Of course, according to popular mythology, this is not a problem for feminists. Like Miss Muffett's spider, they are always depicted as unashamedly "hairy-legged".

But I will let you in on a secret. It is not feminism that causes hirsuteness, but hormones, or rather lack of them. "It's caused by a drop in oestrogen as you get older," says Madam Zap.

However, feminist author Dale Spender, blames The Problem on men. The Problem would not exist, she once wrote, if men did not equate being feminine with being hairless.

But it's not the husbands who usually complain about their wives sudden lack of femininity, says Madam Zap. "Usually the kids will tell them." When you get a shaver for Mother's Day instead of a peeler, you know its time to wax lyrical.

For some, rejecting the electrolysis wand is rejecting ageism. The "bearded toothless hag", the caricature of the aged woman, haunts us all.

As Germaine Greer says in *The Change*: "Even those of us who look good know that the secret marks of age, the witch-marks are there. The proliferation of moles and wens,(sic) the sags and wrinkles at knees and elbows, the pads on our knuckles, the spurs on our heels, the thinning of our hair, the bristles that sprout on our chins, all are easily hidden, but we know that they are there."

Ms Greer, whom I might otherwise regard as a mentor, adds: "If we were to be hauled off and stripped naked at our witch-trial, they would be seen."

Over my dead, perfectly hairless, body.

A SMALL SPACE THAT'S ALL MY OWN

22 March 1993

"I CAN'T hear you!" I screamed to my son, Johannes, as I resolutely plunged my hands in the soapy dishwater, determined not to leave my post.

"What?" he screeched back.

"Don't shout from room to room. If you want to talk to me, come here!" I yelled, practising just what I was preaching against.

It seems our house is too big to allow conversations to be conducted comfortably from room to room, yet never big enough for our needs. Or should I say my needs.

It is all very well to share the marriage bed, but why do we have to share the whole house, particularly a house that doesn't have a study?

In *The Wit and Wisdom of Australian Women*, by Margaret Geddes, writer Elizabeth Jolley says: "I think it's barbaric when people get married and they lose their privacy. Houses should be built with lots of little rooms so everyone can have a room with a table in it." Far away from the cold night air, with one enormous chair . . . ah, wouldn't it be loverly!

Of course, in our parents' and grandparents' day, houses never had studies. They had spare rooms, which were often sewing rooms, or rooms where the ironing was piled and washing was aired. "Paperwork", as family business was known then, was mostly done on the kitchen table.

But we have neither spare room nor study, so contrary to Virginia Woolf's decree that "a woman must have money and a room of her own if she is to write fiction", I have a corner of the lounge—the same corner that my two-year-old daughter, Greta, finds herself banished to when she blows raspberries and stamps her foot instead of doing what she is told.

I, too, have been banished. When Greta graduated from a cot to a bed, I graduated from the nursery to the lounge where, for two days a week when the children are at school and creche, I have a corner of a room of my own.

The rest of the time, I have a corner in my head.

The Japanese, I once heard, cannot afford the luxury of personal space, so they must develop the capacity to create personal inner space: a type of mental privacy. So it is with me.

For years, women have joked about men and their sheds, where weary husbands could escape family dramas.

Those of us without sheds must use their heads.

But even then there are space invaders. We had planned to hire a skip for the garden rubbish, but my husband, Rob, who had volunteered to organise it, had lost the piece of paper with the phone number on it. "Perhaps you've got it?" he suggested.

"Me? How would I have it?"

"I just thought you might have seen it lying around. You're the keeper of papers."

And the keeper of lunch dates, birthdays, anniversaries, cheque books, bills-payment dates, and shopping lists.

In the debate about sharing housework, one important factor is often forgotten: sharing responsibility for remembering the domestic trivia of family life. Telling someone: "Relax and I'll cook your dinner" is not relaxing for them if you are calling from the kitchen "Where's the can opener?" or "Do we have any tomatoes?"

Man has not yet conquered outer space, but for years he has dominated our inner space.

I will get a room of my own eventually. We are planning to build one in the garden.

But a room of your own with a table and a chair, where you may leave the clutter and drama of family life behind, is no good if the clutter is still all in your head.

FUNDRAISING—IT'S AND EDUCATION

28 March 1995

HEY, I've got a great idea for raising money. Let's you and me make some cakes and set up a table in the middle of the street and sell them.

Of course, if we add up our labor and the cost of the ingredients, and our time, and the cost of hiring the trestle table, or if it was borrowed, the time and petrol to pick it up, and the time each person is rostered on the stall, we'd have to charge $20 for the cake, not $2.

But since no one would buy a lop-sided chocolate cake for $20, we'll have to keep prices low, and if the lop-sided chocolate cake is melting and sweating in the sun at 11.55am, five minutes before the last person rostered has to go and pick up their kids from basketball, then it should surely be offered at a discount? Perhaps $1?

And if there are still no takers, you can take it home free.

Free? That's a $20 chocolate cake you've got there!

Still, the box of donated donuts sold well, and with the raffle tickets for the dinner-for-two at the local restaurant, $150 was raised—almost enough to put two flywire screens on the windows of the portable classroom at the local primary school.

Phew, I'm glad it's all over for us at least. But don't forget to buy a sausage at the high school sausage sizzle next week. It took Mrs Kafoops, the secretary, 20 phone calls to get the meat donated, and somebody's cousin who owns a bakery in Reservoir donated the bread, which had to be picked up by 8am so that they could set up the stall in Belgrave by 9am.

And then there was the barbecue, and the time and cost of refilling the gas bottle and the roster for picking up the kids so that they can learn that two and two is not enough.

Of course, it rained, but that just added an extra sizzle to the sausages, which, if all costs were taken into account should have to be sold for at least $4 each, but who's going to pay $4 for a lousy sausage? So they sold for $1 in bread, and $1.30 with coleslaw or onions.

Mrs Kafoops stayed up till midnight chopping the coleslaw, but then she always does, to make up for all those rotten sods who insist on going to bed early so they can get up in time for the kindergarten working bee.

Thank goodness for Mrs Kafoops, and thank goodness for Chocomalts, which come in a big red handy fund-raising pack of 20 that the kids can carry down the street and sell to the neighbours—that is if they don't bump into the neighbors' kids coming up the street to sell Chocomalts to us. Wait till Nana and Pa visit, dear. I'm sure they won't mind parting with $3 from their pension to buy a packet.

Then when you've sold them all you can go triumphantly back to school and write a nice little essay about A Day in the Life of a Penny, and how the penny, or dollar, or whatever you like to call it, starts out to buy ingredients for a lopsided chocolate cake, then a packet of Chocomalts, and eventually ends up paying for flywire.

But if no one can stomach any more Chocomalts, get Daddy to take them to work, where nicotine is banned, but caffeine is welcomed.

Mummy will make a sign: "Sick of Sultana Bran? Weary of Weeties? Try NEW Chocomalts! The perfect office brekky! Only $3. Just like a chocolate milkshake only crunchy."

Of course, if you add up the time it took Mummy to make the sign and Daddy to flog them in his lunch hour, they should have cost $5 a box, but hell, who's going to pay $5 for a box of Chocomalts when they sell them at Kmart for $2.50?

Etc, etc, etc . . .

A TOUCHY SUBJECT WHEN
WOLVES ARE AT THE DOOR

4 April 1995

THERE it was, silvery gleaming, with a long phallic hose and a "power head" that was penetrating deep into my carpet and spurting forth two years of accumulated dust.

"What would your husband say if you just bought it?" the demonstrator was saying.

"The same thing I'd say if he went and spent $900 without consulting me," I said.

But she persisted. She was offering me a simple "payment plan" or alternatively, I could pay for half on my credit card now and half later, "so that you can get it in your home immediately," she said seductively.

I hadn't realised it was that urgent. When I woke that morning, I was blissfully ignorant of the fact that I was endangering the health of myself and my children by not spending $900 on a vacuum cleaner.

It had occurred to me, however, that I would endanger their health and welfare if I didn't pay the rates and the mortgage, as there would be no carpet to vacuum as there would be no house to put the carpet in.

It's all a matter of priorities. Hers was to sell as many vacuum cleaners as she could. Mine was to keep the family business in the black, a roof over our heads and food on the table.

Working from home makes you vulnerable to those people who also work from home—your home or anybody else's in which they can get their foot in the door.

The quick familiarity with which she established herself and the urgent authority in her voice was disturbing but predictable. What was more disturbing was the encouragement to buy now and pay the price for deceiving my husband later. It is an old trick that bore disastrous results for low-income families dealing with the former department-store giant, Waltons, 20 years ago, a friend who is a consumer advocate said.

Wives were encouraged to buy goods on credit without their husband's knowledge. Such contracts were coded HDNK (Husband

Does Not Know) so that travelling salesmen collecting payments (often $10 out of the fortnightly pension) could be discreet if hubby was home.

These days, of course, most couples are much more democratic about the family finances.

But for women of my generation, who saw the "house keeping" money doled out to their mothers in the form of $20 left under the sugar bowl, keeping your own money has been even more vital than keeping your own name.

So how is it now that I find myself without my own money?

The truth is that my husband has no money of his own either, for like most couples, after paying the mortgage and the bills there is nothing left.

Going Dutch on bills and going on a spree with the rest might be all very well for couples without children. But when one is bringing home the bacon and the other is cooking it, it is very difficult to assess each person's financial contribution to the marriage.

There is no financial independence in these circumstances, only financial interdependence.

But money is a touchy subject and my consumer friend says couples are often more open about what they do in the bedroom than what they do with their money. In fact, it seems for some couples, sex and money are inextricably linked.

Another older friend was complaining recently that since her husband had lost his job, he had also lost interest in her. "He is so cold," she complained. "No cuddles! No nothing." It was a case of no cash, no pash.

So she stormed out in search of someone with a great big fat . . . wallet.

THE TROUBLE WITH DAME SLAP'S SCHOOL

11 April 1995

ONCE upon a time, naughty little pixies and brownies were sent to Dame Slap's school but, as few of them were ever rehabilitated by the constant humiliation and pain of physical punishment, this is no longer recommended.

Still, Dame Slap was an influential educator and most parents will find themselves at least tempted to resort to her methods, especially when they are tired and provoked. And most older brothers and sisters will be tempted too.

"I just gave her a little slap," my 10-year-old son, Johannes, said recently, after I found his two-year-old sister, Greta, wailing.

Admittedly, an unprovoked attack of pinching and kicking by a cranky two-year-old is unpleasant, but from my experience, hitting back magnifies rather than solves the problem. "Use your head not your hand," I said. "Move away and ignore her. If you can't, then call me and I'll remove her."

Of course, I am ashamed to admit that I have not always practised what I preached.

Like most parents, I have occasionally lost my temper, and I have always regretted it. As I have a bad temper, the punishment never fitted the crime and the fear and anger in my children's eyes at the time shames me still.

After one or two outbursts like that, I learnt that it was I, not them, who needed disciplining. How could I teach them self-control if I could not control myself?

While EPOCH, a London-based campaign to end physical punishment worldwide, says "hitting people is wrong and children are people too", a recent American survey showed that this continues to be a common child-rearing practice among American parents.

The report, published in *The Washington Post*, cited a survey of 200 mothers of young children that found 42 per cent had spanked their children in the previous week. Not surprisingly, two-year-olds were the ones most likely to be spanked, or if we use the term that we would use if adults were treated in this way—physically assaulted.

The article went on to say what most guilty parents fear—that the only lesson this teaches is that hurting people is the best way to get what you want, and children who are hit are more likely to grow up to be serial killers, alcoholics and child abusers.

EPOCH says it's not a matter of parents' rights versus children's rights, but of upholding human rights.

The trouble is that if you don't advocate smacking as a form of discipline, some people presume you don't advocate any discipline. The study concluded that the best discipline was a combination of rules and procedures, such as time out, reasoning and rewards for good behavior.

Which means parents who do not smack should also be rewarded for their good behavior, because it takes time, energy, patience and a sense of humor to outwit the average toddler, something that is often sapped in the wee hours of the night when the average toddler is keeping the average parent awake. And children whose parents favor negotiation often become expert negotiators themselves.

Trying to get Greta to sleep the other night, I lay down beside her in our bed, calmly refusing her pleas to get up. Finally, she came up with a plea I couldn't ignore, especially as she was thrashing around on my side of the bed.

"I need nappy change! Change my nappy!" she demanded.

"I'll bring a nappy in here," I said.

"No! No!" she wailed. "On my table in Greta's room."

Reluctantly, I allowed her to get up. Triumphantly, she marched out down the stairs to where Rob and Johannes were "playing Simpsons" (chess) and, predictably, she did not need a nappy change.

All I wanna do is dream

18 April 1995

IT IS a beautiful night. A beautiful night for cruising down the highway, radio blaring, the rhythm pounding in my brain, or is that my heart?

The sun is setting behind me, shedding a soft pink glow over the sky, the road is clear ahead. Think I'll pack it in and buy a pick-up . . . la la la . . . start a brand new day.

It's a beautiful night for listening to music, for sitting in a sun-dappled beer garden, sipping wine and letting the wine and the music seep into my limbs and soul.

Remember those nights? Remember when you were young, you shone like the sun. Shine on you crazy diamond. Where everything seemed magnified and, literally, magnificent? Those were the days, my friend, we thought they'd never end . . .

Those were the days when there was nothing that had to be done, but anything could be done—grasshopper days, when the cycle of toil in family life, the cleaning, the wiping (the endless wiping) was unknown to us.

These were the things our mothers did—all mothers did. That was their job, their destiny, even those who rankled against it and reminded us that they had been tricked into it. Trick or treat, they were stuck with it.

They may have created us, but we were the creators now. They were the ones who prepared the canvas. We were the ones who painted it and the town red, blue, yellow. Yellow is the color of my true love's hair . . .

Their wings had been clipped but ours were ready to unfurl. We didn't worry about getting them burned. We did not see ourselves as moths, or even butterflies. We were not fragile, temporary creatures. We were birds: strong, sharp-eyed and free. Some day I'll fly away! We went where we wanted. We went all the way.

Tonight, this starry, starry night, I want to go all the way, again. All the way to the city, to its throbbing heart and groin, where every stranger is a potential lover, and every street is a new path to glory.

110

I search for a sign . . . sign, sign, everywhere a sign . . .

Finally, I see it flashing and winking at me in a come-hither fashion as I pull into the car park, my car pulsating with music, loud and rude.

Some youths are parked near the entrance, their car doors open, like great birds with wings raised to let the cool evening air pass through. They stare. Maybe they're looking for a hard-headed woman but it ain't me, babe, I think as I glide past.

I saunter inside, pushing through the crowd to the front. Dream up, dream up, let me fill your cup.

I lean against the counter. There is a silence as the woman who is serving looks up. "Yes?"

"I'll have a packet of large disposable nappies and a packet of Gastrolite," I say nonchalantly, as I hand over my last $22 and head back home in the family station wagon to Rob, who is in bed with a bug, and Greta, whom I have left running around the lounge room, dangerously naked.

The sun has finally set, pink has turned to black. As I glance into my rear-vision mirror, I see the sign I was searching for flashing goodbye at me: Chemist: Open 9am to 9pm.

I'm homeward bound. Home, where my thought's escaping, home were my music's playing, home, where my love lies waiting, silently for me . . . even if he is lying waiting with a bucket and a towel handy.

Survival of the Freest

25 April 1995

MY husband loves programs on food—food cooked by men.

While most family cooks these days are still women, most of the television cooks are men. Take Floyd. There he was, crouched in a 16th-century kitchen fireplace (which looked twice the size of my entire 20th-century kitchen), about to pour a litre of wild boar's blood into the wild boar stew for authentic thickening.

As the chief cook in our household, I am considering being offended. Not about the boar's blood, but about the impossibility of ever being as fabulously exotic as Floyd, or Gabriel, or Geoff, or the two Ians, or any of the great chefs of Europe and Australia.

Even if I found some cute little gourmet butcher in Victoria Street or Glenferrie Road who would sell me some dainty fillets of wild boar, I'd still have to boil an egg for the kids, or open a tin of spaghetti.

The trouble with Floyd, Geoff, the two Ians and Gabriel is that not one of them tells you how to make "sun-dried tomato and garlic risotto with stewed mushroom caps and parmesan" while staggering around the kitchen with a two-year-old attached to your leg.

Nor do they tell you what to do when the 10-year-old admits he prefers baseball caps to mushroom caps, or what to do with the leftovers after scraping them off the high chair. Or what to do when your toddler's consuming passion is "yoyyies" (lollies)?

There is always one vital ingredient that these super chefs leave out when they demonstrate the fine art of cooking: the baby-sitter.

It is left to the female super-chefs to discover that a toddler in the kitchen at mealtime is a recipe for disaster.

Sure, there may be more men in the kitchen these days but, as one friend commented while sweating over a hot stove recently, it is still mostly the women who do the survival cooking and the men who do the gourmet cooking. She cited her French friend as an example. "Once a week, he cooks this fabulous dish for friends. But she shops for it and cleans up and claps afterwards."

Mon dieu! This man is one smart cookie, I thought. Survival cooking is a chore because the diner is usually more interested in what's on the telly than what's on the plate. Gourmet cooking is fun because your guests will actually eat the main course without being bribed by dessert.

In our household, Rob is too busy out hunting the wild boar to get home in time to cook it, so I am both survival and gourmet cook, (although he does occasionally make a great pizza).

The trouble with being a survival cook is that everyone thinks that their survival depends on you. And I mean everyone even those who are perfectly capable of feeding themselves.

In our house, it starts with the kookaburras in the morning and ends with the possums at night. In between there are the parrots, the cockies, the pigeons, the magpies, the bush birds and, of course, Rob, Johannes and Greta.

I used to have an open-door policy, until one mother possum came bounding into the lounge room recently and scuttled up the video cabinet. We bribed her out with a banana, which she ate while perched on the back of a kitchen chair before being escorted out.

Bob Geldof's song *Feed the World* was designed to raise money, but with me it only raises ire. It is all very well for a do-gooder rich bloke like him to demand that we feed the world, but who's going to do the cooking?

LET'S DO IT, LET'S FALL ASLEEP

2 May 1995

"I THINK I might come home for lunch tomorrow," my friend's husband told her nonchalantly one day. Naturally, she presumed she was lunch.

The children were at school, so she got the best wine glasses out and was ready to slip into something more comfortable, like bed. But when he walked in the door, he made a beeline for the fridge, not the bedroom. "I think I'll just have a ham sandwich and get going," he said.

My friend was furious and frustrated: not just because he preferred ham to cheesecake, but because he had failed to seize the moment. And let's face it child-free moments are hard to come by.

Family therapists may caution that families who play together, stay together. But it is not just family time that keeps a family together, it is couple time.

Most couples, though, don't get anymore than a couple of minutes.

"What became of romance?" chorus the singing group Manic Mothers in their tape *Now Playing At A Kitchen Near You*. It is a chorus repeated by many couples with children, particularly young children.

It is ironic that most couples begin their sex life furtively and in confined spaces and end up the same way. The front seat of a Volkswagen looks like the Grand Canyon compared to the shower in the ensuite, (which, complete with plastic chair, is beginning to look positively erotic).

Most books on sex tell you how to do it, but not how to get the time and opportunity to do it once you are married with children. It's all very well to say do it after the children have gone to bed, but what if they don't stay in bed?

"I need a glass of water," Johannes says, re-emerging for the fourth time after going to bed. "I need a cold shower," says Rob.

The American sex therapist Dr Ruth, in the Guide for Married Lovers, makes brief reference to "kidus interruptus", in answer to the question "What if the child walks in on you when you are making love?"

114

"This is nothing," she says dismissively. "If the child asks what you are doing, just say you are making love and let it go at that."

You will have to let it go at that because everything else will have gone too, especially your desire to get caught in the act again.

In our youth, sleeping together was a euphemism for "doing it"; now it's just a euphemism. We may share the same bed, but there's no guarantee that we will be in it together.

"Go big bed?" says Greta at bed time. "Just one minute?"

Eight hours later I wake up to find I have been taken advantage of again, but alas, not by my husband.

It seems the only times we get to share the bed together are when we are sharing a bug. I had started swimming to try to get fit, but all I got was a fit of coughing.

However, all was not lost, according to one family member old enough to know better. "They say a sneeze is one-eighth of an orgasm," he said encouragingly, as I sneezed for the seventh time.

A few days later, when the only thing turned on was the heater, Rob and I sat sharing our colds and a movie. We had planned to share a bottle of wine, too, but both felt too out of it, so we decided to go to bed.

"I'm going to get some cough mixture. Do you want some?" I offered.

"Can we drink it from the same glass," he asked, as we snuggled down for a sleezy, er, sneezy, night together.

Diet of bananas is enough to drive anyone fruity

9 May 1995

Bananas in Pyjamas are coming down the stairs.
Bananas in pyjamas are giving us nightmares . . .

OKAY, so I changed the words . . . but wouldn't you after the six millionth time?

While everyone else is listening to . . . hey, what is everybody else listening to? Having children has created a cultural generation gap in our household. One minute my generation was bopping and hopping to *Hey, hey we're the Monkees!* and the next we were bopping and hopping to "Three little monkeys jumping on the bed, one fell off and hurt her head, Mummy rang the doctor who came and said . . . . Turn that bloody thing off!"

But what happens when it's not the tape or the telly that's been turned on, but your child?

"I wuv you, you wuv me, we're good fwiends as fwiends should be, wiv a great big hug and a kiss from me to you, won't you say you wuv, meeee, tooooo!" Greta croons, singing the theme song for Barney (a purple dinosaur, for those not familiar), the minute she is strapped into her car seat. This is soon followed by Bananas in Pyjamas, Dinga Danga Darecrow (Dingle Dangle Scarecrow) and a string of others.

When she first started doing it, we were enchanted. Now, 10,000 renditions later, we long to be un-chanted.

"Bloody Barney!" curses Rob. "American crap!"

"Sesame Street is American, too," I point out.

But I admit that when I hear the song, I wish Barney were extinct. However, as babysitters, I find Barney and Big Bird indispensable.

Robert Franklyn, who has been at the frontline of kids' culture in the city's ABC shop for the past six years, says kids like Australian bananas as much as they like overgrown birds and dinosaurs from America. "The children's culture concept has really exploded in terms of

116

material available and Australian gear is right up there in standard and presentation."

Most of the countries at the recent conference on children's television in Melbourne had already snapped up the Australian-made Bananas, he says. "America was the last to sign. The Bananas are a world unto themselves." A world driven by a marketing campaign that would rival a US presidential election. Which makes me wonder what effect this has on kids and their culture, as well as parents and their sanity?

Dr June Factor, the author of a string of books on Australian children's folklore, such as *Far Out Brussell Sprout!* says there has always been a culture for children, provided by adults, that runs parallel to the culture of children, which is what children do among themselves. The difference today is that in a market society like ours, some of it becomes a commodity.

Children are very influenced by commercial culture, agrees Dr Factor, but while some people bemoan the influence of American "cultural imperialism", they sometimes overlook that before that it was British imperialism. "But that isn't to say that local children don't take the stuff and put their own spin on it. While they mimic, they also mock."

That's true. Johannes, who agrees with Rob when it comes to Barney, likes singing the Barney song too, but changes the words to: "I hate you, you hate me . . ."

While he quite enjoys the Bananas, and Australian children's entertainers Franciscus Henri and Peter Combe, his taste is a little more sophisticated these days. "What's *The Brady Bunch* like?" he asked eagerly, always looking for another reason to stay up past his bedtime.

"Like Barney for adults," I said.

That was enough, he darted upstairs to do two hours of keyboard practice.

OUT OF THE MOUTHS OF BABES

16 May 1995

I HAVE never been one of those parents who made it a policy not to swear in front of the children. I reckon people like that are bloody hypocrites.

You either swear, or you don't. And if you do, you make it clear to your children that what may be acceptable behavior in your home is not necessarily so in someone else's.

That is, until your two-year-old makes it clear to you that she thinks swearing is unacceptable behavior anywhere.

"Don't say that, Mummy! You naughty girl!" Greta admonished me the other day, after I had impolitely told her and Johannes to be quiet while Rob and I were trying to have a chat.

"I'm sorry, Greta," I said, embarrassed and contrite for the first time in many years.

Rob and Johannes were ecstatic. "Good on you Greta!" Rob hooted with pleasure. "At last, she'll sort you out!" he gloated.

I admit things had got out of hand. Swearing was the only vice I had left, and I was bloody well determined to keep it.

For me, swearing has been as cathartic as a double brandy, but a lot safer. For a start you can swear and drive. In fact, for me it's as mandatory as wearing a seat belt, but designed for release not restraint.

Jeannette Harrison, a lecturer in early-childhood development and parent education at Swinburne University of Technology, says an open-policy on swearing is fine as long as the child understands when it is inappropriate.

"I don't believe that as parents we have to change everything (we do)," she says. However, she says problems may arise if an adult takes offence at the child swearing and becomes autocratic about it and makes it an issue.

"Then the child sees, 'Wow! Look at the attention that got me. When I want attention, I know exactly what to do.'"

But what happens when the children, not the adults take offence?

Greta has always been sensitive to my moods, so my perverse pleasure in swearing has been diminished by the realisation that the anger associated with it makes her genuinely upset.

A few days later, searching vainly for a car park, I let forth again.

Greta, who had been singing "I'm a dinga danga darecrow!" in the back seat, suddenly stopped mid-song and waved her finger at me again, saying: "Don't say that, Mummy! I happy!"

Again, I felt contrite and guilty. My anger was spoiling her happiness. It was not the words that upset her. She is too young to understand them. But she understood the emotions behind them. Which is why I am quitting swearing—or at least trying to.

I am not planning to supress my anger in front of my children in future, but I will try to save it for the really important things, like poverty in the Third World and mud on the carpet.

And when I do express it, I plan to follow the lead of one of my own childhood heroes: Winnie the Pooh.

The other day when I banged my head on Johannes's bunk, I merely winced and said. "Oh bother!"

But like anyone trying to break a habit, I was keen for a little encouragement.

"Did you notice anything, just then?" I hinted to Johannes, as I rubbed my head.

"No," he said, snuggling down with a book.

"I didn't swear," I said triumphantly.

He smiled encouragingly, then told me how at a friend's place recently the adults had been talking about what to do when children use "magic words".

That's the crux of it, I thought later. "Oh bother!" doesn't have the same magical effect as F . . . . s . . . !"

But no matter how much bother I get into on the road to reform, I am trying.

I swear.

A DICKLER FOR CORRECT PRONUNCIATION

23 May 1995

LEARNING to talk can be a difficult and disconcerting business. While Greta has no trouble with her Rs, she cannot say her Ss yet, substituting either F or D.

"Go and see Hunni," I say sleepily each morning, trying to fob her off to see her older brother, Johannes, as she bounces all over "big bed".

"Hunni afeep," she says, ignoring the fact that, until she came in, I was also "afeep".

But while she says "fring" for swing, for some reason she has no trouble at all saying "Simpsons", "Dow!" and "I didn't do it!" All very cute, except when she substitutes D for S.

While walking down a bush track with Johannes and me recently, she announced loudly: "I want a big dick like Hunni!"

We were rather taken aback, until we realised she wanted a big stick like Johannes.

Later in bed that night, as she was sucking her bottle, she announced: "Hunni got a big dick. I got a little dick."

"Say stick," I prompted.

"Dick", she replied triumphantly.

The next day, Rob persisted. "Did you have a big stick when you played in the puddle," he asked.

"No, I have a little dick," she corrected. "Hunni have a big dick."

"Say sssssnake," said Rob, trying to change the subject.

"No 'nake, I catch fish," she corrected again. Which only goes to show that how much and what your toddler can say is all a matter of interpretation.

"Paul can say chocolate," a friend's husband said of their two-year-old son, when she came home from work one day.

"What word does he use?" she replied sagely.

"Lottie!" said her delighted husband.

To us, Greta can say anything, but to really understand her you have to be around her a lot.

"What did she say?" asked her Nana recently. Although she sees her Nana and Pa almost weekly, it is still not enough for them to grasp Greta talk. In the old days, they'd call it baby talk, but don't tell Greta.

The secret to encouraging language is to accept that while she says she wants a big dick, I know she really is talking about a big stick, so that's what I reinforce. (Perhaps this is where Freud got confused?)

Dr Cheryl Semple, of the Department of Languages and Literacy Education at Melbourne University's Institute of Education, says adults are continually presenting correct language models and, as long as they respond in a way that supports and encourages, then children will learn happily. Constantly telling children they are "making mistakes" only encourages them to shut up, she says. Children need to hypothesise about language, to take risks and experiment, she says.

Fortunately, most parents seem to know naturally what to do to encourage language. But that doesn't mean all children will respond equally. Some will start experimenting early, others may not talk until later but will then use more complex language, depending on individual ways of learning, Dr Semple says. "You have to have input before you get output."

But before you get on the blower to start boasting to friends and relatives about what your child can say, remember verbal skills come long before telephone skills.

"Say 'Hello Nana'," I prompt Greta, holding the phone out encouragingly.

Delighted, Greta stops trying to interrupt me, grasps the phone eagerly, and is immediately struck dumb. All Nana gets is heavy breathing and a lot of head nodding.

"Say goodbye to Nana," I say, giving up.

Greta drops the receiver on the floor and runs out of the room shouting, "Hunni, I talk to Nana!"

MAKING TIME FOR PLAYTIME

30 May 1995

IT IS a beautiful autumn day, too beautiful to stick to our original plan of shopping and bill paying. Instead, we have gone to the playground. Greta is standing inside an enormous tyre, playing shop.

I admit it was my idea. "Is this your shop?" I asked, handing her an old two-cent coin and the scrunched-up plastic wrap from my newspaper.

For the next 15 minutes, we traded the carefully wrapped coin for many imaginary purchases, accompanied by a constant babble of commentary from Greta.

We could have played the game anywhere, but the big tyre, waist-high for her, captured her imagination. However, it did little for mine, and I must admit I tried to read the paper between purchases and felt frustrated and guilty about all the paid work I had to do at home that I couldn't do until Greta's creche days. Then I felt guilty again: why couldn't I enjoy these precious moments?

Later that afternoon, I was tempted to turn on the television for her, but I resisted, telling her to look in her toy box instead.

Out of the corner of my eye, I saw her wrapping her doll, Olivia, in an old cloth nappy and singing a lullaby that I used to sing. Then, using the footrest of her high chair as a nappy table, she said: "I wipe 'Rivia's bum!"

"Say 'bottom'. It's nicer," I said.

"Bottom," she said obediently, then inquired, "You got a dirty bum, Rivia?"

For the next hour, she enacted this routine, as I washed dishes and made tea, fascinated and guilty once more that I had earlier tried to rush her through her play.

In trying to keep up with my schedule of housework, shopping and bill paying, perhaps I had been preventing her from the equally important work of play?

Kay Plowman, author of a new book called *Let Children Play*, published by the Victorian Playgroup Association, says play is vital to a child's physical, emotional and intellectual development. But a parent or adult should be a partner in the process, rather than an initiator.

As the title of the book suggests, Ms Plowman believes many children these days are seldom allowed to just play. "They (adults and parents) don't give them enough time, they don't dress them appropriately and a lot of backyards these days are so sterile. Now they get taken to this and that. When is there time to play? It's so natural, so essential for a child just to work out what they're thinking, even when they are tiny."

We also have to get away from the idea that play for a baby or a small child has to involve a lot of plastic toys, Ms Plowman says.

Twigs, leaves, the hose in the garden, the pots and pans in the kitchen cupboard, rice and other dry ingredients for pouring, or any (safe) object around the home are all good toys. "Real things are more important to a child than the plastic miniatures of everything, although they are sometimes good too," she says.

Real things like my earrings in the special jewellery box that Johannes gave me for Mother's Day.

"What are you doing, Greta?" Rob asked the other night when he found her on tiptoe, standing at the dressing table with the box open.

"I just putting them away," she said, reluctantly closing the lid.

But even moments like these, caught red-handed with my precious earrings, are precious moments gone all too soon, according to Kay Plowman.

"Stop and look every now and again and record a memory. My children are in their 20s now and I speak from experience," she says.

TIME FOR THE PATTER OF MORE LITTLE FEET

6 June 1995

WE ARE thinking of adding to our family. Now that Greta is growing up and I am mostly working from home, I feel there is room in our hearts, if not our house, for another family member.

In short, it's time we got a dog.

I had wanted to get one for the children's birthdays in March, but Rob was adamant: we were not going to get something that needed toilet training until Greta was toilet trained. ("Don't make me sound like a tyrant," he says when I read him this.)

But as far as Greta is concerned, using the toilet is just a means to an end: you sit there for 20 seconds so you can push the button for half an hour. So, it looks like our dog will be a long time coming, which is why I am taking this opportunity to work out the appropriate breed for us.

And that's the problem. It seems everyone you talk to thinks their dog is the perfect dog for you.

We had considered a Jack Russell—a perfect choice according to other Jack Russell owners. But according to golden retriever owners, they yap all the time. Golden retrievers are the perfect family dog, we are told, if you don't mind retrieving all their hair from the couch every week. Which is why I should consider a miniature poodle, a miniature poodle owner advised, adding that they are also very intelligent.

"I'm not having a poodle!" declared Rob, who is not really a tyrant, but favors dogs with a mission rather than a mince, such as cattle dogs. Just like Sam, his family dog, or Sergeant Sam, as he is known these days.

Sam was plucked out of retirement recently to help Rob's younger brother ward off potential burglars in his job. However, Sam is so short-sighted he can't see a ball coming, let alone a criminal.

But it's appearances that count and Sam, who will happily chase a cat, looks like he might also chase a cat burglar. And if he doesn't, no matter, you could just pick him up and wave him in front of the burglar's nose—the smell would be enough to frighten anyone off.

But as much as I love Sam, I do not want a dog that is inclined to round up small creatures. I want something small enough for Johannes to handle, but gutsy enough to frighten off intruders. Something that is, dare I say, a little macho, like Macho, a friend's Maltese-Chihuahua cross.

But Macho is too micro to cope with the stairs at our place. I need something small enough to control, but big enough to climb up a mountain without oxygen. Not like my mother's dog, Possum, a tiny long-haired Chihuahua who died several years ago and is still sadly missed.

Possum was lovely to look at and lovely to hold—if you didn't mind holding her for 12 years. Possum, we concluded later, was not a dog after all, but a dog-shaped brooch.

Perhaps I should get a Chinese hairless crested dog, my sister, Juliana, suggested. "They don't get fleas, they don't get ticks, they don't moult, and they don't smell. You don't even have to bath them," she said.

"But think of all the suncreen you'd use," I wailed.

"But they're little dogs. They stay on your lap. They only have to go out side for two hours a day so their pigment doesn't fade. It's the canine you want when you don't really want a canine."

But, doggone it, I want a canine that looks like a canine, even if I don't want it to behave like one.

A SNAG IN HIS IMAGE

13 June 1995

MY husband Rob is worried about his image. He swears he is a New-Age Man, but grumbles that he doesn't come across that way in this column.

"It makes me sound like all I want is my food, my house clean and a bit on the side, and that I dictate what sort of dog we have," he complained when I read him the latest instalment.

Click, click, click, ever the opportunist, I type his concerns into the computer.

"Don't write that down!" he says in exasperation.

Click, click, click, I keep writing.

"Stop it!" he says, trying not to laugh.

Click, click, click. This is getting interesting, I think.

"Stop writing!" he orders, trying to sound cross. "I mean it!"

"Got any other ideas, then?" I ask.

"Nothing to do with me," he says firmly.

Click, click, click, I keep writing.

"Stop it! Stop it!" he pleads, helpless with laughter and frustration.

OK, OK, I'll stop it. Nothing to do with him? Let's talk more generally about the New-Age Man then, or the SNAG (Sensitive New-Age Guy), as he is sometimes known. Is he a myth or just a mythtery?

But in thinking about a particular SNAG that I'm not allowed to mention, I hit a snag. It's hard to be a SNAG when you're heading for the office at 7am and heading back at 7pm.

If I waited for this SNAG to put on the snags for tea and bath the kids, we'd all be eating at 8pm and the kids wouldn't be in bed until 10pm.

When I worked in town, I had a photo on my desk of my SNAG doing the dishes while carrying the baby in the back pack. It hadn't occurred to me that this was anything extraordinary until a colleague said: "That's priceless! Talk about a New-Age Man."

But now I am at home every day, I must admit our roles have become surprisingly traditional.

If you had told me this five years ago, I would have thought you were talking about the wrong woman. I was used to the starring role, not the supporting role. But here we are now playing mothers and fathers in the traditional sense.

Both of us would be happy to reverse roles (especially as Rob complains that by the time he gets home, all the chocolate biscuits are gone), but it would really not be practical. He does not have the flexibility I have to combine paid work with child care. And because of the way we have both been raised, our home-making skills are traditional: I am better at home management and he is better at home maintenance.

The difference, I suppose, between us and previous generations is that this is a temporary choice. And choice is the key word.

The trick for us both will be to avoid getting locked into these chosen roles. I see many "retired" couples, where the husband is the only one who has really retired, because his wife still does all the relentless unpaid work.

And these days there is another snag in the struggle to be a SNAG.

While Sensitive New-Age Guys may be on the increase, Sensitive New-Age workplaces are still rare. Perhaps the best some SNAGs can do for their families in this age of stiff competition and high unemployment, is to keep the wolf from the door, even if that means by the time the SNAG walks in the door at night, the baby is tired and grumpy and all the chocolate biscuits are gone.

A TOY CATALOGUE OF DISASTERS

20 June 1995

IT SEEMS like the answer to your prayers—the new toy catalogue. Here is new hope that your toddler will be entertained by something other than you.

But it only takes a quick flick through to discover that the price of buying quality toys to replace quality time is too high.

Anything highly recommended is usually also highly priced, which is why we joined the toy library.

If you don't mind a few hours library duty now and again, and spending the last few days of every fortnight crawling around your lounge-room floor in search of stray pieces of Lego, marbles, cars or any of the other 211 pieces toys seem to come in these days, the toy library is a joy library.

Not only has it been a money saver for us, it has also been an important lesson for me in just how few toys really seem to interest children or perhaps I should say, my children.

At first I thought the problem was me. I was just choosing the wrong things. Perhaps I was choosing what I would have liked to play with as a child, rather than what Greta preferred? The dolls' house, for instance, I found charming and so did Greta—for about two days. For the other 12 days of the fortnight, we took turns in tripping over it. The same went for most other toys I chose.

But according to English experts, Dr Pam Harris and Toni Arthur, authors of *100 Ways to Amuse Children,* the reason Greta wasn't playing with them was because I wasn't playing with them.

"Many of the bought toys that children acquire and tire of quickly can be made more interesting if an adult sits down with the child and thinks of novel ways of using them, and once into the swing of things children will often be extremely inventive," they advise.

In other words, toys alone are not enough. What children seem to prefer is someone to interact with them and the toy. Perhaps in the days when families were bigger, this burden did not fall so heavily on parents, or perhaps, parents did not feel pressured to play with their children.

But Jeannette Harrison, a lecturer in early child development and parent education at Swinburne University, says it is also important for children to learn to play alone. "In those first two or three years, the most valuable toys are the ones children can do something with, without an adult: things they can put things in and out of, explore, or open and close—what we call 'open-ended' toys."

However, she concedes that most children do prefer an adult to sit with them. "That's where you have to set limits. Tell the child you need to do something else for half an hour and you will play with them after that. Make it a short time and stick to it," she says.

Just as importantly, make sure you follow through with your promise.

Despite our toy catalogue of disasters, there has been one toy from the toy library that has been a spectacular success: the bubble car, a huge plastic Flintstone-style car. The only problem is Greta insists on parking it right in the middle of the lounge room.

I suppose some manufacturers figure any toy bigger than the average television at least stands a chance competing against it.

I was at the toy library again last week, wondering whether it would be politically incorrect to borrow the wooden chainsaw, when it occurred to me that what I really wanted to borrow was not just a toy but a toy room.

"I'll have this," I said, pushing forward a gigantic garage. "And can I borrow the lounge room to go with it?"

THE IMPORTANCE OF NOT BEING EARNEST

27 June 1995

PARENTING is one big contradiction. You wait breathlessly for your children to learn to talk, and then can't wait for them to shut up.

And when you talk, you mostly talk at them rather than to them. "Have you cleaned your teeth? Have you done your homework? Have you got a singlet on?" and "Have you done your piano practice?" seem to be all I say to Johannes these days.

So in a rare moment sitting on the couch watching telly alone while Greta allowed her father to put her to bed, I was glad when Johannes came and sat beside me, cuddled up and asked: "What's 'imperial' mean?"

Having had chats in the past about items on *Behind the News*, such as apartheid and trade wars, I assumed a political context. I explained clearly and concisely about the difference between imperial and metric measurements, which countries still had imperial measurements and why.

Then, inspired by his interest, I started on imperialism, colonialism, cultural dominance and arrogance.

I was just heading into how this, combined with economic problems and racial prejudices, had contributed to the rise of Hitler and the Third Reich, when I began to wonder what had prompted the question.

Was it some school assignment due in tomorrow, or had he seen something on telly to stimulate his thirst for knowledge? Had *The Simpsons* or *Neighbours* touched on one of these weighty issues perhaps?

"Why do you want to know?" I asked.

"It said 'Imperial Leather' on the soap," he said, as he wandered off to make himself a drink.

I felt like a drink, too—one that made me forget what a pompous fool I'd been. It reminded me of that joke about the child who asks: "Where did I come from?" After a lengthy explanation about sex and birth, the mother asks why the child wants to know. "Because Johnny comes from Greece," the child says, or some such thing.

It just shows how easy it is to assume that our children's lives are as complicated as our own, and how even easier it is to complicate things for them.

Talking to Children about Things that Matter, by Sheila and Celia Kitzinger, discusses how parents might approach profound moral and political questions that are raised by their children.

"The way we respond to children's first questioning is a rehearsal for all the other questions that come later, and through encouraging children to question, we prepare the ground for discussion and for sharing ideas about values and human behaviour," they write.

True. But after 10 years of parenthood, I've discovered that it is just as important to talk about things that don't matter and a lot harder.

I don't find it difficult talking about politics, or sex, or death or morals because these are things that interest me. I do find it difficult talking about every frame and every line of dialogue in the latest episode of *The Simpsons,* or the most recently borrowed *Garfield* book, or what you have to do at certain levels of the Monopoly video game, or why we should buy chocolate ice-cream rather than vanilla.

These things, fascinating to the average 10-year-old, are not quite as fascinating when you grow up. But it is these things that are important to Johannes and just as interesting, if not more so, as the meaning of "imperial".

Children do occasionally ask profound questions, and when they do, if they are too profound for you, you can always refer them to a book, or refer to one yourself. But mostly, I have found if you want them to talk to you about the things that matter, first you have to talk a lot about the things that don't.

SEEKING A SISTER, FINDING A FRIEND

4 July 1995

"This is a real family postcard. This is Jane's real family, not her extended family. This is Jane's root family. And this is Jane's sister speaking."

Yes, this is my sister, Juliana, looking very suspicious.

"She feels very suspicious. You can't trust these journalists even if they are family," says Juliana.

We are sitting here, each nursing a brandy, writing this while Greta sleeps.

I want to tell you about my sister. I want to tell everyone about my sister, because for 15 years I have hardly even admitted to having a sister, and now . . . I have not only discovered my sister, but I have found a friend.

Due to the behaviour of our father, a gulf was created between us and the more time passed, the wider it seemed to grow. The wider it became, the riskier it seemed to cross it. Finally, our mother urged us to build a bridge.

It took courage to build it, and even more courage to cross it. But here we are, suddenly on the same side, with that yawning gulf behind us, not between us, getting sloshed together.

"Hi, Juliana Cafarella in her own right (and write) here," my sister says.

She's smart, streetwise, slim (the bitch!) and sassy, my sister.

It's been nearly a year since we first met again. Why did she agree to cross that bridge, I wonder?

"Maturity. Because I was with Macca (her partner) who had a family life and you see family as different. I felt that we had to make the family complete. Unless you put the pieces together, it's not going to work. You have to be strong to go through the process. It's bitter and it hurts but you'll be a better person."

While it was bitter, it was also sweet. I liked her. She liked me. Surprisingly, we had a lot of fun.

But liking each other was not the only shock. "I was shocked when I met you," Juliana said after our first meeting. "You were more woggy looking than I thought. You are a lot like Dad. You're good at twisting words around, like Dad."

Thanks—I think. I had an admission of my own. I was terrified. I'd been told all the time how different we were. Now, the biggest shock was that we weren't. "You seemed like somebody I already knew," I told her.

At that first meeting, we talked for hours and then met over the next few months to talk again, and sing all the old songs of our childhood. Between memories, songs and brandies, we made a tape.

"I play our tape periodically and I get great enjoyment from it," Juliana says. "The music, you're coughing, Greta wakes up . . . we sing one good song and one shitty one, the talking. The concept is nice."

For me, that tape, with me fumbling along on Dad's old guitar, was part of the healing process. But part of the healing, also involved howling. After that first meeting, I was angry and upset over all we'd missed out on together.

But Juliana is more pragmatic: "I don't think we would have got on anyway (earlier). We really were different. I think it's due to the family separating that we have become alike—growth, independence, career paths, broken marriages . . ."

In conclusion?

"In conclusion, we can thank Mum. If it hadn't been for her, we wouldn't have gone through the process of seeing each other."

"Why are you writing this with me?" I ask.

"Because it's part of Jane's postcard from nowhere."

"You don't mind other people reading this?"

"It just doesn't matter."

"So you don't mind?"

"If you don't twist it, I won't mind."

Greta wakes up. We must finish writing this postcard from nowhere.

Having a wonderful time, love
Jane and Juliana.

THE HIDDEN COST OF A HEALTHY FUTURE

18 July 1995

"SHE'S getting tall!" everyone seemed to be saying of Greta all of a sudden.

Rob was shattered. "I don't want to be the shortest in the family," he wailed. He was hoping Greta would take after his side of the family, where platform shoes are mandatory.

As I am tending towards width rather than height myself these days, and Johannes is already up to my chin, it appeared neither of our children would be looking up to us for long. So it was off to the maternal and child health nurse with Greta to see if our great expectations were correct.

Actually, I look forward to my chats with Liz, our local maternal and child health nurse. After weighing and measuring and discussing Greta's development, we talked about which secondary college Johannes might attend in the future, my job, Rob's job and, inevitably, Liz's job.

With all the changes brought by municipal amalgamation, I admit I was relieved to see her still there. Our local council is still implementing the old maternal and child health program which allows unlimited visits.

However, under the new system, overall State Government funding for the maternal and child health program remains the same, but is tied to a program called Healthy Futures, which funds nurses to see children at specific developmental stages. Any additional visits or programs have to be paid for by the council.

According to Liz, some newly formed councils have gone further, making 20 per cent cuts across all community services, including maternal and child health. "People have to pay a subscription to get services which were normally free," she said sadly.

The Government says Healthy Futures improves the service by ensuring that children are assessed at important stages of their development. But Liz and the Maternal and Child Health Consumer Group say Healthy Futures alone is not enough.

For Liz, and other nurses like her, the job is much more than checking developmental milestones; it is about developing a relationship with the parent and child and supporting them when they need it.

We live in a very anti-baby and mother society. The shock of new motherhood and the apartheid and isolation that often goes with it makes these wise women a godsend. Under Healthy Futures many new mothers exhaust their allotted number of visits within the first few months.

Although our local service is continuing at the moment, there is a chance it might be tendered out to private contractors.

"I might have to look around," Liz said. "If local government doesn't fund it, I just think it would be a job that wouldn't have the caring element in it and I wouldn't like it."

After 20 years, leaving would be a huge wrench. But not being able to do the job well would be even harder, she said. "There's so much more to it than eight visits in two-and-a-half years. You really feel you know people. You wouldn't be able to help people if you didn't know them."

As for us, and thousands like us, our healthy future depends on Liz and all her colleagues. Parenting is such an unpredictable job, and often our own parents are so far away that we frequently need someone to turn to we can trust.

Nurses like Liz have supported families for years. Now it is up to us to support them.

PS: We have nothing to worry about. Greta is still just below average in height and weight—and way above average for head size!

A TIME FOR EVERYTHING—INCLUDING RIGHTS

15 August 1995

ELIZABETH, a business acquaintance of mine, is expecting her first baby in three months. Elizabeth is planning to take one month off work before the baby is born and two months after through choice, not circumstance.

She did not tell me this. Another business acquaintance mentioned it for the same reason I mention it now. She, like me, was in awe.

As mothers doing paid and unpaid work, we know how difficult it is to juggle both jobs when children are older, let alone when they are infants.

But it is not just this knowledge that puts us in awe. It is the notion that bringing a new life into the world, and all that it entails physically and emotionally, could be treated in such an unremarkable fashion.

Having a baby is a profound, life-changing event or am I the only one who found it so?

Perhaps Elizabeth, or more to the point, her boss, thinks that having a baby is like taking long-service leave, or some kind of sabbatical; a kind of work break that, if you are organised enough, will not make a huge difference to your life?

Perhaps she fears that if she chooses to stay home for six or 12 months, she will be forced to do so forever? Perhaps she fears the marginalisation, alienation and powerlessness that are often the price of motherhood in our culture?

These are all legitimate feelings. It is difficult for women to acknowledge the monumental effect that the birth of a child can have on them when this brief need to nurture and be nurtured has been turned against them throughout post-industrial history to exclude them from so many fundamental rights, such as the right to paid work.

It is also difficult to acknowledge this when maintaining the right to work means competing with others who do not need this time out.

The International Labor Organisation Convention 156 on Workers with Family Responsibilities upholds the right to parental leave. But sometimes, because of economic circumstances, the expectations of employers or peers, or because women themselves are trying to be "equal", this right is seen as a privilege.

And privileges are so much easier to decline in the interests of company loyalty and profits (and so much easier to take away, for that matter) than rights.

No woman knows how she is going to feel after the birth of a child, particularly a first child. Much depends on the type of birth, your age, the physical and emotional support you have and, of course, your own character and personality.

That is why I believe that those like Elizabeth, who are lucky enough to have the choice, may be wiser to make it after the baby is born, rather than before. It is much easier to return earlier than to extend your leave.

Women need reassurance that taking up one right will not cost them another. But it is difficult for mothers to tell other women this when political correctness requires that we respect each other's choices even if experience tells us that such choices are not as easy as they seem.

I have great sympathy for mothers who must return to paid work soon after the birth of a child. I had to do it myself for 10 weeks when Greta was just 16 weeks old, and I found it traumatic.

I do not believe men or women should be locked into particular roles. And given the time and permission, fathers can also nurture an infant, even though they cannot breastfeed.

My instinct is in tune with Pete Seeger's song, and the words from the Book of Ecclesiastes, "To everything there is a season and a time for every purpose under heaven".

POSEURS, PROPHETS AND THE SEARCH FOR WISDOM

22 August 1995

I SAT up in bed as if struck by lightning. The voice on the radio was introducing a newspaper columnist who wrote about her life and anyone else's that she could exploit.

The interviewer was sycophantic. The interviewee was egotistical, smug, twee: everything I fear I am becoming. The readers loved her, the columnist gloated, because she was just like them—ordinary.

Then she went on about her overseas trips and her new condo.

Perhaps I am dreaming that somebody is parodying me, I thought? Perhaps somebody is parodying me?

"Who is it? Who is it?" I kept demanding of Rob, as Greta, who had come between us in the night as usual, prattled on.

But this was not a parody. This was reality; luckily, somebody else's reality. I felt relieved, then depressed. I had recognised something of myself in a fellow writer, and I had not liked either of us for it.

The only trip I can afford is the weekly one to the supermarket and, until recently I thought a condominium was an exotic spice.

But still, the fact that I am writing this now, the fact that I have this little soap box, puts me in with them: the middle-class media poseurs whose biggest worry is whether they like Hermitage wine, or whether to renovate now or later, or how to tempt toddlers with clown faces made out of sausages, cherry tomatoes, alfalfa and carrots.

I whinge to Rob about the fact that I have nothing really to whinge about—yet I have the nerve to write about it.

"Hang on!" he says. "There's a difference between posing and sharing a common experience."

Besides, those who are aware of these contradictions know, too, that there are no simple solutions, he says.

"That's why we have people with answers: telling us what we should be eating, and how we should be living. It makes us feel secure because we have got some answers to some problems. They may be irrelevant to the bigger issues, but the problem is we've got to live."

My aunt, Tess, agrees with Rob when I complain to her that I am fiddling while Victoria burns. "If you didn't have your fiddle, your wine, your movies or whatever, you'd go mad," she says. She is right. If I went mad it would only add to the collective madness.

Paul Chadwick, media commentator and director of the Communications Law Centre, helps me get things further in perspective.

"You ought to trust the readers," he says. They understand that we have to shift gear, that we can talk about ethnic cleansing on one page and toilet training three pages later.

Still, I wonder. What provides security for some must provide alienation for others.

But what's the good of wondering. I should be doing something about it—about everything! Trouble is, I am too tired. I lay down to read a book with Greta at night and invariably fall asleep, waking guiltily three hours later. Guilty that I didn't manage to fit in a cuddle with Johannes or Rob, guilty that I didn't ring anybody, guilty that I wasn't fundraising, demonstrating or whatever.

We all have limits; it is a mistake to read the media and feel a call to action every time, Mr Chadwick says.

For him, the poet T. S. Eliot summed it up in *Choruses From The Rock*: "Where is the wisdom we have lost in knowledge? Where is the knowledge we have lost in information?"

Mr Chadwick says: "One of the comforting things for people bewildered by the media is to try to sort through in your own mind, according to your own experience, how much of what is being shovelled at you is just data, or slightly refined information, or better still, some kind of valuable knowledge, or finally, what is wisdom distilled."

What is wisdom distilled? That is, Mr Chadwick, that is.

Accepting what can't change, fighting for what can

29 August 1995

"HELLO. My name is Meredith. I am 32, a trained primary teacher on family leave . . . I spend my time with my daughters Erin, four years, and Jai, two years . . . Oh, by the way, I have epilepsy. My daughter Erin has it too . . ."

So begins Meredith Hendy's story in a new book *Epilepsy—I Can Live With That!*

I am riveted by her story. Having had epilepsy myself as a child, I am interested in how others cope, and even more interested in the fact that the children of epilepsy sufferers can sometimes suffer from it too.

I scan the page, searching for more references to Erin's epilepsy. How and when did it start? Is it under control? How did Meredith feel? I am disappointed. Meredith tells her own courageous story, but not Erin's.

Sue Goss, the editor of the anthology, says the focus of Meredith's story was living in the country, rather than being the parent of a child with epilepsy.

I admire Meredith's strength and cheerfulness. She accepts what she cannot change, but fights for what she can, such as the right to retain her driving licence, essential for life in the country.

But I am left wondering about Erin, and about my own children, too. Of course, I am happy for them to inherit my good looks and charm, but not my childhood epilepsy.

Suzanne Yanko, the author of an earlier book, *Coming To Terms With Epilepsy*, reassured me that while it was possible for Johannes and Greta to develop epilepsy, it was not inevitable.

"What doctors tend to say is that it's not inherited, as such; however there can be a genetic predisposition," she said.

For example, the child of an epilepsy sufferer who fell off a horse and banged her head, would be at risk, she said.

This does not mean that falling off a horse causes epilepsy. Rather, it means that a head injury can be a trigger in those with a family history of it. (Remind me to get Greta a crash helmet for Christmas.)

These days, however, a diagnosis of epilepsy is not as devastating as it once was. These days, there are new drugs and new attitudes.

Drugs can help keep epilepsy under control and positive, understanding attitudes can help sufferers and their families cope (although most of the people in this anthology do much more than "cope").

However, real understanding can only be imparted by those who have epilepsy. This is why this anthology is so important.

There are 20 stories like Meredith's in the book. While some types of epilepsy can be controlled through surgery, for most it is a life-long condition and, therefore, lives and lifestyles must be adapted.

"Am I the only one who grew out of it?" I asked Suzanne Yanko. I have had no problems since the age of 14.

"You were very lucky in that way," Suzanne said. "In the teenage years, it can go for better or worse."

Hormone development has a lot to do with it, she said. That's why menstruation, pregnancy and childbirth can also be times when women who have epilepsy may notice changes in their condition or when it may begin.

As for Johannes and Greta, I sincerely hope that neither of them develops epilepsy. But if they do, I know from experience that it will be all right.

Sue Goss says people who are diagnosed with epilepsy sometimes ask: "Is there life for me after epilepsy?"

As an author, editor, teacher, mother, wife and a person with epilepsy, Sue Goss replies: "A strong positive answer can really only be provided by someone else in the same situation. Of course there is—look at me."

Confessions of a Bad Sport

5 September 1995

THE subject on telly all weekend was sport, as it always seems to be. Sport, it seems, is central to the nation's economic, physical and emotional development and ego. Sport is wonderful, sport is essential, sport is fantastic, sport is . . . dare I say it? BORING!

The only thing that fascinates me about sport is the endless hours that otherwise seemingly intelligent people can spend discussing, watching and playing it.

I realise that in our culture and our city, arguably the sports capital of the nation, this constitutes treason. However, I can no longer play ball, so to speak.

I am coming out—right out into the middle of the footy oval to make a point or two. My goal is not to be a bad sport, but to tell my opponents what it's like for people like me, for whom a mark is something your two-year-old has made on the carpet, a hamstring is something you buy at the supermarket along with gelatine for the apricot glaze, and a behind is something you sit on.

For Dr June Senyard, of Melbourne University's department of history, it is sport to observe unsporty people like me.

Dr Senyard lectures in Australian sporting culture, among other things. "For one of the essays, I actually did pose the question about why don't people like sport," she said sympathetically.

Dr Senyard is sort of on my side. Sport, she admits, does not increase life expectancy, only the quality of life generally (although this depends on how many teeth and noses you break, how many shoulders you dislocate and how many knee operations you can tolerate).

And though it may be a national obsession, only one-fifth of the Australian population actually plays organised sport. The rest just watch, getting fatter rather than fitter.

The division between the arts and sport only occurred in about the 18th century, Dr Senyard said. Previously, sporting acts of prowess were part of the theatre. "In Australia, that division became very entrenched."

Sport is also popular because it gives people something in common and provides a social link, Dr Senyard said. "Then there's your family and your peers . . . Once you're into it . . ."

It sounded disturbingly like religion. If they get you before the age of seven, they've got you for life. Thank goodness my children had been spared, I thought.

"It's just as well Johannes isn't interested in football," I said to Rob one night, describing how another non-sporting friend had managed to spawn a basketball-loving son and had been forced to actually watch a game every Saturday.

He was more the arty type, I explained, like his father and me and Rob for that matter.

Rob scoffed. "And why do you think he's like that? What about all those nights sitting up in bed eating chocolates together and watching musicals?"

It's true. I am interested in mixed doubles and scores of a different kind. When Johannes was small our Friday nights were spent watching Fred and Ginger, Gene and Cyd, Kathryn and Howard.

However, Dr Christopher Ball, an appropriately named sports psychologist at Melbourne University, says an obsession with sport should not be confused with a love of sport. Sport psychology is about improving enjoyment, skills and motivation.

But what if you are just as unmotivated to do it as you are to watch it?

"I guess you have to find out what sort of physical activities you enjoy doing and encourage those," Dr Ball said.

A few weeks ago, my sister, Juliana, gave me an exercise bike and a chocolate cake for my birthday.

It took a few days, but I know which physical activity I prefer.

JUST ONE OF THOSE BAD SWEAR DAYS

19 September 1995

I WAS having one of those days, I swear.

I mean I don't swear.

That is, as you know, I am trying to give it up. But I had lost my keys and there is nothing as provocative as being all dressed up and having nowhere to go because you've lost the bloody car keys.

It was a Saturday morning and Rob was out shopping-and-dropping—buying essential items, like another wine cask, and taking Johannes to squash (yes, there is a sporting chance for him after all.)

Greta and I stayed home to rest, but instead I was restless. "Let's go to the video shop!" I said.

Any kind of shop is fine with Greta, so half an hour later, we were ready to go.

"Where are my keys?" I said half to myself, as I searched among snotty tissues and credit card receipts in my handbag, through my coat pockets and then frantically under cushions and newspapers.

"Where are they?" I repeated in exasperation.

"In the toy box," Greta piped up helpfully. "Did you take them?" I asked, turning around with a mixture of fury and relief.

"I did," she said bravely.

Together we turned up the toy box, but there were no keys.

"Did you put them somewhere else?" I coaxed.

"In the cubby!" she said again helpfully.

This time we turned out the cloth cubby borrowed from the toy library, but found nothing except a stale peanut butter sandwich and a doll's cradle full of Lego.

"Where did you put them?" I coaxed again.

"In my room," she said. So off we went to search under the doona, under the bed . . . anywhere.

"Bloody hell, where are they?" I yelled, beginning to feel irrational. I searched the rubbish bin, under the couch, in Johannes' room, in the bathroom, on top of the fridge exclaiming at each post "BLOODY HELL, WHERE ARE THEY?"

"Helen took them!" said Greta, looking triumphant.

I was baffled. "Helen, who?" I demanded, wondering vaguely if I had left them at my neighbor Helen's house.

"Bloody Helen!" offered Greta.

I stopped looking and started laughing, realising that as long as I was demanding a solution to the problem, poor Greta had felt obliged to offer one.

I also realised that my plan to give up swearing was as lost as my keys.

I am trying to set a better example, but some things, like my language, are out of my control. Nature conquering nurture is the key argument in this debate. As for those other keys, it turned out that Rob had taken them by mistake.

A week later, after I had written this, concluding that losing keys is enough to drive anyone crazy, I received a letter from the City of Hobson's Bay, written on behalf of the Altona North Police Community Consultative Committee (PCCC).

The letter referred to my previous column on swearing. "The issue of bad language has been one that has disturbed the committee members and the committee would like to express its support of your stance on bad language and would be pleased to see a follow-up article," the secretary, Mr Damien Reeves, wrote.

The committee is setting up a forum on bad language, inviting schools, police, church groups and the public. "The Committee is also interested in whether you would accept our invitation to speak at this forum," Mr Reeves wrote.

Me? At first I thought it was some kind of joke but, no, the council seal appeared to be authentic. I did not know whether to be flattered or insulted. Then, I thought, why not?

Perhaps I should begin my speech: "Hello, my name is Jane and I'm a swearaholic."

Just let me wash my mouth out with soap first.

Recipe for Whining and Dining

3 October 1995

IT STARTS in one of those rare moments when life seems to be in order. The house is tidy and relatively clean, something wholesome and plentiful is bubbling on the stove, there are flowers in all the vases and the children are playing quietly.

I am on the phone catching up with a friend and have just finished my third glass of wine. Suddenly I hear myself saying, "Why not come up for lunch sometime?"

Anyone who has been here for lunch recently should put this down and go out and do some gardening or shopping. Right now! For the rest of you, this will be a lesson in never entertaining the thought of entertaining while you have little children, a little kitchen and precious little time.

How can I have forgotten that visitors, especially ones who have trekked an hour or more from town, require more than a boiled egg and a peanut butter sandwich? How can I possibly have forgotten that the mere mention of visitors sends Rob into a frenzy of whipper-snipping and burning off, only to emerge 15 minutes before the guests arrive covered in grass and sweat?

After the initial panic, I do the only sensible thing. I make lists: lists of what to do, what to make and what to get. I pore over recipe books searching for a dish that can be made a week in advance, served cold if necessary and looks like something that should be photographed rather than eaten.

I list everything I will need, and then I usually go out and buy a quiche.

Naturally, I have lots of help from Greta, who helps me remember jelly beans and forget quiche at the supermarket.

I decide to make a vegetable curry, forgetting that there are only two settings on our electric stove, on and off, which makes both the food and me stew. I yell at the stove. I yell at Greta. I yell at Johannes. The phone rings. It is my guests.

146

I hope they have gastro and can't come. "We're really looking forward to it. What shall we bring?" they ask.

"Something to drink," I say, reaching for the wine cask.

The big day arrives and I am like a general issuing orders. If it is too late to clean up, I cover up, throwing clean and dirty washing into the cupboards and anything else in the toy box.

I need bread, milk and flowers and Greta needs a sleep, so I take her with me. I drive around and around the block waiting for both Greta and the flowers to wilt. Finally, she nods off, and I head home only to be greeted by my visitors, who have beaten me there.

Rob pours them a drink; he pours me a drink. By the third drink, my face is flushed and I have forgotten to put the dinner on. By the time the visitors go, I am feeling very warm and relaxed and can't remember what we had for dinner.

"Thanks for coming," I hear myself say. "We'll have to do it again sometime."

A week later, when I can't find any of our clothes and there is an awful smell coming from Greta's cupboard, I remember what we had for dinner—visitors.

Holiday without Hunni is only half as sweet

17 October 1995

THE word "half sister" is sadly appropriate for Greta during the school holidays, because without her half brother, her world is incomplete.

At first Rob and I thought she had suffered a personality change; she was so cantankerous during the first week of the school holidays while Johannes was visiting his father. Then we realised that she was bored and lonely.

I should have realised earlier because the first night without him, she woke about 2am and said: "Where my Hunni? We have to go and pick him up from Harald's. Harald's a big daddy. Hunni loves his daddy. I love my daddy, too. Harald's a big daddy," and then promptly went back to sleep.

Then in the morning, as we got into the car, she said: "We have to pick up Hunni?"

"Hunni's gone on a holiday to Harald's," I explained yet again.

She should be used to this by now as Johannes goes every weekend fortnight, but the longer holiday break was made much more difficult this time by the fact that she is now older and more appreciative of her big brother.

There are problems, of course, having children with such a big age gap, because the needs of one are often incompatible with the other. But there are benefits too: less rivalry and more companionship. Rob and I try, but Johannes joins in her imaginative games with much more gusto and creativity.

Of course, there are often times when he would rather be playing with his friends, or better still, sitting at this computer with his friends. And he often rails against the fact that much more is expected of him than of her.

"She's a dominator!" he complains when I let her watch The Wiggles so that I can have some peace while I make tea. That's why it is so important for him to have that special time with his father where he can be the dominator for a change.

Jeanette Harrison, a lecturer in early childhood issues at Swinburne University, says that the changes brought by the children of blended families coming and going between households can affect family dynamics dramatically.

For example, at his father's house where there are two older children, Johannes is the youngest, displacing the youngest child there who then becomes the middle child. When he returns here, he takes on the role of eldest again.

"It can affect the family balance," Ms Harrison said. Even if everyone adjusts happily, they must still adjust.

As for Greta, she goes from being youngest to only child.

While it can be nice for a change, after a while she misses him, just as we miss him.

So what can we do? "Don't try and push it aside," Ms Harrison said. "Let her know it is OK to miss him. Ask her what she would like to do. Does she want to telephone him each day? Would she like him to phone her?"

At the same time, understand bad behavior, but don't reinforce it, she said.

Time away from Greta is essential for Johannes, she said, and probably highlights how much Rob and I depend on him to meet Greta's needs.

It is true, I'm afraid. He's playing with her in the bath right now while I am writing this. That's why I'm planning on an extra day of creche for Greta next year.

Meanwhile, with Johannes home it is just as the Shirley Temple song says: "An ordinary day is like a holiday, when I'm with you."

We counted the sleeps until he came home and when he walked in the door Greta threw her arms around his neck and repeated over and over, "I wuv you, Hunni!"

Going potty on the way to grandma's

24 October 1995

THE horse-drawn cart rocked and rolled along as the driver explained that in the gold rush days, it would have taken five days to reach Melbourne from Maldon, travelling in this way.

I could well imagine, having taken almost as long to get to Maldon myself, thanks to Greta.

We had gone to visit Grandma and Grandpa for the weekend. Throughout history, visiting Grandma has always had its hazards. In the old days it was the wolves waiting in the woods, today it's potties in the grass.

"I need to do wees," declared Greta 20 minutes from home.

"Do it in your nappy," I said, breaking every rule about potty-training. I had insisted on a nappy, despite the fact that she had been successfully using the potty and toilet on most occasions recently. A nappy, I had thought, would help avoid the need to stop and find a toilet every half an hour or so on our four-hour journey.

But my toilet training had been more successful than I had realised. Big Girls do not do it in a nappy even if they have to do it in the potty on the side of the road instead.

A woman walking her dog barely noticed us. I supposed that she was used to things that needed to urinate on the nature strip every 20 minutes or so.

Back in the car, I hid the bottle of drink and drove on.

Another 20 minutes later, Greta announced again, "I need to do wees!"

I did not know how much capacity she had for hanging on, but I knew how much capacity she had for letting go, especially as she had found that bottle of drink, so I stopped at a service station as soon as I could.

Unfortunately, the service station toilet had not been serviced in a while. "It smells in here!" declared Greta as she ran out crying. I took her back to the car and got out the potty.

"Fill 'er up!" I commanded, as Greta sat down beside the petrol pump.

We headed for the freeway. "No stopping except in emergency", the signs said. I wondered if the sort of accident I was envisaging would be considered an emergency by VicRoads. Fortunately, she fell asleep.

At Grandma's, the toilet was the third biggest attraction (Grandma and Grandpa being the first and second).

"I'm doing it! I'm doing it!" she cried triumphantly, followed by "I done it, I done it."

"I *have* done it," I corrected.

"Me, too!" she replied.

For toilet training you need a sense of humor and no sense of smell. There are a number of contradictions to start with.

First of all, this is essentially a private act, made public by the fact that, to start with, your child cannot do it independently.

In an article on stress-free toilet training in the August issue of *Parents* magazine, Dr Paul Roy says a child is usually ready for toilet training when he gives his primary caregivers the signal that he is looking for a place to urinate.

But what happens when you get the signal three hours from the nearest toilet?

Despite all this, we had a nice break. But next time we venture away, I will certainly bring the potty and leave the bottle of juice at home.

I have always taken heed of the Transport Accident Commission's campaigns, but now I know what they really mean by: "If you drink, then drive, you're a bloody idiot."

WHEN IT'S ONLY MAKE BELIEVE

8 November 1995

GRETA sat in the big black upholstered chair at the cinema, clutching a carton of popcorn. "I excited," she said as the lights dimmed and the film began. We had taken a chance, Johannes and I, a chance that Greta, who loves videos, might just last through a whole feature film at the cinema.

Johannes had wanted to see *Power Rangers* but we had settled on *Pocahontas*. Still, that did not prevent Greta from getting a burst of *Power Rangers* during the previews. I put her hands over her eyes but fortunately she was more interested in the popcorn than the preview.

"You're not allowed to talk during this. If you have to talk you whisper, like me," I said as it started.

"Okay," she said.

Things went well until about three-quarters of the way through, when the popcorn ran out. She got up from her seat and wandered into the outside aisle where she sat on a ledge, swinging her legs. The cinema was not crowded and there was no usher, so I decided to leave her there. Besides, the Indians and the White Men were preparing for battle.

Greta made her way back just as John Smith, Pocahontas's boyfriend, copped it in the chest from a rifle shot. Not knowing the ending, I explained that he was dead.

"Don't be deadibones, John Smiff!" she called out, making the moment even more dramatic.

Back home, playing Pocahontas became her latest favorite game. Whether it is *Pocahontas, Pinocchio, Beauty and the Beast, Bambi* or *Cinderella*, watching these animated videos at home has not stifled her imagination, as one might think, but stimulated it.

"You be John Smiff, Hunni," she commanded Johannes later that day.

"I love you, Pocahontas. Will you marry me?" he dutifully asked.

"I have to ask my farder." she replied and trotted off to find the imaginary chief.

I know all this sounds terribly politically incorrect, but Greta has no qualms about role reversal. Sometimes she orders Johannes to be Pocahontas, who dutifully asks again: "I love you, John Smith. Will you marry me?" to which Greta replies: "I have to go back to my ship and find a doctor."

This is all very charming while Johannes is around, but a little tiring when he is not, especially as I never know when she is going to metamorphosise into one of her fantasy characters.

"Stepmudder, stepmudder! Don't be mean!" she pleads, following me around the kitchen. I daren't visit our local shopping centre, lest she suddenly turns into Cinderella and I am arrested by the child protection authority.

Other times she asks, "You be the fox from *Pinocchio*, Mummy?" and I have to waylay her on her way to school and stop her from becoming a real boy. "High diddly-dee, an actor's life for me!" she sings.

The only worry is to make sure she knows the difference between fantasy and reality. "It's just pretend," I say to her if she looks worried while watching TV.

But how do you explain pretend that is so effective that it is almost real?

I thought I would give both Johannes and Greta a thrill by taking them to see ventriloquist David Straussman and his friends Chuck Wood and Ted E. Bear. What could be more charming than a doll and a teddy bear?

I had not accounted for the alien. When Mr Straussman introduced Kevin (that's what the alien name translated to), a cross between E.T. and Alf, Greta decided it was time to go home.

"It's just pretend. It's just a puppet," I explained, trying to restrain her. But it was no good. Pinocchio was just a puppet, but then he became a real boy.

There was no telling what Kevin might do.

A FATHER AND CHILD RENUNION

15 November 1995

"YOU look older. You've put on a bit of weight?" he said, when I met my father again after many years.

I hardly recognised him either. After all, where were the horns, the tail and the pitchfork? It is often the case however, that when we confront our demons, they stop being demons.

How could I not recognise him anyway? The wave of his hair, although thinner now, the curve of his forehead, the veins, blue against the brown of his hand—all these things have been imprinted on my memory since birth. We can choose not to forgive, but we can never forget, even if those memories are locked away deep inside.

It seems apt that in this International Year of Tolerance, our family is in a conciliatory mood. For years, we had focussed on our differences. Now we are learning to focus on our similarities.

To prepare myself for this reunion with my father, I borrowed a book from my local library, *Family Harmony*, by American journalist and author Denise Lang. As it happened, I didn't get time to read it before the big event, but later, I found some pearls of wisdom.

Ms Lang quotes someone in a similar position to me. "When someone had blown up with another member of my family, the solution was just to cut that member off," says Lanie, a 46-year-old English teacher.

"My whole family was that way," she said. "I grew up not knowing whole sections of the family. As a kid, you wonder about them. As an adult, to try to contact them looks like an act of treason. As you can imagine, I have a very small family."

I know how she felt. I had made family of friends to fill the gaps, and of course had been lucky enough to have a wonderful stepfather and wonderful parents-in-law.

But when I saw my husband become a father I wondered more and more about my own father.

I am not the only one, of course, to find that I had been mothered, but not fathered, so to speak. In the past, many men were more often providers than fathers. Some, sadly, did not even manage that.

Later, with the increase in divorce (a good thing, in my view if unhappy people can have a chance at happiness again), many children grew up fatherless in other ways.

But as any adopted child will attest, no matter how much denial there is, as a child grows, the need to know the biological parent grows too. In some ways, knowing the parent is like knowing yourself.

Ms Lang offers some advice: "To cut off one's arm, will of course, solve the immediate problem, but the results will present long-term problems of greater magnitude. Life goes on, and sometimes ends during a period of non-contact, and no amount of remorse can recapture those moments that contribute to the full picture of family life."

It is that full picture that I am trying to piece together now. Poor old Dad! Just as he has reached that stage in life when memories begin to get a little blurry around the edges, I am at him to pull them into focus.

Slowly, my picture of our family life is becoming clearer. At the reunion, we enjoyed lunch and, surprisingly, each other's company. I asked some important questions and got some important answers.

Some of these my father gave me. Others I worked out for myself—like you cannot hate someone for being unable to give you what you wanted; like you can forgive one parent without being disloyal to the other; like recognising the humanity in your parents is part of growing up.

It seems from the moment we are born, we are striving to grow up. Already Greta knows there is more status in being "a big girl" than a little girl.

What she can't know yet is that sometimes, even big girls have a lot of growing up to do.

Out and About Under Cover

22 November 1995

WHAT don't you do on a wet weekend? Install a garden watering system, that's what. But when, like Rob, you've waited all week to install a garden watering system, you install it come hell or high water.

But as the rain continued to come down, he eventually had to give up. "I feel a bit ridiculous," he admitted, after coming in wet and muddy.

Poor Rob! While spring gives me hay fever it gives him garden fever. "What's it like up there today?" he asks wistfully if he telephones while he is at work.

"Terrible!" I lie, as I watch a panting cocky gargle some water from the tray on the sundrenched verandah. "It's grey and overcast and I think it's going to rain."

He immediately cheers up. "Perhaps it will clear up by the weekend then. I really need to get out into the garden."

It's true, the spring rains make things grow at a phenomenal rate, but the garden doesn't need Rob half as much as Rob needs the garden.

That's why we all felt tired, grumpy and cooped up when it inevitably rained all weekend recently.

As usual, there were toys and washing all over the house. We could either clean up or clear out, so we decided to clear out. But where? Landing on other families cooped up with kids on a wet weekend just halves your space and doubles your kids.

Nana and Pa were both unwell, so we decided to employ a great Australian family tradition and go for a drive. Anywhere.

We picked up Johannes from his friend Rhys's house on the way. Rhys's father looked tired and frazzled when he answered the door. "It's been wall-to-wall kids here," he said. "We've got to get out!"

I sympathised. "Where are you going?" I asked.

"I don't know," he replied.

Neither did we. I didn't care as long as Greta fell asleep so Rob and I could have a rare conversation. But no, amid cries of "Where are we going?" she sang at the top of her voice, her latest obsession—Belle's song from *Beauty and the Beast*. "I want adventure in the wide blue yonder! I want it more than I can tell!" she crowed.

We wanted it too. Desperately. Preferably alone. Eventually, we all got it at Victoria's Farm Shed, in Tynong. George, Rocky, and other sheepish friends, as well as some bulls and some cows, all made their big entrance to their own special theme music in an informative display obviously geared to the overseas meat-eating and wool-buying tourist market.

They were so endearing that for me the promotion backfired in part. As Alice found in *Through the Looking Glass* when she was faced with an amiable leg of mutton, it is difficult to work up an appetite for something to which you have been introduced.

I admit, our main reason for seeking out this attraction was that it was under cover. There are so few places that families can go on a wet day that are under cover and cheap.

When Johannes was small and we lived in the city, many a wet afternoon was spent wandering around the National Gallery or visiting the museum. In those days, the museum, at least, was free. These days it seems you have to buy the right to spend money, as even our local undercover market now charges an entry fee.

But families are very resourceful. On any wet day you are likely to find my friend's husband, Denis, at Tullamarine airport.

It's Melbourne's largest undercover playground and a great place for Denis to let his two-year-old take off.

Perhaps one day the idea of wet-day entertainment for families will take off too?

Hark, the Two Wise Men Arrive Early

29 November 1995

REMEMBER when we were kids and we couldn't wait for Christmas? Well, our kids don't have to wait. It is November and Santa has already arrived at our local shopping centre, much to Greta's delight and my horror.

"Look! Santa!" she said, and sure enough, there were children queuing to sit on Santa's knee and have their photo taken.

"Santa's coming 'morrow!" Greta said confidently, as I tried to divert her. How was I going to explain that it would not be "tomorrow" for about another five weeks?

It may help retail sales to bring Christmas on early, but it does not help children for whom every day is an eternity when they are anticipating something as exciting and bewildering as Christmas. It did not help to count sleeps either, as the number of sleeps between late November and 25 December was just as unfathomable as the idea of a short, fat man scrambling down our very long, thin chimney.

I am not a religious person, but the sight of the Christmas marketing machine being cranked up and wheeled out so early convinced me that Greta needed to know the real story.

"Christmas is Jesus's birthday," I said as we drove home.

Greta understands birthdays completely, so this was a good start, or so I thought.

"Happy birthday to Jesa, happy birthday to her!" she sang.

"Actually, Jesus is a Him," I said, half to myself.

"Happy birthday to Jesa, happy birthday to him!" she sang obligingly.

"I'll tell you a story about Jesus, if you like?" I said, hoping to shed some light for her.

"Okay," she said, happily.

And so I began my own adaptation to suit her level of understanding, and with apologies to biblical experts.

Naturally, it began with "Once upon a time there was a lady called Mary and a man called Joseph. One day an angel visited Mary . . ."

The angel who visited Mary was sort of like a fairy, I explained.

And well, there were no hospitals in those days, so Mary had to go to the pub, which was full, so then she had to go to a stable. To cut a long story short, it ended up more or less happily ever after as Jesus grew to be a great and kind king.

I thought I'd wait until Easter for the gory bits, so I told her that when Jesus died everyone was sad and decided to remember him on his birthday by giving each other gifts, and that Santa helped by giving presents to all the good children.

It seemed to satisfy her, so much so that she asked me tell the story over and over, each time singing "Happy birthday to Jesa".

"I know a song about Jesus," I said, hoping to vary her repertoire.

It was too early for Christmas carols, so I taught her *Jesus Bids Me Shine*, which she sang at the top of her voice for the next few days, much to the amusement of others. All she needed was a hat and a tambourine and we would have been able to pay off last Christmas.

It seemed incongruous for a family that doesn't go to church to be teaching such things, but I suppose no more incongruous than Santa coming in November.

Regardless of whether the population practises Christianity or not, most of our calendar is still organised around Christian festivals and it seems only fair to explain to children why they are held.

That's the easy part. I still haven't worked out how to explain that Santa isn't coming tomorrow.

GENDER IMPASSE AT THE CHOOK SHED

6 December 1995

LET ME tell you a secret. It is not sex that divides men and women. It's chooks.

Chooks make lots of my women friends all clucky. As far as men are concerned, chooks are messy, noisy creatures that require maintenance, a place to live, and are certainly nothing to crow about.

If men are indeed from Mars and women from Venus, then chooks on Mars are probably vermin, while on Venus they are probably sacred.

My own preference for chooks comes from all those images in childhood books where the ample-bosomed farmer's wife scatters grain for some plump red hens, and happy children collect the eggs in a little basket.

This was a city child's fantasy image of country life and probably would have remained so if Greta hadn't been such a poor eater. If I wasn't able to recycle Greta's leftover broccoli by offering it to Rob, I was determined to offer it to a more appreciative audience. After all, chooks will eat anything.

However, we have moved to an area more suited to goats than chooks, so the plan for the chook shed has had to go on hold until we can afford to get part of the back yard levelled.

But first I am trying to straighten out Rob. He enjoys eggs. He just doesn't enjoy the idea of coming home from work and having to tramp down the back yard with a torch to feed or put the chooks away.

I reassured him. All he had to do was put up the chook shed and bring home the bacon. I would clean the shed, feed the chooks and collect the eggs.

He was sceptical. "Even when it's the middle of winter and cold and dark?"

"I'll go down when it's still light," I replied.

Our neighbors, Helen and Morris, are equally divided. "What's the point, when you can go and buy a dozen free-range eggs for $3 or whatever?" says Morris. The point is that we won't have to buy them, and at the same time we can recycle all Helen's homemade bread that Morris won't eat.

How could Helen and I make Rob and Morris understand? Sure you can drive anywhere, but sometimes it's nicer to walk. It is an environmental and spiritual issue. It is also an issue of health and economy, which is why Helen and I are thinking of following another friend's plan. To avoid embarrassment, I'll call her Karen, and her poor hen-pecked husband, Ken.

A few years back, in their previous house, when Ken was a high-powered executive, he and Karen were also divided over a chook shed. One day, when he came home from work, she told him that there was a surprise for him in his garden shed.

When he opened the shed door, he was greeted by three good-looking birds. But they were not his type. "There were chooks and crap everywhere," he moaned.

He built the chook shed that weekend. And after a while, despite his initial protests, Ken didn't notice the chooks.

In fact, when he woke early one day and decided to sit in the garden to dictate some letters he didn't notice them at all.

Back at the office a few days later, Ken's boss dropped by, tears of laughter streaming down his face. "Listen to this!" he crowed. Amid the "Further to your letter of . . ." and "Yours faithfully" was a cacophony of crowing and clucking.

These days, Karen doesn't have any chooks. And Ken doesn't have a garden shed either—just in case

WHY PARENTS ARE DRIVEN TO DRIVE

13 December 1995

WE FORGOT it was Thursday last week. If we had remembered it was Thursday we would have remembered that it was time for art classes for Johannes. Instead we bought take-away and watched a video.

No one was too perturbed. After all, the art class is just for fun. But it reminded me of a letter I read in a magazine once where a grandmother was lamenting all the extra activities her grandchildren seemed locked into.

She had been looking forward to caring for them—relaxing, chatting, reading, and perhaps cooking while their mother was away—but found herself being a replacement taxi service instead. There seemed to be no time for fun and relaxation.

It is a scenario that is usually frowned on by childcare experts. Children must be given the chance to be children and playing is as important, if not more so, than playing the piano or whatever, they say.

True, but I can understand the feelings behind that frantic schedule.

Every parent wants their child to discover something they are passionate about: something apart from television, computers and chocolate. Something creative that will enrich their future lives. That's why we get caught up in that endless taxi service.

But what happens when we start driving our children too hard? What happens when what was thought to be encouragement is seen to be pushing? What happens when your child wants to get out of the taxi?

If you agree that the child should give up the chosen activity, are you giving up on the child? Will the child later complain, as we all seem to do, that if only they were pushed a little they could have been a great artist, pianist, ballerina or cricketer? Or will the child develop a pathological hatred of the very thing that you wanted it to be passionate about?

It is one of the milestones of parenting to suddenly recognise the emotional investment you have in your children's abilities and interests, even when you vowed you wouldn't.

When that happens, you must sit down and try to nut out how much of whatever your child is doing outside of school is your agenda, and how much is the child's, according to Dr Mary Dawn Ainley, a lecturer in psychology at the School of Behavioral Science at Melbourne University.

"You have to sort out to what degree is that being imposed on the child as opposed to the child's genuine interest being supported," she says.

"Is it something about their past that the parents are reliving, or trying to, through the child as opposed to providing the conditions to support the interest the child has? As parents we often load other things on top of that, so that no longer is the person being supported to do an activity, and develop it for its own sake. It becomes a pointer to something else. Often, not always, it can undermine the initial interest in the activity itself."

Dr Ainley does not use the word "push". "That gives the wrong edge to it," she says. "I call it supporting. You might be doing exactly the same things as someone who is pushing, but pushing implies that the person doing the pushing has decided the goal." As the child progresses, the goals should become more and more their own, she says.

Of course, most of us are not wise enough or fortunate enough to find such good advice until after the event. And meanwhile most of us have still got the motor running on that taxi, providing opportunities and support for our children as best we can.

As for me, I am a driven person, so I tend to drive others, including my children. But in future, I will try to remember Dr Ainley's advice and allow them to decide the destination.

FROM FRANKINCENSE TO NONSENSE

20 December 1995

I AM sitting here with my feet up, sipping a glass of chilled wine, Christmas shopping.

What? Don't tell me you actually went to the shops to buy your Christmas presents, when all you needed to do was go to your letter box?

As every parent of a young child knows, the only sensible way to shop for Christmas is by catalogue—not those relentless catalogues from the Mega Toy Store, but those genuine mail-order catalogues where you can only hope that what you see is what you get.

There is much to be said for avoiding the Christmas crush and shopping at home. On the first day of Christmas, you can give your true love a partridge in a pear tree without having to visit the forest or the nursery or, indeed, even your true love.

And shopping by catalogue is not only guilt-free, but positively saintly. Lots of worthy organisations provide catalogues of dual-purpose gifts. You can give your mum an embroidered tablecloth, for example, and provide a well for 50 villagers in Africa at the same time. Or why not buy a fridge magnet for your friend and help pay for an HB pencil at your local school?

Dual-purpose gifts like that truly live up to the old adage that it is better to give than receive. But there are some catalogues that seem to be full of no-purpose gifts.

Like the Suction Cup Dent Puller. Perfect for the family member or friend who is apt to lean against a new car occasionally.

In the old days, these suction cups were handy to clear a blocked sink, but these days I believe that when carefully handled, they may also be used to cure migraines.

If you are the type who is apt to lose control, especially your remote control, perhaps you'd like a special Remote Control Organiser. You probably already have a special place, such as a bookshelf, to which the control is seldom returned. But for $10 you can get a special Remote

Control Organiser, to which the control will probably also be seldom returned.

However, the ideal mail-order catalogue present for me (hint, hint) is the pair of shorts I plan to eventually look good in. No exercise is necessary, other than zipping them up and breathing in. These amazing sauna shorts do all the work for you so you can "get rid of that tummy bulge, those chubby thighs or spare tyre". Unfortunately, they only come in small, medium and large—not grotesque.

Better still, if your eyes are tired from scanning all those catalogues, why not try the new eye massager? It may look out of this world, according to its advertisers, but it is specifically designed to release tension through gentle stimulation.

The massager stimulates the blood flow and nerves to improve the flow of oxygen and refresh tired eyes—but it doesn't do much for your love life.

Or why not spoil the gardener in your family by splurging on a pair of lawn aerator sandals? These amazing sandals allow you to poke holes in the lawn and get your daily walk at the same time. And for the adventurous New-Ager, just turn them inside out and they double as massage sandals!

However, the ultimate gift for the person who has everything must be the Big Toe Straightener.

"This is an absolute boon to sufferers of inclined big toes," the catalogue boasts. Depends which way you are inclined, I suppose. For that little number you only have to hang $10.

It's a small price to pay for a little Christmas cheer.

The Three Wise Men were obviously not wise enough, travelling so far bearing gifts. But then we've all come a long way since then. After all, what's gold, frankincense and myrrh compared to a Big Toe Straightener?

LESSONS IN LOVE

27 December 1995

WE ARE in mourning this Christmas. You see, our little Jack Russell puppy—Johannes's Christmas present—died.

We had bought her from a breeder's co-operative and she had come with a vet check and her first immunisation, so there was nothing to indicate that she was not well. In fact, when she stood up and wagged her tail at Johannes, in a "Choose me!" kind of way, she looked the picture of health.

We had chosen both the breed and the name very carefully before we even went to look at puppies. We had originally wanted to name her after the star of the movie *Mask*—that little brown-and-white Jack Russell called Milo. But we hesitated to lumber a girl with such an unfeminine name.

"You can't call a female dog Milo," I said to Rob.

"Yes, you can," he said. "What about Venus di Milo?"

"Because she's 'armless?" I quipped.

Rob groaned. But somehow, Milo stuck, even after I kept suggesting that we change it to Bonnie. "I like Milo," said Johannes, who had naming rights.

But Milo was not the active little puppy I had imagined. For a start, she shivered and shook, and didn't seem to want to get out of bed—hers or ours.

She would not eat any of the special puppy food we had bought, and I found myself cooking up chicken and rice and throwing it out for the dog, as well as Greta.

"That's the third person in this household who won't eat what I cook!" I lamented.

"Perhaps she was too young to leave her mother," Rob said.

However, it soon became clear that Milo needed a doctor, not a mother. In that week, she had five trips to the vet and, finally, despite being put on a drip at the veterinary hospital, she was moaning and bleeding and it became clear that it was cruel to prolong her agony.

Johannes was glum as he went off to school that morning, and even glummer that night. I was in tears and poor Greta was confused and miserable. First she had trouble adjusting to Milo's presence—particularly as she was taking all my attention. Then she had trouble adjusting to her absence.

"I don't want my Miro doggy to die. Bring her back to rife!" she cried, when I told her the sad news.

"Darling, she can't come back to life. She was too sick," I explained. "The doctor gave her some medi to help her but it didn't work and she died."

It seemed so final and such an inadequate explanation, but what else could I say? Later, as she was sitting on the footstool, drinking a bottle of milk and looking at the Christmas decorations, she turned around and asked: "Why did Miro have to die?"

"Because she was too sick. The doctor couldn't help her."

"But I want her to come back to rife," she said, beginning to cry.

"Darling, she can't come back. She's gone," I said lamely.

"Where has she gone?"

Before I knew it, I found myself saying, "She's gone to the angels in heaven."

"Are the angels fixing her?"

"No, they can't fix her. She has to stay there. She can't come back," I said.

The breeder and the vet were both wonderfully supportive and sympathetic. Milo had free vet care and we got our money back with an apology. Two tests for parvo virus both showed negative, so we will get another puppy soon.

But under the Christmas tree, courtesy of my sister, Juliana, wrapped in gay Christmas paper were a pile of dog toys, a bowl and a lead and, beside them, two children who had learned that no one, not even Santa, could give them what they really wanted for Christmas.

1996

Days of chops and repair

3 January 1996

WHOEVER wrote about days of wine and roses was obviously not Australian. As any fair-dinkum Aussie knows, in the weeks after Christmas it is days of beer and chops, and sausages and "dead horse" and simple salads, and fruit and ice-cream.

Epicureans may enjoy more exotic fare but for families with little children, this is the ideal meal—even more ideal when it is served on left-over paper plates with Christmas motifs.

I had originally opposed the idea of buying a barbecue. "What's the point?" I had asked when Rob talked about paving an area just outside the back door, creating a kind of carnivorous shrine. With a perfectly good stove just a few metres away indoors, it seemed a bit ridiculous to be firing up the coals outside.

But now I see the point. Of course, the point of a barbecue is that the men cook.

So what if it means that we eat the same thing for three weeks—as long as I don't have to cook it. And while the chops cook, the other cook chops: lettuce, celery, tomatoes, anything I find in the bottom of the fridge.

Of course, the barbecue is much more than an easy, cheap meal. It is a symbol of a lifestyle, a holiday lifestyle. Ordinarily, Rob does not get home in time to eat with us, let alone cook for us. But since Christmas, we have not only had tea together but breakfast and lunch, too.

It is quite a novelty. Who needs to go away on holiday when sitting on your own veranda and eating breakfast is a rare event? I suppose the difference is that when it's your own veranda, you notice that it's covered in possum poo and the window frames need painting.

So it wasn't surprising that, on the fifth day of our holiday, Rob came home with color samples from the local paint shop.

Some holiday, you think. Yes, but that's what holidays at home are like. A time of relaxation and repair. You repair your home, your own health, your relationships with friends and family.

By repair, I mean restore. You restore your own sense of well-being, your perspective on work and life. You fall in love again, with your partner, your kids, your own back yard and yourself.

Why don't we do any of this any other time, we wonder? The reason, of course, is that at other times there is no time, only timetables.

It is sad, even tragic, to think that most people who actually have to "go to work" undergo this restoration during only three to four weeks a year. And it's even more tragic and ironic to think that those without jobs, who have no timetables, are unable to do it because they lack the power and self-esteem that money and status provides.

What, then, is the answer? From a reading of *Manhood*, the latest offering from Sydney family psychologist Stephen Biddulph, the answer seems to be for men at least to seriously re-evaluate and, where possible, change their priorities.

Of course, some priorities are almost impossible to change, such as making your mortgage payments, and in some ways Biddulph's solutions seem a little naive, in the short term at least.

For example, he advises men to "burn your tie or use it to tie up the tomato plants". Some ties, in my opinion, should be used only to tie up the tomato plants. But some jobs are such that if you don't wear a tie, you will find you have nothing else to do except tend the tomato plants.

But there are many truths in the book, too, like "love, fun and idealism have as much place at work as in any other aspect of life".

As we have found, a holiday can just be a state of mind. You don't have to "go away" to go away.

The trick is to be able to do this when the barbecue and the holiday is over.

A LONG JOURNEY WITHOUT ARRIVAL

10 January 1996

YOU see them sometimes, while you are idly scanning the birth notices wondering if any of your old school friends have become parents lately. Among the "thrilled", "ecstatic", "excited" and "pleased" new parents are those who quietly announce a birth—and a death—in one.

It seems such a shocking and surprising thing, accustomed as we are to seemingly risk-free pregnancy and birth. But these tiny notices, which seem so understated and inadequate, are sobering reminders that, even today, birth is not necessarily risk-free for mother or child.

I have read enough birth notices to expect one of these every now and again, but it is always a shock. So it was when I cast my eye over them again recently and read about the arrival of Briana Jane, followed by seven sad words: "Our precious little daughter now in heaven."

Even heaven must be small comfort compared with the hell of losing a baby. I cannot presume to understand the pain this must cause. But I know that when a baby is born, so too is hope, optimism and a sense that you have a future, as a couple and as a family. When a baby dies, do these hopes and dreams die, too?

There are hundreds of books on pregnancy and birth and while most advise that death, through miscarriage or stillbirth, may be a possibility, few deal with the reality. That's why I was pleased to see that Sheila Kitzinger, the world-renowned expert on pregnancy and birth, has included two experiences of stillbirth in her most recent book, *Giving Birth—How It Really Feels.*

Ms Kitzinger says: "Many birth educators are reluctant to explore feelings in their classes about death and what will happen if a baby is stillborn, because they are anxious that they will make pregnant women unnecessarily frightened. Yet, in Western countries, roughly one baby in every hundred dies before labor starts, during childbirth or soon after."

In some ways, she says, no one can ever really prepare themselves psychologically for an experience like that. But listening to other women and men who have been through it can "help open our minds to the possibility and give us strength and confidence to cope with the loss of a baby".

In the book, one mother, known only as Deborah, tells how her baby died in utero at about 32 weeks and how the attitudes of the midwives turned what should have been a "ghastly" experience into a "positive, memorable and meaningful" one.

"I will never forget the midwife wrapping the baby in a cloth and cuddling it with a lovely smile on her face. To her it didn't matter that the baby was dead . . ." Deborah writes.

The other story is by Kenneth R. Freeston, who describes how his daughter died in utero after eight months of trouble-free pregnancy when his wife suffered severe undiagnosed toxaemia. The story was originally published in *The New York Times*. "A father's pain is no less intense, just different," he writes.

Death is difficult enough to deal with at any time, but when for nine months you have prepared for life, it is all the more terrible. "Catalogues for children's toys come in the mail and I cry," he writes.

The message is clear: even today, life and death remain bitterly entwined.

But, for me, there is another message: it is easy—and wrong—to assume that people who do not have children now have never had them.

It is easy to imagine the pain of a parent who sees a child without a toy, but it is far more difficult to imagine the pain of a parent who sees a toy without a child.

DEALING WITH PRIDE AND PREJUDICE

17 January 1996

EVERY morning, when I get out of bed, Greta and I have the same conversation. "I don't rike your yukky reg," she says (meaning leg), as my warm feet hit the cool carpet. "I rike your better reg."

"I like my better leg, too," I say, and then she adds, "I tiss your better reg," and promptly plants a kiss on my knee.

It is a rather rude awakening, you might think, to be reminded of one's shortcomings so early in the day. But this is a big improvement. The first time I tried to hop into the bath with her she recoiled and sat cringing in the corner crying "Get out!"

Greta is right. My "better reg", the one without the swelling and scarring, is much easier on the eye. In many ways, her revulsion is natural, even if it is socially unacceptable.

However, in my view, it is no good telling children at this age that they are hurting someone's feelings with these attitudes.

That might cause them to feel guilty, but it won't change their attitudes, because such attitudes are not born of malice, but of fear. At least, that is what I recognised in Greta.

Perhaps it is a natural reaction, a type of instinctive self-preservation against any disease that might have caused the deformity. That's my theory now, because few books on raising children seem to deal with this issue.

That's why I was so interested in Hugh Mackay's discussion on how we judge people's physical appearance in his recent book *Why Don't People Listen?* Mackay, a social psychologist, talks about the "cage" that we each construct around ourselves to help us interpret and cope with our world. "The bars of our cages are all the things that life has taught us: our knowledge, our attitudes, our values, our beliefs, our convictions," he says.

This cage is essential for our mental health, Mackay argues, and far from being a prison, inside it feels bright, airy and comfortable. But at the same time, the bars impose their own pattern on what we see.

Mackay argues that one of the most obvious ways that the cage distorts our view of the world is in our personal assessment of each other. He says: "Prejudice about personal appearance can strongly influence our response to each other . . ."

So how do we overcome this in teaching our children to accept people who are different? Mackay argues that our experience shapes our attitudes, which in turn shapes our behavior, pending new experience.

Looking back, I suppose this is what Rob and I have tried to do for Greta, reassuring her, so that her experience of difference was positive rather than negative. This did not mean lying. Rather, it meant lots of reassurance.

Soon, the fear changed to sympathy. Then sympathy changed to acceptance, but not without our early-morning reminder that, like most people, she prefers not to be confronted with such differences.

That's why we prepared her well before she met my father, who lost the fingers on one hand in an industrial accident some 20 years ago. We carefully explained that he had an accident a long time ago and had only one hand, but it no longer hurt him and it couldn't hurt her either.

But it wasn't his hand that sent her running to me crying; it was his comment about "not having eaten any little girls lately".

He didn't realise that we had been reading Raymond Briggs's wonderful book *Jim and the Beanstalk*, which features a giant who remembers better days when he enjoyed three fried boys on toast for breakfast every morning.

Greta had expected her new grandpa to stay for lunch. She was rather taken aback to discover that she was the main course.

WELCOME TO THE HELL-RAISERS' CLUB

21 January 1996

DON'T you hate all that back-to-school stuff that advertisers throw at us poor parents as the holidays draw to a close?

It's not the cost of the new school gear that horrifies me, it's the thought of all those relentless notices about raffle tickets I will never sell, working bees I will never attend and Parent Teacher Association (PTA) meetings that always seem to be on the night I had planned to get drunk with a girlfriend.

Yes, I admit it. I am a member of the Bad Mothers' Club. You can tell our kind. We are the ones who know the other mothers only as "Billy's Mum", rather than by their own first names; who walk through the school gate only when it is compulsory, such as on parent-teacher night; and who use the backs of school notices for finger-painting and shopping lists.

I admit, too, that I am following a family tradition. My mother forsook the Good Mothers' Club and refused to do canteen duty.

However, she did organise a musical evening that was so popular it became an annual event.

Like Mum, in the past, I have tried to do my bit in my own way. For example, I once made my own Mother's Day cards to sell at a school stall. I had them copied on special card and included the original cartoon in case they wanted to run off extra copies.

On the day of the stall, when Johannes came home from school, I asked eagerly: "How much did they sell my cards for?"

"Oh, those! They gave them away for free," he said.

That's why, unlike my mother's musical evening, my Mother's Day cards are unlikely to be an annual event.

But that's not the reason I have forsaken the Good Mothers' Club. It is lack of time and patience, and the sheer frustration and futility of it all.

Don't get me wrong: we bad mothers are full of admiration for the good mothers. We are amazed at their patience and understanding about the lack of adequate Government funding for schools.

We are amazed that they don't get good and mad and march together to the Government and say that it is a disgrace that the quality of their children's education depends on the quantity of cakes they are prepared to bake.

We are amazed that they are not outraged at having to spend their evenings tasting and endorsing processed food produced by multinational companies or flogging chocolate on behalf of other multinational organisations, just so the school can buy another book for the library.

Of course, some good mothers are not quite so appreciative of us bad mothers. If only we'd support them, the library could have two books instead of one, they lament. We should all pull together to provide a better future for our children, they say.

To the bad mothers, however, the future under these conditions is the same as the past: an education system struggling to provide even the most basic resources for society's most precious resource—its children.

However, apart from being shockingly politically incorrect, being a bad mother can sometimes backfire. Like the time, last term, when I kept Johannes home from the school walkathon.

The idea of having him walk around the block 10 times to help pay for his education made me furious.

So, instead, we had a lovely day together, despite the fact that it rained.

I was surprised, however, to see him drag himself through the door after school the next day, looking pale and wan. "What's wrong?" I asked in alarm.

He looked at me mournfully and panted: "The walkathon was postponed until today."

It's almost enough to make a bad mother reform. But not until the PTA reforms, too.

Like the good mothers and fathers, I want the best for my children and I am quite prepared to stand up for state education. But I'd rather raise hell than raise funds.

New twist in a dog's tale

31 January 1996

"IT'S like going to the orphanage," I said, as the whole family trooped up to our local vet recently to choose a new puppy.

After the death of our previous puppy, Milo, we were all a little nervous. Although we had not had much chance to bond with her before she became ill, Milo's death had made a big impression. Puppies, we had learnt, could be delicate creatures.

That's why we chose the fattest one this time. "He's fine. He's just a glutton," the vet assured me when I asked why our chosen one was all stomach.

How true. This was a boy who always wanted more. So we called him Oliver Twist, Ollie for short.

For a few days we lapsed occasionally and called him Milo, but it was soon apparent that Ollie was nothing like poor Milo. For a start, Milo never bit Greta on the nose. "Do you wuv me and are you sorry?" she demanded between sobs.

There was no real damage. In fact, in a few weeks Ollie has done more damage to our couch than Greta's nose.

It didn't take him long to work out how to open the sliding doors between the kitchen and the lounge room and, although he is too small to jump on the couch, he figured out that if he climbed the stairs he could jump from the landing above.

"Bad!" we all roared at him in turn, following the advice of Danny Wilson, the author of *Curing Your Dog's Bad Habits*. "My own theory on reprimanding is based on the way one dog would reprimand another," Wilson writes.

"We all know that a dog will respond to a growl. We therefore use a short, harshly uttered word such as 'bad', that the dog would not hear in normal speech.

However, Ollie was either deaf or defiant. "Say it like a dog," I urged Rob one night.

"BAD!" barked Rob, with such a roar that poor Ollie ran and cowered under my desk.

Despite this deference and despite the fact that he is officially Johannes' dog, Ollie soon worked out who is the most important person in this family. "If it's not Greta, it's the bloody dog," groaned Rob, as Ollie whimpered pitifully when I left the room.

It was even worse when I left the house, as we discovered after returning home one afternoon.

"There's a note on the door and Ollie's gone!" cried Johannes in alarm, when I sent him down the driveway to let the dog out of the house, while I retrieved Greta and the shopping. The note, in big blue letters, said: "We have your dog . . . If you want him back . . . PS: We know who you are."

Remembering an incident in our street some years ago when someone had taped the muzzle of a barking dog and it had choked on its own vomit, I immediately thought the worst. Some sadistic maniac had stolen our poor Ollie, I thought.

I don't know what made me think of our neighbor, Morris, but I quickly turned to Johannes and said: "Run over to Morris and Helen's house and see if they know anything."

With great relief, we learnt that Ollie had not been stolen, only rescued. Morris, well known for his animal magnetism, had not been able to bear Ollie's howls and had climbed up the veranda and taken him home for the afternoon.

After I had recovered from the shock, I decided it had been a real neighborly thing to do, and one that should be encouraged.

That's why when Greta starts howling next time, I'm planning to go out for the afternoon and leave her on the veranda.

THE GAME OF LIFE ON CD-ROM

7 February 1996

WE WERE having yet another of those conversations, Johannes and I, about how he went to this amazing place and had to go into this forest and fight that ogre and use this rope and climb that tree.

But while he was doing this and that, all he was really doing was sitting in a chair, twitching his fingers.

Until recently I had scoffed at computer-game critics. Anything that kept my son's brain ticking over so furiously couldn't be too bad, I thought, as I watched him ring his friend Rhys at all hours of the day and night, trying to nut out solutions.

But when I picked him up from a friend's house on a 32-degree day recently to find him pale-faced and still wearing a windcheater, I realised that reality had made way for virtual reality.

"Aren't you hot?" I asked.

"No," he said, looking surprised.

He hadn't exerted himself enough to be hot, despite trekking thousands of kilometres over uncharted lands on a strange quest.

I felt annoyed. How could he wear a jumper on a day like this? A few days later, I realised what was really annoying me. We were on our way home from the pantomime *The Magic Faraway Tree*, and while the real live performance had generated a few appreciative comments, it was not long before the conversation turned to computer games again.

Suddenly I blurted out, "Doesn't it ever worry you that you are not really doing any of these things? That there are real worlds you could be adventuring in, real trees that could be climbed?"

"It's not the same," he said.

Certainly not the same as *Myst*, our latest CD-ROM acquisition.

"*Myst* is real," the blurb says. Johannes had been lured by the graphics; I had been lured by his claim that it was "sort of educational".

"The puzzles you encounter will be solved by logic and information—information garnered either from *Myst* or from life itself," the blurb boasts.

But will something from life be missed while adventuring in *Myst*? Combined with a fascination for television, will this result in a generation of watchers rather than doers, I wondered, as I saw Johannes shaking a toy for the dog while still gazing at the television later that day.

No, said my friend Lyn, who has two children, a boy and a girl, of similar age to Johannes. Her son loved computer games, but her daughter also lived in a fantasy world, she said. This world was created through books.

"And somehow that's more acceptable to me," Lyn said. "But maybe there's not much difference. She's doing it all vicariously through reading, the same as Johannes is doing it through computer games."

Johannes reads avidly, too, but shouldn't he be out with his sling-shot and his fishing rod, with his dog running at his heels instead of sitting on his knee?

Lyn laughed. "That's your romanticism," she said. Still, she agreed there had to be some sort of balance.

As for the dog, not playing with it today does not mean Johannes will not want to tomorrow, she said. Perhaps, too, a dog does not fit in that fantasy world? As a child, Lyn had been an avid reader of *The Famous Five* books, by Enid Blyton, starring Timmy the dog, and her own dog had been part of her fantasy world as a result.

I feel somewhat reassured. But there is still the question of balance. All I need now is a computer game about a boy and his dog. Does *Lassie* come on CD-ROM?

BETTER CARE FOR KIDS AND PARENTS

14 February 1996

"YOU'RE going to creche tomorrow, because Mummy has to go to work," I told Greta one night, in my cheeriest, won't-this-be-fun voice.

"But I don't want to," she said.

"You'll have a happy day," I reassured her. "You can play with the big girls."

"But I don't want to. I want to stay home."

"But Mummy has to go to work in the city to get money to buy things."

"Daddy can look after me."

"Daddy will be at work in the city too, and you can't stay here all by yourself."

"I will stay here by myself and, and I . . . and I can . . . Daddy can get some money," she retorted.

Child development commentator Penelope Leach was right, I thought in exasperation. In her book *Children First* she said that while day care frees mothers to earn, lessening their dependence on partners and the state, it does not free them from their feelings. "Their children, and their feelings for their children, still exist," she wrote.

But Leach was not naive enough to merely condemn child care, as the outcry about her book seemed to imply at the time.

In the debate about whether child care was good or bad, the fact that she tried to offer some realistic ideas about ways to integrate paid work and family care and some alternative models for long-day care was lost.

One of her suggestions was a central child-place in each community that might serve all the disparate people presently involved. This would also serve as a drop-in centre or informal club for anyone else caring for a baby. The centre would facilitate a gradual separation between parent and child and eventually foster stress-free day care, she argued.

That's why I was so interested in a letter from a new child care centre which has just opened a centre in Collins Street. "Features include a secure rooftop garden and a butterfly house and provision for parents to visit their children to share lunch and other activities," the promotional blurb boasts.

The rooftop garden and butterfly house sound nice, but what sounds nicer is the idea that parents can visit and share lunch. This accessibility is available at many other childcare centres, but usually parents and children are not within lunching distance of each other. For city workers, being a tram-ride away from their children means such accessibility would be a reality.

The centre claims that this flexibility, and the fact that it can cater for children aged from six weeks to six years for up to 24 hours a day, may help some women combine professional advancement with motherhood.

It certainly will help some, but being able to come early or stay late is just one obstacle. There are many others, not least being the child who doesn't want to stay at all.

Sowing the seeds of friendship

21 February 1996

"THEY'RE like strawberries and cream," said Della, the child-care worker, when I went to pick up Greta from crèche.

To my relief, it seemed that Greta had made a new friend.

"They even had to have their little beds together so that their toes could touch at sleep time," Della said.

Michaela, Greta's new friend, confirmed the depth of this new relationship by promptly bursting into tears when I arrived to take Greta home.

It was not the first deep friendship she had formed at creche.

Fiona, impish and outgoing, had been Greta's first real friend at creche and Thursday—"Fiona's day"—is eagerly awaited.

Hearing this and seeing the children's tender embraces at the creche Christmas party last year was both endearing and surprising. It made me wonder how the seeds of friendship are sown. What makes some friendships grow and others die? How do children as young as two and three decide who among their peers will be their friends?

For the answers I had no book, so I asked Greta. "Why do you like Fiona?"

"Because she's pretty," Greta replied. I had to admit that even in friendship there is an element of attraction.

But there are lots of pretty girls and, indeed, some pretty boys at creche, so there had to be more. "Why do you like the other girls?" I pressed.

"I don't like the boys fighting," she said. "The girls, they pray (play) with me. They let me jump on the trampoline."

There were some boys who were nice because they "prayed" too, but she did not like one boy "because he keeps trying to bash me".

I was glad that even at this age she was discriminating.

However, discrimination can work both ways, as she found last weekend when Johannes had two friends around. Initially, they found her a pleasant diversion between sessions on the computer. But when it came to playing Monopoly in the tree house, which is really just a platform a metre off the ground, she was considered too little.

I looked out of the window a few times to see her standing below, looking up pitifully, while the boys threw her down an occasional goodie from the box they were hoarding.

However, patience paid off. The next time I looked up, there she was, sitting among them, clutching the box.

The ebb and flow of friendship can be both joyous and painful, particularly among children, but also among adults. Some friends can outlast husbands, others are formed through circumstance rather than choice and when circumstances change, so does the friendship.

However, keeping friendships, like any relationship, requires work and in these busy days of juggling work and family life, this is becoming increasingly difficult for many people—even little people.

For all the debate about child care, child-care centres have become an important source of friendship for many preschool children and their parents. Indeed some children, like Fiona, are in child care for this very reason.

But this formal contact is not enough. The seed of friendship, if it is to flower, needs more than a once-a-week watering, so we decided to organise a play date for Fiona and Greta.

Organising friendships that require chaperones means that the chaperones need to get along, too. So I was delighted to find myself thoroughly enjoying the company of Fiona's mother. In fact, we were so engrossed in conversation that we forgot to check on the girls who had disappeared, squealing with delight, into Greta's room.

When we called them downstairs, they were as white as ghosts, their faces covered in talcum powder. "We are Blinky Bill!" Greta announced, grinning.

She had been singing "I'm Blinky Bill, my whole rife's a frill!" all week. And now with a friend to play with, who could deny it?

COPING WITH A SECURITY CRISIS

28 February 1996

"HOW'S work?" I asked one of the other mothers as we collected our children from creche last week. She sighed. "There are so few us and we are expected to do so much. We're all so tired."

It seems to be a common feeling among those in paid work at present. This particular friend is a local teacher, so it is not surprising that she feels as if more is expected from less. But it is not only teachers who are feeling tired.

It seems that in almost every workplace, more is expected from fewer people, and for fewer rewards.

By rewards I mean such things as recognition, encouragement and good will, as well as money. However, the most important reward that seems to be lacking in the modern "efficient" workplace is security.

In all the election rhetoric of the past few weeks, the only thing that has really struck a chord with families like us is a comment by businesswoman Eve Mahlab on ABC TV's *7.30 Report*. The real issue for many people was security, Ms Mahlab said.

Since the 1970s, women have had to enter the workforce just to maintain the standard of living that was once achieved on one wage, she said. Workers must now work longer hours to maintain the same entitlements, yet with no guarantee they will keep their jobs.

For families already struggling to juggle work and home life, the thought that this struggle might be in vain is overwhelming. It adds pressure—and despair.

"Families are slowly cooking," said my friend Claire Miran-Khan, who trains health professionals in family therapy. "It's like putting a frog in a pot of water and bringing it very slowly to the boil. If you add the heat slowly the frog doesn't notice. But, of course, it eventually dies."

The cost to families of policies that cut services and jobs—embraced in various degrees by both major parties—is a loss of confidence both personally and in the future.

How can we encourage our children to work hard at school when no matter what they achieve, there may not be a job for them? How can we maintain our own momentum at work when we know that no matter how successful we are, if it is more profitable to do without us, we will be dismissed?

Loyalty among the workers that I know has been replaced by a sense of hurt, distrust and (eventually) cynicism. On the long train ride into work, the topic of conversation among commuters has changed from weather forecasts to job forecasts.

A banker friend who is facing redundancy told Rob in disbelief last week: "At the end of last year, we were told we were valued. Three months later, we are told we're not."

This man has worked for the company for 18 years. Now, at 36, he must compete for other jobs in an ever-shrinking market. Retraining will take three or four years, which brings him to the age of 40 when people, not jobs, are now considered redundant.

I am not naive enough to think that security has been guaranteed in every generation. Depressions, wars, booms and busts have affected families in the past. But was this the result of policy or merely blunder? I, for one, am not interested in election trinkets bought at the expense of other people's jobs.

Call me a cynic, but it seems we are moving towards a world where people no longer matter, unless they are young, can provide cheap labor, wear nifty uniforms and baseball caps and ask few questions other than "Will you have fries with that?"

Depression lifts at the Sound of Music

6 March 1996

I ONCE knew someone who had a very uplifting cartoon stuck on her refrigerator.

It was a drawing of a woman standing on her head, surrounded by miscellaneous bits and pieces. It read: "Mrs Brown was depressed. So she stood on her head and all her depressed bits fell out on to the floor." It still makes me smile, even though I feel thoroughly depressed—and ashamed, as I have nothing to be depressed about, really.

I have a roof over my head, food on the table and people who love me and whom I love in return. So why do I feel as if I have swallowed a lump of sand? I examine my hormones, then my heart and conclude that what is depressing me is not the knowledge that I have a roof over my head, food on the table and people that love me, but the thought that I may not have it tomorrow.

That's why, despite Mrs Brown's advice, standing on my head has resulted only in a headache. The sun shines, I tell myself. But will it shine tomorrow? What can I do to rid myself of this paralysis?

If I cannot be sure of the future, at least I can be sure of the past, so I eschew modern pop psychology and do what they did in the old days, or at least during that other Great Depression. I go to the movies. But I can't afford a babysitter, so I borrow an anti-depressant video instead—*The Sound of Music*.

If Julie Andrews can climb every mountain, then so can I, I think, as I set the children up with lollies to bribe them to stay, and together we join the Von Trapp children in singing about our favourite things.

Rob comes home and walks out again, groaning.

"Don't say anything!" I warn him. "Don't spoil it!"

"I'll watch musicals with you," says Johannes in my defence, charmed as much by the lollies as the music. Greta and I dance around the room, and I sing at the top of my voice, so that even Johannes comments: "Boy! You really get off on this stuff, don't you?"

However five days later, after the 25th rewind of the song *The Lonely Goatherd*, I am only slightly rejuvenated. Paralysis sets in again. Like a drunk who recognises that only the hair of the dog will get rid of a hangover, I realise that having had a good sing and a good laugh, what I really need now is a good cry.

So I borrow *Little Women*, the latest version of that classic tear-jerker about the fortunes and misfortunes of the ever-optimistic March sisters. Furtively, after Rob has gone to bed in exasperation, Ollie Dog and I prepare for a night of pure indulgence.

And it works. By the time Jo, the heroine, seals her matrimonial fate with a kiss, Ollie is sleeping on my knee under a blanket of soggy tissues, and I am feeling much better. That lump of sand in my throat has been washed away by a wave of tears, not to mention a few litres of wine.

Of course, I feel guilty. Not about the wine or Rob, but about the movie. Everything I enjoy is so politically incorrect these days.

When I once confessed dreamily that I had stayed up late watching *Seven Brides for Seven Brothers*, my friend Rosemary looked at me in horror and said, "That sanctions rape." And I do squirm slightly when Maria in *The Sound of Music* marches triumphantly down the aisle to the song *How do you solve a problem like Maria?*

But when it comes to my problems, I'd rather hire a video than a therapist, especially a musical video. Then, like Maria, my heart wants to sing every song it hears.

A BRIDGE BETWEEN TWO WORLDS

20 March 1996

WE LINGERED at the creche gate, my friend Sue and I, after dropping off our children. It was a beautiful sunny day. But for me there were clouds. I had to write this column, among many other things, and Johannes was sick. How would I pack 16 hours work into eight, care for a sick child and get to the doctor?

I felt a sense of rising panic even stopping to talk. Sue, on the other hand, had a free day; she did not have a paid job. How I envied her that freedom. "So ultimately you would rather not work?" she asked, after hearing my litany of woes.

Well, no. My identity and my sense of achievement was so tied up with work. The problem was not my work or my children, but the fact that I had two jobs.

For Sue, this was a reminder that doing one job these days was a privilege. But, she confessed, she had to keep reminding herself of this. "I struggle to put a value on it," she said. The reason, of course, was that her job was unpaid.

As we talked about the problems facing women in paid and unpaid work, it slowly dawned on me that women like me, who have two jobs, are not the only ones feeling that whatever we do, we should be doing something else.

Many women staying at home full-time with young children, no matter how much they believe in it, also feel that they should be doing something else, something that gives them money and status and something to talk about at the dinner-party table.

"A friend of mine once put her finger on it," Sue said. "It's not so much that you have nothing to talk about with other people, as that they don't know what to talk to you about."

Perhaps this is because only the world of paid work is considered of public interest.

That's why Sue is thinking of doing something else. Not for the money, not because there is a particular career she is hankering to pursue,

188

but just for the feeling that "a person should be able to do something to support one's self".

It is true that full-time mothering makes women economically vulnerable. But there is another reason for seeking another life other than caring for others. "Something happens to you if you do it for a long time," Sue said.

"What?" I asked.

"I don't quite know," she said. "Perhaps it was that things got out of perspective," she suggested. "You become consumed by things that others are more properly detached about."

However, we both agreed that paid jobs could also be consuming.

Perhaps it is because caring for children requires a degree of selflessness that is easy to idealise and difficult to achieve.

That day was a case in point. Johannes was feeling better, so we decided to take the dog and walk down to the creche to pick up Greta. I should have known better, I thought later, as I struggled with the pusher, the dog and the Chinese takeaway while Johannes followed behind me, throwing up every six paces.

Thankfully, we were rescued by a friend, but at home Ollie Dog decided to follow Johannes's example and threw up all over the lounge room floor.

When Rob and I finally sat down to cold Chinese food we soon lost our appetites as we were in full view of Ollie, sitting outside the lounge room window eagerly scoffing his own pooh.

It is true, I thought, as I made my way to the bathroom: there is definitely no status in this job. But who says I don't have anything to talk about at the dinner party table?

A PARENT GOES TO SCHOOL

27 March 1996

EXAMINING secondary schools for your child is a sobering experience.

First, because you keep shaking your head in wonder that this person, who only yesterday was walking excitedly inside the primary school gate, will soon be walking inside the secondary school gate.

And second, because you wonder which school to choose. Once upon a time you simply sent your child to the school in your area. Now it is a complicated process of matching your child's needs and potential with your own values and aspirations and the education services offered by the various schools. I am grateful for the choice, but mindful of the need to choose wisely.

Then there is the other vexed question of whether to go public or private. It was this question that sent me on a flurry of school inspections recently.

Many private school enrolments for next year and scholarship applications were closing. Family members who are teachers said that any school, whether private or public, was only as good as its principal and teachers and school community, and these elements could vary over the years. The biggest influence on a child's education, they said, was still the home.

As a product of the state education system and a person who believes that education should be a right rather than a privilege, even thinking about private school education felt like treason to me. However, state schools are great schools only if they are properly resourced and supported.

As a parent, the knowledge that many state schools are now struggling to do more with less made me think what once would have been unthinkable: perhaps we should consider a private school education after all? By we, I mean all Johannes's parents: me, Johannes' father, Rob and, of course, Johannes.

So I called for the prospectuses of half a dozen schools, public and private, and sat poring for days over glossy brochures and pastel-colored booklets, with pictures of smiling girls and boys in neatly pressed uniforms, sitting at computers or in science labs or stepping radiantly into the future.

However, these told me only about the school's self-image. The best way to find out about schools is to ask their students and go there yourself. So I visited a few, and then we took the day off, Johannes and Greta and I, and visited a few more.

At the end of the day, there was no school that was better than another. Each school had something special or unique or a combination of features that made it either suitable or unsuitable.

In the end we chose a school that has music as its focus. "I like this one," said Johannes as we walked out. So did I, and I was delighted that the school that most impressed us was a state school.

But I wanted to keep an open mind, so I suggested we attend a house music festival at the school the following week.

I had been expecting something rather prim and classical, with lots of speeches and polite clapping. What we saw was a high-class performance received with the fervor usually kept for a rock concert or a football match.

The festival was organised by the students, so their enthusiasm should not have been surprising. However, I was surprised at how much fun they were having.

Johannes was won over when they played themes from *The Simpsons* and *The Muppet Show*, but I liked the set song, which was *Never Give Up*. It seemed like a philosophy that these students had taken to heart and an excellent one for any school, particularly state schools.

THE HOUSE THAT JACK BUILT

2 April 1996

IT WAS a warm day and having dropped Greta at her preschool dance class, I found myself wandering the streets of a neighboring suburb with a rare 45 minutes to spare. Although it was only half an hour from our place, it felt like another country.

There were few trees, just houses standing shoulder to shoulder, each one grander than the next. No wind or rain had softened the corners of these brick mansions yet, no sunshine had bleached or scarred them, and it seemed few footsteps had marked the well-swept pathways and cricket-pitch lawns.

I did not like this bold little Lego village, but I could not help looking wistfully at the size of the houses. It would be nice to have a kitchen big enough to actually cook and serve food in, a laundry where you could wash, dry and air clothes, and a bathroom in which you didn't crack your elbows on the shower screen as you dried yourself.

It was these thoughts and the heat that led me inside one of the display homes in the area. The house was certainly big. There was a grand foyer, a powder room, a family room, a living room, a dining room, an atrium, a parents' retreat, a spa. In fact, it was big enough for 10 people. So why did it have a two-person laundry and kitchen?

The kitchen had lots of floor space, but not much bench space. The pantry opened into the thoroughfare between the kitchen and dining room, and the stove and dishwasher were below the bench, which meant bending down or kneeling on the floor, which was covered with cold, hard tiles.

The laundry was no better. As usual, it was also the only access to the back door, with just enough room for a small trough and a washing machine.

As I made my way past the smiling salesman, he asked: "So what did you think?"

I knew it was not his fault, but I was irritated. "This house must have been designed by a man," I said. (Forgive my sexism, but so far most houses are still designed by men, while most housework is still done by women.)

He looked surprised. "We have some very good women designers," he said.

"Well, they must be women who never cook or wash," I replied, explaining my grievances. "Where would you air the washing?" I asked. "In the parents' retreat? I don't want a spa and parents' retreat. I want a house that works. On the two most important rooms in the house, you've failed," I said, pointing an accusing finger and marching out the door.

"So I guess we won't be building a house for you?" he called after me.

No, thank you. I guess one day, I'll have to design and build my own. It would not be a flash house, because I could not bear having to worry about keeping it flash. It would not be too big either, because the more you have, the more you have to look after. But it would be big enough.

The kitchen would be big enough to allow children to get drinks and snacks without getting in the way of the cook. The benches would be big enough to allow for the clutter of meal preparation and serving and all the miscellaneous items that seem to gather there. The laundry would be big enough for several clothes racks and baskets of dirty and clean washing.

No bending would be required in either room and neither would be major thoroughfares.

As for the rest of the house, it would be "closed plan" rather than "open plan", so that family members could work, watch television, read or whatever without disturbing each other.

But this, of course, is not the modern view. The modern family home seems to be designed for eternal entertainment. Architects seem to have forgotten that families need to work—and so do family homes.

When 'no' seems to be the hardest word

9 April 1996

"PARENTS can't seem to say no any more," commented a colleague, after telling me about her visit to a friend's house. Apparently her friend's children had the run of the place, and were still running it at 10 o'clock at night.

It sounded like a familiar scenario and one that puzzles older generations, who are wont to tell us that in their day, children were neither seen nor heard after 7.30pm.

Pondering this on the way home from work one day, it occurred to me that the reason modern parents have this problem is that most of us want to be liked by our children. Older generations wanted to be liked, but they seemed to value respect more.

Wanting to be liked is a burden that usually makes leadership difficult. And being a parent is like being a leader of sorts.

Once, when I was struggling with a position of authority at work, my supervisor gave me some good advice. "You don't have to be liked," he said. That advice helped a lot. It gave me permission to use my head rather than my heart.

Of course, when dealing with children it is usually best to use both, but sometimes this creates conflict. Our hearts tell us that we want our children to be happy, while our heads tell us that getting one's own way all the time does not encourage self-discipline, and a lack of it does not encourage happiness.

Perhaps another reason that modern parents seem to have difficulty saying no is the fear that it will not make any difference. Then what do you do?

These days most parents prefer not to resort to corporal punishment. So we resort to blackmail and bribes. "Do what you're told or you won't get any videos (or whatever)!" we plead. However, most of us know that this sort of discipline only teaches our children how to get videos.

What we want instead is to help our children see the consequences of their actions and act accordingly.

Family therapist Stephen Biddulph writes in his book *More Secrets of Happy Children* that discipline is in vogue again.

He advocates the use of "firm love". "Firm love rests on two main techniques—the first is called 'stand and think' and the second is called 'dealing'," he writes.

Children are removed from the situation and told to think about their actions. Then, when they are calm enough, they are encouraged to talk about a solution and to make a commitment to it. The technique can be simplified for toddlers.

However, it is not just the children who must be old enough and mature enough to use these techniques—it is the parents.

I know because it has taken me three years to use a similar technique to get Greta to sleep in her own bed alone.

Lying beside her one night recently, feeling bitter and resentful that my evening was being whittled away, I suddenly realised that it was not her fault but mine. She had been ready for quite a while to go to bed alone. Now I was ready, too.

Within two nights, she was asleep in her bed.

Saying no is sometimes one of the best things that a parent can do for a child. Saying no at bed times usually means everyone gets more rest. Saying no at meal times usually saves someone throwing up on the carpet later. And saying no can sometimes even save lives.

So why do we sometimes put it off for so long? Perhaps it is because we know it will be difficult, not for our children, but for us.

CHARITY BEGINS AT HOME

16 April 1996

"WHEN I grow up, I'm going to do this," Johannes said as we were driving along.

"What?" I asked in that only half-interested way you manage when you are distracted in heavy traffic.

"This," he said, holding up the latest Pocket Saver coupon book.

In the rear-vision mirror a pair of soulful brown eyes peered back at me from a round brown face. It was the face of a child I didn't know. A hungry face.

At the lights, he tossed the book in my lap. It read: "Free a child from hunger and disease. Free a child from poverty and despair. Just $1 a day."

"I could only afford to do it for five days now," he said, "which wouldn't be any good, and I wouldn't have anything left for my own things. But when I grow up, I'm going to do it."

Here was my opportunity to encourage and reward his desire for community service by suggesting that the whole family pitch in and sponsor a child. But I held back. Perhaps it was the distant memory of an article I had read about a Melbourne woman who had sponsored a child in India? The attention and status conferred by the sponsorship caused conflict between the child and her siblings and divided the family from others in the village.

I knew that real help to people in developing countries was best given through programs that empowered them and gave them independence.

But I also knew that this took time and as a mother I hated to think that, meanwhile, a child would go hungry.

"How much is it a month?" I asked.

"Thirty-one dollars," he said, and then rather taken aback, added: "That sounds a lot." He did a mental calculation. "That's $372 a year!"

Yes, I thought, a decent sum towards the piano we were hoping to buy for him this year—if only we were thrifty enough to save $1 a day.

I immediately felt guilty. How could I withhold food from the mouth of one child, to give another something as ostentatious as a piano? Even so, the thought of adding another bill to our regular mountain of bills felt like a burden.

Then I recalled a scene from *Eight Cousins* by Louisa May Alcott. The heroine, Rose, and her guardian, Uncle Alec, discuss sacrifice. "A real sacrifice is giving up something you want or enjoy very much, isn't it?" asks Rose.

In this case, the sacrifice would not be Johannes's, but mine. I would have to let go of my own desire to be more politically correct. I would prefer to give a donation to an organisation that offered education to all, especially to women, for that has been shown to be the greatest benefit to children. But that would be my gift, not Johannes's. He wants to give to a little boy or girl like himself.

Perhaps it would be enriching for both children? One would have more food, the other more food for thought. Perhaps encouraging the desire to help now would instil it for life.

But what of the adage "charity begins at home"? Should I encourage some local community service instead?

A week has passed. Johannes has not mentioned it since.

Perhaps by vacillating I made a decision. Perhaps by vacillating I missed an opportunity to change not one life, but two.

If the dress fits

23 April 1996

"IT MAKES me weep, coming in here," I told the saleswoman in a local children's wear shop. "All these gorgeous clothes—and she only wants to wear one dress."

It probably made the saleswoman weep too, as she sat surrounded by racks of lovely but unsold dresses.

Anyone thinking of buying a children's clothing business should consider catering only for children under three years of age. After the age of three, little girls, in particular, get very particular.

"Can I wear my favorite dress?" Greta says every morning.

It is the perfect outfit as far as she is concerned, chiefly because the skirt is cut on the bias and spins around when she twirls. The fact that it was a hand-me-down from her cousin, Sian, also adds to its appeal. It is a lovely shade of blue but it is long-sleeved and lightweight, and the perfect dress requires perfect weather. On warm days it is too warm and on cool days it is too cool.

This fickle fashion sense extends to evening wear, too. When I bought Greta a dressing-gown recently, she insisted on wearing it throughout the shopping trip. But, of course, as soon as we got home she wouldn't wear it without being bribed and coerced.

That is, until one day as we were both traipsing down the stairs, me in my white dressing-gown and her in her pink one, and Rob commented: "There goes the big white marshmallow, followed by the little pink marshmallow." To any other girl it would have been an insult, but Greta saw it as an analogy to something sweet, rather than something short and round.

"You can't tell me that that's natural," warned my friend Carolyn when I told her about the favourite dress. "She wants to be like you."

Like me? For the past three years I have worn nothing but pants and a long shirt, chiefly because I once had a fat purse and a slim tummy, but now it is the other way around.

"But I don't wear dresses any more!" I protested.

"No, but you still have that very feminine style," Carolyn insisted.

Being feminine never stopped me from being feminist, so I was not too perturbed. I do not want to encourage "lookism", a term coined by Mary Pipher, an American psychologist and the author of *Raising Ophelia,* a new book about raising girls.

However, I am convinced that Greta's fashion fetish has more to do with wanting to be assertive rather than caring about her appearance.

But perhaps Carolyn is right in one sense. On the rare occasions that I do wear a dress it is always the same one, known as "she's red dress".

This title comes from a family story. When my sister and I were small, my mother often wore an orange cardigan, chiefly because she had nothing else. One day her friend asked her three-year-old son to keep an eye out for my mother. "Will she be wearin' she's o'nge jumper?" he inquired.

She was indeed wearing "she's o'nge jumper", just as Greta is constantly wearing "she's blue dress"—over her shorts, under her tracksuit pants and under her dressing—gown.

She'll grow out of it, I know. Meanwhile, I take comfort from the song that says "Young girls do get weary, wearing the same shabby dress" and from the remarks of Greta's Nana.

When I complained that Greta would wear only her favorite blue dress, Nana's face lit up. "Fiona (my sister-in-law) will be pleased. Her mother made it for Sian, but she wouldn't wear it."

Rekindling lost passions

30 April 1996

NEXT TIME you buy a book for your child, remember that it may change her life. I was given such a book many years ago: *I Can Jump Puddles*, by Australian author Alan Marshall.

I read it avidly, not just because it was a good read, but because I was intrigued by its hero. Despite being crippled by polio at the age of six, he rode horses, swam and did all the things country kids did.

Like Alan, I was different. I had lymphodema, which meant one leg was much bigger than the other. But the thing that intrigued me about this hero was that although he was different, it didn't seem to make much difference.

"Why don't you write to him?" my mother suggested, when I mentioned how much I admired Alan. We rang a newspaper, someone gave us the name of his publisher and a letter was labored over and dispatched.

I can't remember whether I asked him to write back, or whether that was just his habit. But soon I became one of hundreds of children throughout the world who corresponded regularly with him.

Alan died in 1984, and although we met several times over the years, I can't pretend I knew him well, despite our letters.

This wasn't due to any holding back on his part. He was always generous with his words and time, even when he was too sick and frail. He always managed a "'G'day", even if it was by proxy through his secretary, Gwen.

But I was young, lacking confidence and too self-conscious and silly to realise what an opportunity for learning and growth he had given me with his friendship.

I was also painfully aware that the world he wrote about was not my world. At 14, I was studious, a little anxious and a rather serious city child. Yet Alan wrote so powerfully about his love of the land that I wanted to love it, too, even though I was afraid of horses and ignorant of the smell and feel of the earth.

But this was not the full reason I wanted to reach out to him.

More attractive than the country I didn't know was a feeling I didn't know: a complete lack of self-consciousness about his disability. I was reaching out for that. Alan was so interested in and observant of others that he seemed to have no time to feel sorry for himself. It was not pity but passion he inspired.

It is this passion that will be celebrated on Sunday at Alan's birthplace, Noorat, in the Western District, about three hours' drive from Melbourne. The festival, just four days past his birthdate on 2 May 1902, will involve horse riding, folk music, street theatre, a state-wide short-story competition, a photography competition and even a yarn-spinning competition. It's just the sort of thing that Alan would have loved.

Alan was a great talker and a great listener, too. And he listened to the Aborigines in the days when few listened. They called him Gurrawilla, which means song-maker or story-maker.

So much has changed since the days of Gurrawilla. Few of us now talk about "coves" and "buggers", or use expletives like "struth". And all our mates are now "guys".

Not long ago, a visiting American complained on radio that no one had said g'day to him—despite the promises of actor Paul Hogan on the television ads.

In this global village, the culture is lost but the cultural stereotypes survive. That's why, if you're up near Hamilton way this weekend, turn off at Noorat and drop in on the Alan Marshall festival, to celebrate the life of a great Australian and to say g'day.

HEAD OVER HEELS OVER DANCING

1 May 1996

The shop assistant smiled indulgently while she put some blue eyeshadow, a packet of hair clips and some hair nets in a bag.

"Ballet, is it?"

"Yes," I said and tried not to look embarrassed when I had to admit that the dancer had only recently been a toddler.

It was really pre-school ballet, I explained—music and movement with ballet shoes—and she was not so much dancing as falling, as the class was miming Humpty Dumpty for an inter-school competition.

"I'm surprised at you!" my friend Chris cried, when I mentioned in passing later that Greta had started dancing classes. She was surprised, I guess, because she presumed that feminist mothers didn't encourage such feminine pursuits.

I tried to explain: "I hate sport, but I want her to have what I never had: confidence in her body. Dancing will teach her about music, rhythm movement, theatre."

I didn't realise it then, but it would also teach her perseverance and courage.

The competition was on a Sunday afternoon, so we all traipsed off with Greta togged out in leotard and ballet shoes, her hair in a bun, her brown eyes shaded blue with "eye washer" and her mouth a brilliant splash of red "wipstick".

At the hall, dozens of little girls and a few little boys similarly attired, were all jumping on the flip-down seats or running around excitedly, while an adjudicator sat at a table in the middle of the room.

We were a little early, and fearing Greta would get tired of waiting, I gave Johannes some money to buy some lollies at a stall—anything but chocolate, I said.

He came back with a packet of hard fruit lollies and gave one to Greta, which she crunched eagerly. "More?" she said with her mouth full. "Not until you've finished that one," I said. So she started swallowing them whole.

Just as the Humpty Dumpties were lining up ready to go on, she began to scream and retch. "She's choking!" I yelled. "Do something!"

I started to tip her upside down while Rob went to find a drink of water, but just as I turned her upright she vomited a slimy orange spray all over her purple leotard and my new red jacket.

"Is she nervous?" asked someone, while someone else kindly gave me a packet of tissues to mop up the mess. She wasn't to start with, but no doubt she would be now, I thought.

"Do you still want to go on?" I asked as the Humpty Dumpties lined up. "Yes," she said, her blue "eye washer" now washed with tears.

All went well—until Humpty had to sit down and cry. Greta was so busy rubbing her eyes that she forgot to get up again. I think it was probably her doing that earned them equal third with the Wee Willy Winkies, but we were all delighted anyway.

"I'm the winner," she said on the way home.

"No you're not. You came third," Johannes said matter-of-factly.

"I'm the winner. I'm free," she said, holding up three fingers and waving her green ribbon around excitedly.

Okay, okay, I know what you are thinking: she's too young for hard fruit lollies and far too young for dancing classes.

But from the moment she could sit up, she was rocking to music and would have started ballet sooner if not for the ban on nappies under leotards.

However, I have no illusions about her future. As far as I'm concerned, que sera, sera.

Her favorite video may be the *The Nutcracker Suite* but as long as she likes to watch it while gnawing the fat from a chop bone, she is more likely to be a pudding than a Pavlova.

BREAKING THE RULES ON KEEPING MUM

7 May 1996

"I'VE had enough!" I yell at my children as I herd them off to the bath after a day that has ended with all of us feeling tired and grumpy.

I have had enough of them and they, as usual, have never had enough of me.

But I am tired. Tired of talking, tired of giving—and besides, on the table is a new book with which I was planning to retreat to the bedroom. It's called *Motherlove—stories about births, babies and beyond*, edited by Debra Adelaide.

Such are the contradictions of motherhood.

It is these contradictions that make writing about motherhood and Mother's Day, in particular, so difficult. The relationship between a mother and child is arguably the most intense human relationship, so it is understandably fraught.

Most people love their mothers, but mixed with this love is anger, disappointment, frustration, sadness, a fierce pride and a terrifying empathy.

In some ways, no matter how much we deny it and strain at it, that umbilical cord connecting us to our mothers remains. As infants, our mothers appear omnipresent and omnipotent. As we grow up, they become more human, and a large part of growing up is forgiving them for their humanity.

For daughters, this connection is strengthened when we have our own children. We understand how the need and desire to nurture and give totally and without hesitation competes with the need and desire not to give too much, in case there is nothing left for ourselves.

We understand the anger and guilt when we find our children's needs impossible, insatiable and outrageous, mixed with recognition that this is not only their right, but an ancient tool of survival. Here, too, there is fierce pride and terrifying empathy—and awe as we acknowledge the miracle of life.

But these emotions are rarely aired. As Adelaide says in her introduction to *Motherlove*: ". . . who has ever talked or written of such things without feeling self-conscious, out of place, ridiculous or plain soppy?"

This is not surprising; in talking about it, we make ourselves vulnerable. In *Motherlove*, 17 women, (including actors Noni Hazelhurst and Rachel Ward, and fellow journalist Adele Horin) most of whom are better known for their paid work than their unpaid work of mothering, make themselves vulnerable by talking about their experience of motherhood.

In commissioning stories for the book, Adelaide gives the contributors permission to do what most dare to do only among trusted friends and family: tell it like it is.

Baby and parenting books abound, but as Adelaide says, these "do not tell the real story of what it is like to be pregnant, give birth, handle a baby and raise a child. The real story, as anyone who has had a child knows, involves a lot more blood, dreams, tears, laughter and screams than the authorities are prepared to reveal."

There are few outlets for these real stories, except in parenting magazines. Even journalists like Adelaide are reluctant to use their craft in this way. "It's self-indulgent. Boring. Only of limited interest," she says when describing the reaction of others to her desire to write about what she describes as "often the most compelling experience of one's life".

Perhaps journalists feel this reluctance because writing about motherhood would require them to be subjective rather than objective. Yet those of us who do write such things know that we are not only writing our own stories, but everyone's.

We are not just saying our experience is important, but that the experience of giving birth and raising children is important, and so is our experience as mothers—not just on Mother's Day, but every day.

WHY BARBIE IS A NERD

14 May 1996

IT HAD to be a set-up. There was TV presenter, Jo Beth Taylor, on *Hey, Hey, It's Saturday*, wearing a Celebrity Head sign that said "Barbie".

When she asked "Am I somebody very intelligent?" the audience erupted in loud guffaws.

Unless they have been surfing the Internet, few among the audience would know that Barbie's image as a bimbo is about to change. According to an anonymous source—in Los Angeles, naturally—Mattel is about to introduce "Hacker Barbie".

"The aim of these dolls is to revert the stereotype that women are numerophobic, computer-illiterate and academically challenged," wrote the anonymous Internet user.

Hacker Barbie has all the right computer equipment and wears "a dirty button-up shirt and a pair of worn-out jeans with Casio all-purpose watches and thick glasses that can set ants on fire".

Aided by her sidekick, Ken, she aims to offset the damage caused by a previous Barbie who said: "Math is hard."

Of course, it's a joke. But then that's what Barbie has always been, except to her millions of fans, Greta among the youngest.

For most Barbie fans, it is fashion fantasy that is the main attraction. Barbie has the figure and the finances to wear what most real women can only dream about.

But for Greta, undressing her is more fun than dressing her. "Look at her big milk bars!" she gloats. Ever since she was reluctantly weaned Greta has had a perverse interest in "milk bars".

As a feminist, I had no qualms about her playing with Barbie. Despite some women's claims about Barbie being a powerful role model, I consider myself a more powerful one.

Besides, girls who do try to use Barbie as a role model usually find it an unsustainable one. In the latest issue of the feminist magazine *Refractory Girl*, which is dedicated to debunking fashion, writer Lang Goodsell recalls that "once, in what now seems like a former lifetime, I was in danger of becoming a Barbie doll. I was anorexic and very, very blonde. I even considered getting breast implants."

Now, she is pleased to report, "I'm one of those so-called 'ugly' feminists, with hairy legs and underarms." The reason for her conversion: ". . . my brain kept getting in the way of a perfect Barbie existence."

But over the years, Barbie, like Lang Goodsell, has changed. Along side Baywatch Barbie, there is Astronaut Barbie, Teacher Barbie and Doctor Barbie, to name a few.

Still, the notion that you cannot have a brain and big breasts persists, even for dolls. Until Barbie was created in 1959, no other mass-produced doll tried to represent a real woman in such unreal proportions. As Lang Goodsell comments: "If Barbie were real, she would be disabled."

To be fair, Barbie's most important accessory, Ken, is also somewhat disabled. "Ken and Barbie's creator, Ruth Handler, did initially request a penis for Ken, only to be shouted down by the mostly male marketing department. They finally settled for a little bump," claims Beauregard Houston-Montgomery, a writer for the US interactive magazine *Urban Desires*.

Perhaps this is why Ken has never been as popular as Barbie. What is a little bump compared with two big "milkbars"? Perhaps this explains why every second every day, two Barbie dolls are sold somewhere in the world.

Still, there are some who are yet to be convinced. "Tell them anything except a Barbie," said eight-year-old Hannah, when asked recently what friends could give her for her birthday.

A few days later, at my request, Hannah's mother asked why she didn't want a Barbie for her birthday. Her answer was a fair dinkum triumph for those who fear that Barbie and American culture are taking over the world.

"I suppose I wouldn't mind," Hannah mused. "Barbecues are all right."

THE PUBLIC PRIVACY OF A FAVOURITE RETREAT

25 June 1996

THERE is a section in Robyn Davidson's book *Desert Places* where she describes with grim horror how the Western notion of privacy is alien to Indian culture.

Although she went to India as an observer, it was the feeling of being constantly observed herself that she found most difficult.

But you do not need to have travelled to India to know exactly what she means. All you need is to be the parent of a small child.

In preparing for parenthood, parents expect to be fascinated by everything their child says or does, at least for the first few years. What the parenting books don't tell you is that your child will also be fascinated by everything you say and do, no matter how intimate. Parents are the only workers (apart from politicians) who are frequently caught with their pants down.

That parenting is relentless is a common lament. But the hardest part, I find, is not the endless drudgery, the sleepless nights or the exasperation of dealing with a small irrational person. It is the complete lack of privacy, especially intellectual privacy.

"Quiet now, Greta," I say as we are driving along. "Mummy wants to think."

There is a brief moment of silence. Then she begins to sing a Shirley Temple song that I used to think was cute: "Sometimes I ought to hate you, you make me feel so blue . . ."

What makes me feel so blue is that I was looking forward to this day together, so why do I suddenly find it so oppressive?

"It's the old introvert, extrovert thing", commented my friend, Jan, who classes herself as an introvert. "If I'm here in the house, Anna wants me to be her companion, but often I just want to go off inside my own head."

I knew exactly how she felt, yet I would hardly describe myself as an introvert. Perhaps, I thought guiltily, this need for privacy is a symptom of my generation, the "me" generation, where the needs of the individual are valued above those of the group.

Older women, especially those who have made their families their careers, do not seem to have the same expectation, and therefore the same frustration. Is this because they are selfless, or because they were raised with more realistic expectations of family life?

Whatever the reason, and regardless of how profoundly I love my children, I often find the lack of intellectual privacy in family life depressing and debilitating.

Perhaps this is why I have always been attracted to the idea of a retreat (in the religious rather than the military sense). Webster's Dictionary describes a retreat as: "The act of retiring or withdrawing from any place; state or place or retirement, privacy or refuge . . . a period of retirement with a view to self-examination, meditation and special prayer."

These days, the need for retreat is rarely acknowledged or accepted, but it still easily recognised: by moods that create emotional distance; or habits that create physical distance, such as working late, staying up when everyone else goes to bed or even reading on the toilet.

These have become our little retreats, to the amusement or irritation of other family members.

I have several little retreats. A favorite is a long shower. I shut the door and let the water and my thoughts wash over me. But just as a river always has a destination, so too must these thoughts.

So, over the past few years, the perfect retreat for me has been a popular pursuit for women through the ages: writing.

In her book *Writing a New World: Two Centuries of Australian Women Writers*, Dale Spender refers to the letters and journals written by convict women as a "means of conceptualising and comprehending the strange and the new and of conveying the experience to a distant audience".

I know what she means. Writing is both an essentially private and public act. But ultimately for many, it is a form of retreat.

That's why, in the past few years, whenever I have felt the need to make sense of what it means to be a woman, a wife and a mother in the '90s, whenever I have yearned to become the observer instead of the observed, I have sat down and written a postcard.

ELECTRONIC COTTAGE IS HOME SWEAT HOME

24 June 1996

These days, when people ask "Where do you work?" I am greeted with a mixture of curiosity and envy. "Lucky you!" they say, when I tell them that I work from home.

In many ways, they are right: the computer age has brought the office home for women like me, allowing us to fit our paid work around our families, rather than the other way around.

Doing paid work from home is nothing new in itself: so too, does the woman who sells homewares or cosmetics, or takes in a bit or ironing, or minds other people's children.

However, the image of the "professional" who works from home is much more glamorous. As British sociologists Annie Phizacklea and Carol Wolkowitz point out in their book, *Homeworking Women*, the common view is that this heralds the era of the "electronic cottage"—the modern equivalent of the pre-industrial ideal when work and home were integrated and harmonious.

Unfortunately, their research does not tally with this view. They say that while homeworking allows some more flexible working hours, saves fuel, and cuts commuting time and pollution, it also gives employers the opportunity to cut labor costs, benefits and other overheads.

The reality for most homeworkers is that the pay is often low and unpredictable; there is more mess, longer hours and a good deal of isolation, and it requires incredible will power—especially if your desk is close to the pantry.

Phizacklea and Wolkowitz focus on both the new and old type of outworkers—women in the clothing and textile industries or those doing clerical or craft work as well as professional women—and find some disturbing parallels.

Of the professionals, they say ". . . our impression is that many women working at home have been vulnerable to cuts in income during the recession and would welcome help and support in setting their rates for customers and clients, for instance."

They suggest a minimum wage and better organisation and collection of data on homeworkers. They also suggest that, among white-collar workers, there is scope for more networks, so they would no doubt be pleased to know that there is a new network for homeworking mothers operating via the Internet.

WAHM, or Work at Home Moms, is an American organisation which aims to provide information and support for homeworking mothers all over the world.

WAHM is the brainchild of Cheryl, a computer programmer from Folsom, California. "This is something I started and it has become my crusade," she said.

She decided to work from home after her seven-year-old daughter was diagnosed with diabetes just three days before her little sister was born.

"I love being home with my girls, but I really like to make money, too," Cheryl said.

She also missed the intellectual stimulation of her workplace, so she started a home business designing websites.

"As I started to meet other women, online and in my community, I realised what a huge pool of talent is going to waste."

There were very few opportunities for women to work from home, other than in sales, she said. WAHM aimed to give women who want to work from home legitimate ideas (not get rich quick schemes) and also provide tips for making a home business work.

"Working from home is working out well for me, although there are extra challenges. In many ways, going to a job was easier," she said.

It is not surprising that so many homeworkers are women with small children. But doing paid work when you have small children is difficult, whether you are working from home or not.

A friend who was forced to work from home recently when her children were sick, organised an important meeting in her lounge room.

"But only those who had had chicken pox, or didn't mind getting them, could attend," she said.

NIGHT OF A THOUSAND STARS

17 July 1996

It was the sort of advertisement that makes every parent publicly wince, but privately answer "Yes!"

"Is your child a star?" asked the Victorian Youth Theatre, its advertisement for a theatrical holiday program in Kew leaping out at me from the middle of the newspaper.

Ordinarily, I would have passed it over, but the school holidays were looming and the thought of trying to work in the lounge room with a tribe of 11-year-old boys traipsing in and out of the house, was making me desperate. Here was my chance to make time and space for my work while encouraging Johannes's passion for the theatre.

However, for the past few years I had so little need to go the city that I had forgotten where Kew was—somewhere in the eastern suburbs, I had thought.

"You'll be driving half the day!" Rob had said, and he was right. Now, a week later, I not only know where Kew is, after four hours a day in the traffic to get there and back, I think it should be spelled Queue.

Just as Adelaide is known as the city of churches, Kew must surely be known as the city of schools—private schools—schools so big and grand that the gates as well as the students must be numbered.

The holiday program was based at the Montague Theatre at Xavier College, and 100 children aged from eight to 18 were unloaded at Gate 4 each day at 9am and collected again at 5pm.

On my three work days I turned around and came home and then set off again at four with Greta in tow. But on the other two days, I hung around.

I had no money—having given it all to the Victorian Youth Theatre—so I trudged up and down Glenferrie Road and High Street, ducking into book shops every now and again to keep warm, and occasionally indulging myself with a coffee, wondering if this is what it felt like to be homeless on a cold winter's day in Kew.

Even the Holy Trinity church, whose door had been open invitingly, could offer no comfort. The big bluestone church was empty, of course, with only the sad and silent faces of Jesus and his followers etched in stained glass, gazing down at me; reminding me that in the past, real glory had been found by fishermen and shepherds rather than actors.

"How was it?" I asked Johannes each day when I picked him up.

"Good," he said, just as he always said about anything.

By Friday night, when I turned up for the gala performance, I knew all the short cuts to Kew, so was able to get there early enough to get a good seat. The Montague Theatre was packed with excited parents, and Patrick Conlan, the Victorian Youth Theatre's founder and director, was understandably a little hoarse.

It had been a big week, he explained. Here were 100 or so kids who had met on Monday and who by Friday were performing, singing and dancing together. They and his staff had worked solidly for about seven hours a day, so it was up to us to show our appreciation, he said.

We needed little further encouragement. From the first of the three one-act plays written by talented staff member Alan Dickson we were engrossed. The plays were complex little vignettes, full of tongue twisters and clever ironies, written around the songs that guest director Denise Drysdale had chosen. As these included such disparate numbers as *The Good Ship Lollipop* and *Big Spender*, the plots were interesting to say the least.

Theatre is the ultimate in team sport. If you forget your lines, the next player is caught out and the game is up. But with the exception of a few of the very young ones, who had the occasional prod from Patrick, lines, movements, dance steps and positions were all remembered.

They had been taught to open their mouths and sing and speak clearly. They had been taught to dance. They had been taught to act. But mostly they had been taught to give—and they gave it all they had.

By the end of the night, I, too, was hoarse from cheering, and my hands were raw from clapping. This time the drive home was not long enough for all the talk that was going on about the show, so we stopped for a coffee.

"What did you think?" Johannes asked yet again, urging me to "be critical".

What did I think? Was my child a star, I wondered, remembering the ad? I thought of all those eager-faced kids packed on to the stage

singing "This is what we call Denise and Co!" to the *Muppet Show Theme.*
I thought of all that relentless driving—not just by me, but by Patrick,
Denise and Co, who had driven them to strive for excellence.

The night had been cold and cloudy, but here in Kew one hundred
stars had shone.

PS: *This was the last Family Postcard published in The Age.*

*From 1997 to 2002 the columns appeared bi-monthly in Quality Time
Magazine, published by Telling Words Pty Ltd.*

1997

READY OR NOT?

January 1997

My four-year-old gave me a book for Mother's Day, but it is the title page that I am enjoying reading most.

Driven by my own mother's rule that a book given as a gift must be signed by the giver, I urged Greta to write in it for me. She can write half a dozen shaky letters, including T, O, G, A, and M, so together we wrote, "To Mum from Greta", with me filling in the letters she has yet to master.

This delights me because I read it as yet another sign that by next January she may be ready for school.

I know that the trend these days is for children to start at six rather than five, and that studies have shown that those who are older cope better in the long run. But I admit that I am not only considering how Greta will cope if she starts school at five, but how I will cope if she does not.

After four years of being immersed in family life while only dabbling in my career, I am ready for something more. I am not quite sure what it will be yet, but with that in mind we are moving house—closer to the station and shops to give both me and my son more independence. As a result, I am investigating primary schools in our new area.

This in itself has been an education. In both the state schools I have visited so far, the warmth and caring shown by both principals for their school community has contrasted sharply with the coldness of the corridors, the shabbiness of the buildings and the meagreness of the resources.

In Jeff Kennett's Victoria*, where the hardest lessons for some are learned at the casino, it is obvious that sending your child to a state school is becoming more and more of a gamble.

For us there is no other choice, financially or politically. We are adamant that state education should continue to be available both for our children and their children and their grandchildren. This means making a commitment to support the school as much as possible.

So either way, you pay: those who can't invest money in their children's education, must invest their time.

Still, having decided where, the question remains: when? School readiness I know, depends on a lot more than copying letters. With the trend for most children to start at aged six, when they are obviously more mature and capable, I worry that starting Greta at five will put her at a disadvantage. As a friend commented. "Only those who can't afford another year at creche, are sending their kids at five, which means that the poor start earlier and continue their disadvantage."

But what do you do with a bright eager child if she does not start at five? I am very happy with the kindergarten/creche where Greta now attends three days a week, but another year of this would not be enough academically for her, and frankly would be too much financially for us.

I am trying not to let my own readiness cloud my judgement. There are still another eight months to go, and that is a long time in a child's life. As her kinder teacher says: "Let's wait and see."

Meanwhile, there is no harm in a little encouragement. So lately, when she says "That's S for Snake," I gently add, "And S for School, too!"

---

*   *Jeff Kennett is a former Premier of Victoria.*

PRIDE, PRONUNCIATION AND PREJUDICE

Like my mother, and I suppose because of her, I am a stickler for correct grammar and pronunciation.

So when Greta came home from creche saying: "Look what I done!" instead of looking, I glared and corrected: "Look what I DID. Only morons say 'done'!"

Every time she lapsed, I would prompt with: "What did you say?" and after a while, she would hesitate and correct herself, saying triumphantly: "Look what I DID!"

Call me a snob, a pedant, or a pain, but I am in complete agreement with Henry Higgins when it comes to teaching children how to speak. "Why can't the English teach their children how to speak?" he laments in *My Fair Lady*.

Mispronunciations, like "everythink" or "sec-e-tary" or "lib-ary", or as one former friend used to say "obvissly" can also set my teeth on edge.

"Don't say it like that. You sound like a moron," I chide relentlessly and politically incorrectly to both my children.

In my view, children who are not taught correct grammar and pronunciation are not only disadvantaged, but they must surely be confused? They are taught to read and write English—but not to speak it. They are also taught that proper grammar and pronunciation is important in Languages Other Than English, but not in English itself

However, I admit that sometimes, just sometimes, one can go too far.

Take the other night. I was sitting on the edge of Greta's bed reading from *The Bedtime Book—Stories and poems to read aloud*, chosen by Kathy Henderson and illustrated by Penny Ives.

In it, there is a poem about ghost stories, called *I Like to Stay Up* by Grace Nichols, which goes like this:

> *I like to stay up*
> *and listen*
> *when big people talking*
> *jumbie stories*
> *Ooooooooooooooooooooh*

I does feel so tingly
and excited
inside—eeeeeeee
But when my mother say
'Girl, time for bed!.
Then is when
I does feel a dread.
Then is when
I does jump into me bed.
Then is when I does cover up
from me feet to me head
Then is when
I does wish
I didn't listen
to no stupid jumbie story!
Then is when
I does wish
I did read me book instead

The picture showed a little black girl seated under the table with a blanket and a book, bug-eyed, while her mother and friends sat around a table talking.

Greta loved it. "Read it again!" she urged, giggling and squealing with pleasure.

But after two or three nights of this, she had obviously had time to reflect. When I finished reading, she stopped laughing and asked: "Are they morons?"

I was speechless. Here was all my class prejudice thrown back at me. How would I explain that slang was sometimes a cultural phenomenon that had nothing to do with intelligence? How would I explain that the real morons were those racists who prevented poor black children from getting access to education?

Of course all this was too complicated for a four-year-old, so I blushed and said: "This is called slang, and sometimes it's used for fun."

Still, the incident made me realise how easy it was to pass prejudice on to children. In trying to pass on my love of language, I had inadvertently passed on a distrust of those who use it badly, for whatever reason.

In the light of this, I have relaxed my standards slightly. There is, of course, I tell me self, such a thing as poetic licence.

That's why I decided to teach Greta a new poem. As the spring brought our daffodils out and wreathed our weeping cherry in the front garden in a crinoline of white blossom, I felt it was timely to teach her an old favorite from the school yard.

Spring is here,
the grass is riz.
I wonder where
the birdies is?

A Tiny Tina bit embarrassing

As a parent, there are many memories I cherish—and a few I would like to forget—like the time my 12-year old son, Johannes, asked to go to a rock concert with his friend Tom.

My first instinct, of course, was to say no. To me, rock concerts meant mass hysteria, fights, and possible brain damage.

But my sister-in-law Barbara, a veteran parent of teenagers, had tutored me that it was a no-no to actually saying no to a teenager, or even a sub-teenager, even if that was the intention in the end. What you had to do was to show that you were prepared to at least take their attempts at independence seriously, and then perhaps suggest a compromise, such as "Maybe when you're 25".

So eventually, after a long conversation with Tom's parents, in which I extracted the pick-up times and venues, his family history for the past three generations, his mother's maiden name and his father's shoe size, it was arranged—Tom's parents would take them to the concert and pick them up and my husband, Rob, and I would sit home and worry.

On the night of the concert, we watched television until 11 and then went to bed, were I planned to worry more comfortably.

"You'll fall sleep," warned Rob.

"No, I won't," I said.

He went to sleep and I lay awake—or so I thought. Shortly after, I looked at the clock. It was 12.30—surely they'd be home soon?

I got up and looked out the window, which overlooked the street. "They're not home yet" I hissed to Rob.

"He'll be fine, Jane. It probably went a bit later," he mumbled and went back to sleep.

At 1am, I went downstairs to the office, which offered an even better view of the street.

At 1.30pm I had diarrhoea and the visions of Johannes sitting on my bed happily relating the events of the night had been replaced with ones of me weeping by a hospital bedside.

And by 2am, I was hysterical. "They're not home yet and it's 2am!" I shrieked at the sleeping Rob.

"Well why don't you ring Tom's parents?" he said, sounding worried himself.

So with shaking hands, I went down to the office and dialled the number. I was surprised when a woman answered. After all, I had expected them to be smashed up in hospital, not home in bed asleep.

"Yes?" she said, groggily.

"I'm sorry about the time, but it's Johannes' mother here and he's not home yet," I said, my voice shaking.

"Hang on, I'll get David," she replied.

"Hello?" said a sleepy David.

I explained and apologised again.

There was a moment's silence. "But we dropped him off at 11.30," David said in surprise.

I froze.

"Hang on!" I said.

I tore across to the other side of the house to Johannes's room, flung open the door, flicked the switch and with my heart beating wildly saw him curled up fast asleep, oblivious to the fact that he would be the laughing stock of the whole school tomorrow.

I ran back to the phone, feeling sick with relief and embarrassment.

"I'm so sorry," I stammered. "I didn't hear him come in. I just presumed he'd come and say hello. I guess we shouldn't have bought a bigger house. Thank you!" and, laughing and crying I stumbled back upstairs to Rob.

"What!" he yelled when I told him what had happened.

"They dropped him off at 11.30. I must have fallen asleep. I can't think why I didn't hear him. I just presumed he'd come up and say hello," I rambled.

"Didn't you see his shoes in the hallway?" Rob asked, incredulous.

"No, I was too busy looking out the window!"

For the rest of the night, I lay awake wondering whether I could get away with not mentioning this to Johannes. But Tom would no doubt tell him, so I decided to come clean casually over breakfast.

He took it rather well, considering. "You are so embarrassing," he said, shaking his head in disgust.

What could I do but apologise and agree and order him to come and tell me he is home next time—no matter the hour.

We bought him the Tina Arena CD *In Deep* for Christmas, and my favorite song now and for the next seven years is *If I didn't love you*—especially the line that goes "If I didn't love you the way that I do, I wouldn't put up with what you put me through."

A ROOM WITH A DIFFERENT VIEW

In our lounge room, there's a little window that gives us a view of the whole world—and lately it has not been a pretty picture.

The usual sufferings of people who are victims of war, poverty and environmental disaster that we had callously come to regard as "other" have been overtaken by sufferings of people like us—people who are not usually victims. The world has changed, they say, and we, inevitably, with it.

Terrorism is no longer something that happens to other people in other countries. It can happen anywhere, as the service at our school church for a local victim of the Bali bombing showed. We are no longer just watching other mothers in foreign countries weep for their children—we are weeping for our own.

But through other windows in our lounge room, the view is entirely different. There are roses, hollyhocks, poppies, cinerarias, rhododendrons and camellias. The birds are nesting, the lawn is soft, new and green—the product of many weeks of reseeding by my husband—and fruit trees, leafy and laden with small green fruit, are promising summer pleasure.

My own children are healthy and thriving and amid the frenzy of exams and end-of-year concerts and parties we are planning for a future that many others in the world dare not dream about.

It is a confusing contrast. I feel a mixture of relief and guilt as we shop at our newly renovated local shopping centre amid the Christmas glitter. Here, where consumption is king, the Christmas story of birth, death and renewal is played out in a different level. The catalogues come, we shop, we consume and we throw out in readiness for the next wave of consumption.

This is heightened by a trip to the tip. Although our local tip is also a recycling centre, it is sobering to watch car after car back into a parking bay and dump its trailer load of junk—everything from old plastic trikes to broken lawnmowers.

What will happen to it, I ask? How will the earth digest and process such seemingly indestructible things?

"Landfill," my husband says. Bulldozers crush it and force it down, hoping it will not be regurgitated sometime in our now uncertain future.

"This is the other side of all those furniture and home wares shops in Whitehorse Rd," I say as we drive away.

My husband agrees. "It's all just consumption," he says, then adds. "You know the X family? They saved their Christmas money and bought an environmentally friendly low-energy heater for a poor family in a developing country."

There is a moment's silence as we contemplate the sacrifice of those who could least afford it among all our friends and the very expensive bike we have chosen for Johannes's Christmas present.

We decide that charming as it is, self sacrifice is a little naïve as a political tool. Besides, the other side of consumption is jobs and growth, as an economist will tell you.

Anyway, such sacrifice reminds me too much of the *Pilgrim's Progress* by John Bunyan, a popular 19th century American school text book about the journey of Christian, a lonely pilgrim, from the City of Destruction to the Celestial City.

In Louisa May Alcott's book *Little Women*—staple diet of all young girls of my generation—the four March sisters were given a personal copy each for Christmas by their mother. This was very helpful in trying times, as the sacrifices they had to make as a result of the Civil War and their fathers' absence, were nothing compared to that of the struggling Christian.

But if not self denial, what message do we give our children when they, too, can look through each window and see such contrasting views? Is it eat, drink and be merry, for tomorrow we die? Do we add a gravy of guilt and fear to the Christmas turkey, and tell them to gobble it up anyway?

I don't have any answers, but perhaps the best guide to how to get through Christmas in times of trouble and change is our children themselves. Having had permission to start singing Christmas carols from November 1, my daughter is now in full throttle as she goes around the house planning her celebrations.

Deck the halls with boughs of holly
Fa la la la la, la la la la,
Tis' the season to be jolly,
Fa la la la la, la la la la.

IN A BARBIE WHIRL

"You can have your photo taken with Barbie," the lady at Myer's department store said when I rang during the school holidays to find out about the new Barbie shop.

It seemed like a good idea at the time: trip into town on the train with Greta to see the new Barbie shop and a photo with Barbie to boot. As the *Barbie Girl* song says: *"Hit the town, fool around, let's go party!"*

Next time I have any good ideas like that, shoot me.

First of all we missed the train. I had dashed out to get money, only to find that the station had EFTPOS and that the train had just left.

"Are you sure you don't want me to drive?" I pleaded with Greta. But she was adamant and began excitedly counting and memorising the stations. After six she stopped and asked: "How many are there?"

"Twenty two," I said.

"I haven't got that many fingers," she said, and gave up.

One hour-and-a-half later, having ascended from the bowels of Melbourne Central to the sixth floor of Myer's via a mountain of escalators, we found ourselves third in the queue of tired parents and excited children in a Barbie world, waiting for Barbie and Ken to arrive.

After about 40 minutes, I noticed something about the other mothers. They all had cameras. "Isn't there a photographer coming?" I asked the shop assistant.

"No, you have to bring your own camera," she said.

"Why wasn't I told!" I demanded. The shop assistant kindly fetched an instant camera from another department and kindly waited while I handed over $22.

How could I not? After it's not every day a little girl gets to meeting a walking, talking living doll. I had half expected a person in a Barbie suit, with a giant head and mosquito-net eyes. How else were they going to get anyone who really looked like Barbie?

But they did. She walked in and suddenly the impossible dream was a reality. Admittedly her boobs were smaller, and her legs shorter, but she had the same tiny waist, pert nose, sparkly blue eyes, nylon-blonde hair, perpetual smile and exquisite little dress. I vowed to go home and lose weight—again.

Ken, too, was shorter—and I was sure I'd seen him singing at a few Italian weddings—but he was a real doll.

Barbie, Ken and Greta posed for two photos on a tiny pink chaise lounge, then we followed the signs and the escalators to the Barbie show in the Mural Hall, were we found ourselves at the back of another queue. As we inched closer to the door, I noticed something else about the other mothers. They all had tickets.

"We haven't got tickets," I explained lamely to the man at the door, but he kindly let us in anyway. The show featured 40 years of Barbie fashion, with Barbie never looking a day over 20.

For me it was a welcome and shameless escape from reality, which could only be topped by high tea in the historic Hopetoun Tearooms in the Block Arcade.

My Earl Grey tea had just arrived, when the inevitable happened. "I need to got to the toilet," Greta said. "Fine," I said, gritting my teeth. "Where is the toilet?" I asked the waitress.

"Oh, there's no toilet here, you have to go to the pub down the road," she said.

It seemed that there was a heritage order on the building that prevented them from renovating to include public toilets. "This is ridiculous," I spluttered, so the waitress kindly took Greta to the staff toilets up stairs.

No camera, no ticket, and now toilet—but it had been worth it just to meet the real Barbie. When the fashion for real, young women is anything dark, shapeless, ugly and expensive, life in plastic does indeed seem fantastic.

A RELIGIOUS EXPERIENCE

For our four-year old daughter, Greta, starting school has meant more than learning her ABCs; it has meant learning her prayers, too.

Although we are not Catholic, we chose a small Catholic school above a state school for a variety of reasons, not least of which was class size. With under 200 pupils at the school and only 22 in each of the two prep classes, we felt that she would be part of a team, rather than a crowd.

As for the religion side of things, being a Catholic was not a prerequisite—although I suspect that it may be a repercussion. What I didn't count on was that Greta's Catholic school experience would be an education for us.

It began the first day, when she learned the sign of the cross and a few simple prayers.

Naturally, she wanted to practice everything she had learned when she got home, but I was surprised to find her kneeling by the bed saying: "For what we are about to receive may the lord make us truly grateful."

Later that term she announced: "God made us. God made everything!"

Having told her the week before that we descended from monkeys, I offered a brief amendment: "Yes, but he started with amoebas and worked his way up to monkeys and then people."

I wondered whether this was the start of a creationist push, but was reassured by the fact that the prevailing lesson the class seemed to be learning was to love one another—beginning with the simple notion of what it meant to be a friend.

Then came Lent, which Greta embraced with gusto, declaring nobly that she would give up chocolate for Easter. This was later modified to giving up chocolate *after* Easter, which she did with great success, since there was none left.

But the highlight of the term was the re-enactment of the crucifixion by both prep classes.

Since I was unable to attend due to work commitments, Greta decided to do an encore at home just for me, with the help of her brother, Johannes.

I left them setting up the show while I went down the street and came back to find her kneeling at the foot of the couch, surrounded by a multitude of soft toys, wearing a white scarf and an old black petticoat of mine that had been borrowed for her costume.

A cardboard cross had been cut out from the lid of a shoebox and colored, and Teddy, in the star role of Jesus, was awaiting his fate.

"Do we have any staples?" Johannes asked, adding that Teddy was going to be stapled to the cross.

Luckily for Teddy there were no staples. But before he took his final curtain, poor Teddy was whipped soundly by Greta to represent the beating Jesus suffered at the hands of Caiaphas's scribes and elders.

He was then made to drag the cross along the back of the couch before behind held firmly on it until his final moments.

With much praying and weeping by Mary (Greta), he was laid to rest in a tomb (under a cushion) and where, given the fact that tea was nearly ready, he rose from the dead in three seconds rather than three days.

I have mixed feelings about all this, as I do about my own religious beliefs. I was raised Anglican, and loved the hymns and prayers, but, I confess, the only prayers I say these days are usually at red lights.

As a feminist, I am also wary of any religion which is oppressive to women, and conscious of the part that organised religion has played in war and politics throughout history.

But at the same time, the older I get, the more plausible it seems that God exists, although in what form, I would not presume to know, nor would I presume to tell others. I suspect that this is something each must decide themself, including Greta.

Meanwhile, if one of the lessons she learns at school is to do unto others as she would have them do unto her, then all I can say is "Halleluiah!"

STOLEN: A LITTLE GIRL'S SENSE OF SAFETY

The afternoon had ended on a high note, as we arrived home from seeing Johannes play Ben in the Stephen Schwartz musical, *Rags* staged by the Victorian Youth Theatre.

We opened the front door as usual, made our way into the hall, and then stopped in the kitchen and gazed at the broken door between the kitchen and back porch. For one moment, I thought there had been a storm and something had fallen from the skylight, but then it dawned on me: someone had broken in.

"Oh no!" Rob and I both cried at once, and I immediately ran into the office to see if my computer was still there. But everything was as it should be—there and in every other room of the house.

Rob's Walkman was still sitting on top of the microwave. The tape recorder I use for interviews was still sitting on my desk. The video, the television, the hi-fi equipment, the CDs, everything was seemingly as we left it—except that someone had smashed in a small pane in the front lounge room window.

But among the shattered glass on the carpet was something that made my heart stop. Blood. And silence. My heart sank. Where was our little Chihuahua, Pepe, who usually tore down stairs to greet us?

Quickly Rob unlocked the broken door and the backdoor and I ran outside screaming "Pepe! Pepe!" But he was nowhere to be seen.

"Pepe! Pepe!" I screamed, my voice shaking as I charged upstairs, where I eventually found him, locked in the ensuite bathroom, cowering. He had obviously been terrified, as he had urinated all over the bathroom.

But it was not Pepe who was the most traumatised by this experience: it was our six-year-old daughter Greta. As soon as she saw the broken door, she burst into tears, crying: "I don't want to stay here."

The disarray and bloody fingerprints of the robber on our cupboards and door-handles terrified her. "I want to go home!" she cried.

I tried to comfort her and the dog while Rob rang the police and then went next door to see whether the neighbors had heard anything.

Greta would not stay in the house, so the neighbors looked after her while Rob and I tried to sort out what had happened. It seems the robber had entered through the window, had found the windows locked and every other door deadlocked, so had tried to kick down the door between the kitchen and back porch to find a way out.

But it wasn't until Johannes came home after his second performance around 11pm that we realised his portable CD player had been stolen. We promised him a new one, swept up the glass and the damage was soon fixed, thanks to the skill and kindness of our neighbor, also named Rob.

The police turned up three hours after our first call and after flashing a torch here and there declared it was "just kids" and left.

But those "kids" had done more damage than they would ever realise. It was 4am before Greta finally went to sleep, after sobbing and crying in fear all night.

The next day Rob bought more window-locks, a bolt for the sliding backdoor and wood to fix the broken door. It was a show of strength and defence, for Greta's sake as much of our own. Now, on the outside at least, everything was as it should be.

Johannes eventually got a new CD player and we got a good-as-new door (thanks again, to our neighbor Rob).

But the thing that was stolen and lost forever was a little girl's sense of personal safety and security.

GETTING A HANDLE ON HIGH SCHOOL

The queues outside the classrooms were growing longer, as outside anxious parents waited to hear whether they had passed or failed. I know that this is never the intention of parent-teacher night, but that's how it feels.

So far, I had always passed, but this was the first test of secondary school and well, the darkening shadow on my 12-year-old son's top lip and the number of phone calls to and from girls every night had suggested that this term he may have been distracted.

Inside the classroom, the teachers sat with their books of names, like mini gods on judgement day, waiting to deliver their verdicts. Parents sat meekly at first, then either broke into broad smiles of relief or looked chastened as they discovered that junior Dr Jeckle was really Mr Hyde.

I peered curiously at Miss Prim, the art teacher. According to my son, Miss Prim was a monster, but to my surprise, Miss Prim did not have two heads.

How could an art teacher by a monster, I had wondered. In my day, art teachers were benign creatures who said "That's lovely, dear!" no matter how much mess you made. But I soon found out that art today is serious business and that it was my son, not Miss Prim who was the monster.

"He doesn't hand in his work and he talks to much," Miss Prim said sternly. Not only that he seemed to move around the room all the time, and when she asked him to sit down, he had asked why. That's funny, I thought; at home he asks the same question when I ask him to get up.

Was this the same child who had taken special art classes at the neighborhood centre and who spent hours in his room drawing, I wondered, as I slunk off to see Miss Jolly, the English and drama teacher.

Miss Jolly beamed as I sat down nervously. "Ahh! He's such a dynamic person, isn't he?" she exclaimed. Not only that he was a terrific actor, had a wonderful sense of humor and was a pleasure to teach, she enthused.

Of course I knew he was a pleasure to teach, but dynamic? "He's practically inert at home," I mumbled. But Miss Jolly wasn't listening. "I really like the way he challenges ideas in the classroom," she said.

Miss Jolly was obviously a very perceptive person. "Perhaps you should talk to Miss Prim?" I suggested, as I set off for the SOSE (Studies of Societies and Environment) teacher, Miss Sensible.

Miss Sensible grinned. "He's doing very well, especially with the girls. I don't know whether they've discovered him or he's discovered them, but I had to sit him up the front the other day by himself."

They had discovered him, I assured her, and in the process had discovered me: the mother from hell.

However, Miss Sensible reassured me that the real attraction for him was the piano. She had to beg him to stop playing in front of everyone—while we at home had to beg him to start.

And so it went on—which just goes to show that parent-teacher night can be a real learning experience.

When I got home, I was not surprised to find my son waiting for the verdict too. So I sat on the edge of his bed and we chatted, not so much about tackling homework, but people. "It seems you have Miss Jolly's smooth handle, but Miss Prim's rough handle," I said.

In the book *What Katy Did*, I explained, Katy is in the wars with everyone until Cousin Helen explains that everyone has a rough and a smooth handle. The challenge is to find the smooth one, she advised.

I had found it useful advice, not only to get a handle on school, but on later life. "Doors open more easily that way," I said.

A DANCING LESSON

Sometimes, we are so busy being parents that we forget that some of us are still children too. This was brought home to me recently when my mother became seriously ill. I had always thought of myself as a strong person, but when she rang to tell me the bad news I cried—and found I couldn't stop.

I cried in bed, in the car, and in my office—so much so that after two days my eyelids were shiny and swollen and my skin was so tight I felt like a burns victim.

As my mother lives in the country, she did not see my distress, but I am ashamed to say that she heard it when I phoned, and that, naturally, this added to her own distress. Rather than behave like the friend and mature woman that I was, I had reverted to the wailing infant who fears abandonment.

"Don't cry: you're making me cry too," she said, as she tried to comfort me.

Stupidly, on the day of her operation, I took her advice and didn't visit, reassured by the knowledge that my stepfather would be by her side. "It would distress me more to know that you had to leave your work and the family," she had pleaded.

But I couldn't concentrate on my work, and when I confided in the person I was interviewing, she said bluntly: "So why are you still at work?"

Why, indeed? It was time to stop acting the child, and be an adult again. So my husband held the fort while I set off on the train, laden with books and Florence Nightingale visions of brow-mopping and poetry reading.

As I walked into the hospital with my stepfather, I braced myself for a shock, which is exactly what I got—but not in the way I expected.

There was no time for reading. Instead I arranged chairs and flowers, playing junior hostess to the stream of visitors, while Mum played senior hostess—introducing people, asking about their lives and dismissing her own problems for more interesting news.

While I had expected her to be oozing blood, as usual she was oozing charm. All that was missing was a glass of "vino". But there was no denying that she was in great pain, and seeing how she was tiring, I begged to send the visitors away. "Don't do that, people will think I'm sick," she said firmly.

A week later, she was home entertaining more visitors and writing letters—one each to Lord Mayor Peter Costigan and Premier Jeff Kennett about creating an artists' market in Swanston Street and one to Edwin Maher, the ABC weatherman, complaining about his glasses. "They're all wrong", she said.

She tolerated my advice about home help and my sister's attempts to provide counselling, and then as usual, did things her own way.

Despite her pain, she still went out for dinner on her birthday, and to all the events they had previously booked for the local arts festival. And when I rang at 9 o'clock one night, with apologies in case she was in bed, I found that she was "out with the girls".

As usual, she had just got on with it, leaving me to ponder how well I really knew her, or how well any of us really knows our parents. (The only thing I know for sure is that she never does as she's told.)

But where did she get the strength to fight yet another battle? And who was behind that charming performer, who since the age of four has been smiling bravely through the stage lights?

"Enjoy your life," she has always told me. "It's but a small dance across the stage."

I can only agree and be grateful that she is still dancing and that I am privileged enough to be there to cheer her on.

1998

PLAYING AUNTY DAPHNE

Driving through busy suburban Doncaster today, it is hard to believe that 30 years ago, it was my childhood holiday destination.

Each year during the September or Christmas school holidays, my sister and I would be invited to spend a week with our cousins, Julianna and Richard, on the site of what is now Doncaster Shoppingtown.

In those days, however, it was Uncle Pete's and Aunty Daphne's orchard, and driving from our seaside home at Mentone to Doncaster meant driving to the country.

There, we roamed the surrounding paddocks, played in the coolstores, and enjoyed the thrill of "sleeping over". In turn, Julianna (who shared the same name as my sister, but with different spelling) would spend a week at our house.

Later, when the property was sold to Westfield, Aunty Daphne and Uncle Pete moved to a different orchard at King Street, where we also enjoyed several holidays.

In the new house, as budding teenagers, we took turns sleeping in Julianna's brass bed and reading *A Peep Behind the Scenes* a melodramatic tear-jerker about the misery caused by a Godless life upon the stage.

Life and circumstances divided us all as adults, but the smell of cold, crisp apples and brown pears brings fond memories to this day.

So it was with this in mind that I invited my daughter Greta's cousin, Sian, to stay with us for a few days during these Christmas holidays.

A firm bond had already been established between them because, being 18 months older, all Sians' clothes have been handed on to Greta (who will soon be five). And at every family meeting this bond seemed to grow stronger.

So it was agreed that Sian, who lives at Tyers, near Traralgon, should come and stay for a few days trial.

All went beautifully until the first night when I kissed and cuddled them both goodnight—mindful of the fact that Sian was a long way from home and might need some tender loving care.

But I soon found out that any TLC given to Sian was too much for Greta. Ten minutes after I turned out the light, she emerged tearful and jealous: "Mummy loves Sian more than she loves me," she sobbed, followed by Sian wailing: "I miss my Mummy!"

Rob consoled Sian, while I explained to Greta that I had enough love for both of them, and they soon settled down again.

But 10 minutes later we discovered that they did not have as much in common as we thought, when Sian re-emerged exclaiming "That music's driving me nuts!" It seems that Sian needed quiet and dark to get to sleep, while Greta needed *The Hunchback of Notre Dame* blaring and the hall light on—so we put Sian in the next room.

The next day we found that Sian needed to get up at 6am, while Greta needed to sleep till 8am. Sian only ate the stalks of the broccoli, while Greta only ate the flowers. Sian wanted to watch *Shivers*, while Greta wanted to watch *Rapunzel*, and that having a rival at home was normal for Sian, but a new, rather confronting, (but healthy) experience for Greta, whose brother is eight years older.

I had always thought that the three days Greta spent at creche were enough to help her learn to share and get along with children her own age. But sharing communal toys is a lot different from sharing your own. And sharing Mummy and Daddy is harder still.

But the thrill of having someone nearer her own age to share in her imaginative games more than compensated. Between the small bouts of jealousy, there were giggles galore and a host of hugs and hand-holding.

As for me, "playing Aunty Daphne" was much more rewarding than just providing some company for Greta and a change of scene for Sian. It was a chance to re-create for another generation of cousins the sense of excitement and welcome that I felt during my orchard holidays so long ago.

1999

AN ODE TO PEPE—DOG NO. 4

When I was growing up, we always had a little dog of non-descript breed. Lizzie, the first one, was clever and loyal, while Mini, my companion throughout adolescence, was streetwise and funny.

My mother would probably contradict me, but as far as I can remember, these dogs were not trouble at all. So why has it take us four dogs and an awful lot of trouble, to find the perfect dog for our family?

Our first dog, Milo, a Jack Russell, died of a mysterious illness after two weeks. Our second, Ollie, another Jack Russell, I wanted to kill after two weeks.

Ollie had a serious personality defect, which caused him to shriek with fear and anxiety every time he saw another dog.

The local dog obedience school declared him "a nutter" and told me not to bring him back unless I had sedated him first. Eventually, we gave him away to a retired couple with no children who wanted a canine scarecrow for their fruit trees.

Our third dog, Jenna, a Brittany Spaniel, dug huge holes in our garden and our bank balance and loved to wade through our pond in search of ducks. Eventually, we sold her to a duck and quail shooter, who planned take her wading through rivers.

Then, at last, came our latest canine companion, Pepe, so named because with his white blaze down the centre of his grey-black head, he looks like the amorous cartoon skunk Pepe le Pew.

In fact, as a long-haired Chihuahua, some may even question Pepe's claim to being a dog at all. As one friend said: "He looks like a rare marsupial."

But Pepe does everything that our other dogs did, such as chewing our shoes and socks, piddling on the carpet and digging in the garden.

The difference is from a dog that weighs a mere 900 grams, this is endearing rather than annoying.

Just like our other dogs, he likes to chew the phone books, but after four weeks, he is still on A.

And if he wees on the carpet, it is a mere thimbleful and unless you catch him at it you have to get a forensic expert to find it.

He squeaks rather than barks, and when he bites and mouths (as all puppies do) he is as gentle as a kitten.

However, for spunk and bravery he outweighs dogs 10 times his size. He will bark furiously at any intruder, whether Great Aunt or Great Dane.

He fearlessly bounds up the steep staircase to our bedroom, and he scales the entrance to the large doggy door with the true grit of Sir Edmund Hilary climbing Mt Everest.

And when it comes to sharing the backyard with our four chooks, his courage and sauciness is unlimited. Henpecked? No fear. Pepe manages first serve of their breakfast every morning, stealing tiny morsels from the very same dinner he rejected the night before.

But the best thing about Pepe is that the children, particularly Greta, are in complete control. I do not have to restrain him when she goes outside to play. Instead, I have to restrain her.

So enchanted is she that poor old Pepe's feet hardly touch the ground. Whether he is driving the Barbie car, being tucked neatly into the cradle or simply falling asleep in front of the telly in the crook of Greta's arm, he has replaced Teddy as her favourite cuddly toy.

Luckily, Greta is old enough and gentle enough to heed my warnings about being careful with Pepe and letting him alone enough to rest, but Chihuahua's are not recommended for families with pre-schoolers who may accidentally harm the dog.

That's why this is not a recommendation for Chihuahua's, as such, but rather a recommendation for exchanging man's best *fiend* for man's best *friend* if necessary.

A dog, like a husband, may be for life, but in my view, neither should result in a life sentence.

WHY I HATE HOMEWORK

I have a confession to make. I haven't done my homework. In fact I am about three sheets behind.

No, I am not a mature-age student. I am just a mum, like many others, whose six-year-old daughter gets homework she can neither understand nor complete alone.

My daughter, Greta, is in Grade 1, and is reading very well, and doing fine in all other aspects of the curriculum. But she is not quite ready to measure the length and width of something in her house, or work out how much petrol the family car holds or make up her own groups of equations or find five words related to older people—at least not without my help.

While I realise the object of this is to involve parents in their children's learning, I think it is a little premature. In my view, homework should be for the child, not the parent. If the child cannot read the instructions alone, then she is not ready for homework. I understand the value of learning at home, but at the age of six or seven, I think a nightly "reader" is enough.

To the school's credit, there is no compulsion to do this homework. And any other form of reading or writing—such as the letters to the fairies we have been writing—can be counted as homework instead.

"Don't worry about it," the teacher said reassuringly. And I tried not to. But the fact that the homework sheet is distributed to each child each week and that most of the children return it the following week creates a type of peer pressure that is difficult to ignore

Children are conformists at heart. They like to do what the others are doing. And most parents are the same. While some parents have admitted they find the homework stressful, none has been as rebellious and erratic as me.

Naturally, Greta is happy to ignore it. However, when the homework "project" came home, she was keen to take part, so I followed suit.

The children were asked to design and make something and then evaluate it. We were encouraged to keep it simple, but most of the children produced projects complex enough to suggest parental intervention—ourselves included.

We chose a sock puppet. I tried to teach Greta few stitches, but sewing with her hand in the sock was too difficult. So she sat beside me saying: "This is such fun. I've always wanted to learn to sew," while I sewed diligently.

During the show-and-tell display there was a tacit acknowledgment that most of the parents had lent a hand, and that the round of applause was for family rather than individual effort.

I'm not sure how much Greta learned from it, but I learned that even at this level, in the face of competition, few parents are confident enough to let their child go it alone. A friend and former teacher says that's one reason that homework is often parent-driven.

But I am not the only one who doubts the effectiveness of homework at this age. Harris Cooper who has studied the history and effectiveness of homework in American education found that homework raised student achievement in the higher levels but had no discernible effect in the lower grades. In fact overall, he found that homework could have negative as well as positive effects on children's learning. In the United Kingdom, Professor John MacBeath argues that not enough is known about how pupils do homework or how effective it is in the learning process.

As for us, unless Greta wants to do it, I plan to ignore the homework until I think she is ready for it—except for the excellent advice on Homework Sheet Four, which I am encouraging her to follow studiously. It says: "Remember to go outside and play."

THE HEARTACHE OF PLAYGROUND POLITICS

There is one thing that every parent dreads for their child apart from a life threatening disease or accident, and that is the plaintive cry: "Why don't I have any friends?"

It is these words from my six-and-a-half year old daughter that sent a cold, steel sword of pain through my heart recently.

Greta's best friend left the school earlier in the year, and since then she has been like a star without a constellation, unable to muscle in on groups that became firmly established in the first weeks of the year. This year, too, she has been without her Grade Six buddy, a close friendship she misses greatly.

While at home she is bright and sunny and even a little cheeky sometimes, she has always been quiet at school, which adds to the problem of trying to be assertive in the playground.

It is difficult to know what to do about this. Playground politics can be extremely fluid. No child is perfect and one that may be the victim one minute can easily be the perpetrator the next. One bad day of "Your not my friend" taunts can send a parent into damage control, only to find out that the child has forgotten about the episode the next day and is happily playing—or (shock, horror) happily inflicting similar treatment on another child.

Sometimes it seems it is best to leave well enough alone and let the child handle the problem, accepting it as part of growing up.

But like all politics, playground politics is about power and the abuse of power, Children who appear powerful seem to attract the support of others—even those who do not like them will support them for fear of being ostracised.

When this abuse of power begins to affect the self-esteem of a child, I believe it is time for the parent to step in. At our school, which is small, bullying is taken extremely seriously and addressed promptly, but sometimes it is not so easy to define what is going on.

This abuse is often subtle: a look that tells the other children that that person is out of favor; yelling at children who do not "obey" the bullying child; and comments such as "your hands are too small for writing properly", or "your legs are too skinny to run properly".

However ridiculous and harmless such comments appear, they are absorbed as truth by the small victims.

The obvious thing would be to approach the parent, but when it is also obvious that a major part of the problem is that the parent cannot say no to the child, there seems little point. Instead, the teacher has moved Greta to another table, keeps an eye on things in the playground, and we discuss issues and strategies at home.

Still, sometimes, the effect of this is that Greta gives up trying to gain acceptance with her peers, and attaches herself instead to the teacher on yard duty. Any questions about who she played with that day, are answered evasively or defensively: "Mummy, I LIKE walking around with the teacher."

But lately, she has started to concentrate on doing her own thing on the monkey bars, with the help of an older girl who helps novices and directs the monkey bar traffic. This has given her a focus and some status, as being small and agile her skills are improving.

We are all looking forward to next year, when everyone moves classes. But it became obvious the other day how powerless these little stabs at her self-esteem have made Greta feel.

She was intensely making something out of Lego the other evening, and came proudly upstairs to show me.

"What is it?" I asked, surveying what looked like a crane with a driver.

"It's a (name of bullying child) pulveriser," she said proudly.

A BOOST FOR SAFETY

I should have realised, when my husband, Rob, rang after leaving to pick up our daughter Greta from a party, that something was wrong. After all, the mobile phone—with a flat battery—was sitting in my handbag on my desk nearby, so how and why was he calling?

"We've been in an accident. Someone ran into the back of me and then sent me into the front of someone else," he said, his voice strangely calm. In the background I could hear Greta screaming.

"Is Greta all right?" I stammered, not realising until much later that it would have been polite to inquire after him, too.

"She's fine," he said. "Just a bit upset."

We were expecting my sister, Juliana, and her husband, Macca, for tea any second, so as soon as they arrived, Macca drove me to the accident site.

An ambulance had arrived as one of other drivers had suffered whiplash, and it's flashing lights, along with those of the police cars and tow truck, made the whole scene seem dramatic and frightening.

Greta ran into my arms, crying and clutching a teddy bear that the ambulance officer had given her after checking that both she and Rob were unharmed.

I didn't even look at the car. What did it matter, as long as Greta and Rob were safe?

Instead, we sat in Macca's car while Rob waited for another tow truck. Greta immediately put her seat belt on, and shivering from shock, told me over and over what had happened.

The car was written off but the insurance cheque did not cover the cost of replacement—so it turned out to be a costly exercise.

But the cost could have been far higher had I not decided just a few weeks earlier to keep Greta's baby booster seat.

Without the booster seat, the seat belt came across her neck, rather than her shoulder. When the car hit from behind, the belt would have cut into her neck as she was pushed forward. Although she had a bit of a sore tummy afterwards, this was mild compared to what might have happened.

However, just a few weeks earlier, I had considered doing away with the seat. Few of the other children at school seemed to be still in booster seats, and I wondered if I was being overprotective.

We had also recently done away with the pusher—so it seemed timely to do away with such a baby thing as booster seat, too. But Rob had argued that she was quite small for her age, and it was better to be safe than sorry. As usual, he was right.

According to the RACV, it is not the age of the child, but her weight that determines when a booster seat should no longer be needed. It recommends that children between the weights of 14 kg and 26 kilograms should still use a booster.

Greta, who is almost six, weighs only 18 kilograms, so it looks like she'll be in the booster for another few years yet.

Fortunately, Rob was stationary when the accident occurred, and could not have done anything to prevent it, we are both more cautious—especially as Christmas approaches.

I am also now more cautious about things being left in the car that may become missiles in the event of an accident—like the rotten apple core that flew through the air and landed on Rob's tummy in this accident.

The impact of the crash broke the driver's seat and left him flat on his back. "All I could see was this rotten apple core on my stomach," he said later.

I didn't tell him about the half eaten banana under the seat.

The car became the property of the insurer who sold it for parts—including parts of my lunch.

A POCKETFUL OF FINANCIAL LESSONS

The voice on the other end of the phone was asking me if I would accept reverse charges from my son, Johannes, in Melbourne.

"Yes?" I blurted, breathless with fear.

"Hi, Momma, it's me. My train was cancelled so can you ring Denise and tell her I won't be there till 11.30," he said coolly.

"Why are you ringing reverse charges?" I asked, annoyed at the fright he had given me.

"I didn't have a phone card," he explained.

"Haven't you got any money?" I asked.

"Yes."

"How much?"

"$130," he replied, equally coolly.

"Johannes! You could have spared 45 cents for a phone call," I spluttered, adding that he could have got change at the milk bar and that his $10 weekly pocket money and the large Christmas bonus his father had given him was for *all* his personal expenses—including phone calls.

Teaching children the value of money and how to manage it is a bit like toilet training. You can't cover them for ever—eventually they have to learn to control their urges.

And the way to learn this control, according to my friend Carolyn, is to be given the chance to earn it and spend it at an early age—and bear the consequences.

Her own daughter Hannah, 10, is a prime example of how well this works.

Hannah had been desperate for one of those baby dolls that eats, drinks and then poohs and wees. (Having had two real babies that did just that, I couldn't see the attraction myself.)

Carolyn was not prepared to pay the exorbitant price of $89, but suggested instead that Hannah could do household chores to earn the money to save for it.

Six months of hard labor later, Hannah had her baby doll. But soon after she discovered that the feeding and toileting aspect of the doll was not what it was cracked up to be. (Could have told her that).

The doll was abandoned, but the lesson she will have for life. "She's actually seen what happens if you save up for six months and then waste your money. It's really been a great education for her," Carolyn said.

Now my daughter Greta, who is almost six, looks like getting both the doll and the lesson as a hand me down.

Greta is equally enamoured with the doll and we are equally sceptical about its play value, so we have agreed to buy Hannah's (as new!) doll, at a discount price of $35, with Greta contributing $5 of her own money. That means forfeiting her 50 cents a week pocket money for 10 weeks.

The trick with pocket money, according to Carolyn, is to be absolutely clear about how it may be earned and what the child is financially responsible for. So if you decide your child is responsible for her own treats—stick to it—even if she has to go without because she has run out of money.

"I'm a great believer in letting them waste it and wishing they hadn't," Carolyn said.

Lessons like this require will-power on the parents' behalf too.

Having decided not to do any chores before Christmas, Hannah had no spending money on a recent holiday and had to forego the chance to buy a beautiful little bag.

Carolyn admitted she would have liked to give her the money, but in the end she decided the lesson about consequences was more valuable than the bag.

Still, such lessons are not really absorbed until at least the age of reason.

Saving up nearly $8 for Christmas shopping helped Greta realise the power of money rather than value of it.

Two weeks later, freed from the social obligation of buying gifts for others and finding herself standing in front of a lolly counter without her purse, she begged me to lend her 50 cents.

"But you have to pay me back the 50 cents when we get home," I said, handing her a $1 coin.

She handed the $1 to the shop keeper, took her lollies and handed me the change, saying "Here's the 50 cents I owe you."

PUTTING WOMEN BACK IN THE PICTURE

The question "Where did I dome from?" can strike fear into the heart of any parent. But what do you do when the inquiring youngster really means, "Where did I come from *as a species*?"

It all began with a book called *In the Beginning . . . The Nearly Complete History of Almost Everything*, by Brian Delf and Richard Platt. I had originally bought it to use as a reference for drawing cartoons, as it had great illustrations. (In this game, you never ever know when you're going to be asked to draw a couple of Romans in togas.)

But the section that most interested my seven-year-old daughter, Greta, was on the Origins of Life. "Read it! Read it!" she commanded, although the language and the concepts were mostly beyond her. Still, we persevered, starting at the Big Bang and progressing to Homo Sapiens.

Greta had many questions, which I tried to use the text to answer. But there was one that I was totally unprepared for. "When did the women come?" she asked, gazing at an illustration of Homo Erectus men gathered around a fire at the mouth of a cave.

"At the same time as the men," I answered dumbly.

Greta frowned and looked at me impatiently. "But where are *we*?" she asked. It took me a few seconds to realise what she meant. Then it dawned on me. In the five illustrations from Australopithecus Afarensis to Homo Sapiens, from 5.5 million years ago to 35,000 years ago, there were no pictures of women.

It was a shock to realise how literally she took these pictures. She had not assumed, as I had, that women were also present. And why should she? The notion of man being inclusive of women is no longer assumed in our society. Language that excludes women is being challenged so that governments, the church and businesses have been forced to paint women back into the picture.

But here was a book published in 1995 that had managed to exclude women.

I began to look at the rest of the book more critically. Sure enough, on page 20, which introduced the concept of "everyday life", five of the seven illustrations showing people were clearly of men. The other two were non-specific—doctors in surgical masks and caps and back views of people wearing coats with hoods and boots.

In the section on medicine, whose early history was dominated by men, it was understandable that most illustrations were of men. But even here the patients were men. The only women depicted were Madam Curie and a pregnant woman undergoing an ultrasound. The same went for pictures in other sections.

The obvious reason, you may argue, is that the people behind all these modern inventions—from the steam train to the space ship—were men. But what about the *Encyclopaedia of Women* I bought recently for a friend's 21st birthday? It listed thousands of women of achievement, who rated no mention in *In the Beginning*.

So what, you say? What difference does it really make? A big difference when a little girl, wanting to learn about the world, learns that she has no place in it.

What role models does this book offer my daughter other than that she is the passive and grateful recipient of progress that has been made at the hands of men? Or that she is a mere passenger in life—carried along by whatever means of transport men offer.

Luckily I had another book to counter this. I told my daughter that it was common for women to be left out of books and that there were lots of wonderful women if she read the right books. So I took from the shelf, dusty and forgotten, just like half the women in it, Judy Chicago's book of *The Dinner Party—A Symbol of Our Heritage*, published in 1979.

Judy Chicago and her team of researchers and artists spent five years honoring women's heritage through the creation of china plates, symbolising 39 women of history and mythology, and a heritage floor depicting 999 women of achievement.

The controversy that surrounded this work is still not resolved, partly because of the bold sexual imagery that was used in the work. When I last heard, there was still no permanent home for this amazing work of art.

But thousands of women like me saw it in Melbourne when it toured years ago, and many of us have given the book a permanent home because it shows what women need to know: that women and girls and their contributions are important—in the beginning and in the end.

GAMES IN THE GLOBAL VILLAGE

In the olden days, when I was growing up, we kids relaxed with friends after school by playing Monopoly, Trap the Cap, Mouse Trap (when we could be bothered setting it up) or cards.

These days, my 15-year-old son relaxes after school by playing Wheel of Fortune with his friends and whoever else happens to pop in. The difference is that each of them is sitting at home alone in front of their computer.

Yes, welcome to the new age of electronic communication, where you can go online and play cards, war games or even (virtual) golf with people from all over the world via the Internet. A computer and a modem and a decent bank balance have become the new international passport for those who like to travel all over the world without ever leaving home.

As I glanced over my son's shoulder one night to see how he was faring with Wheel of Fortune, I looked at the messages from the other players. Mel and Lee, I knew, were kids from school and regular Wheel of Fortune hunters, but who was Bozo?

"Don't know," replied my son. It seemed the game was the thing, and who was playing was irrelevant. Bozo could have been from Tamworth, Texas or Transylvania, but who cared?

It just shows, I thought, how the concept of the global village has become so normal and acceptable to this generation. Once upon a time, communicating with someone from another country was akin to receiving messages from outer space. Now outer space is in our inner space, and especially in my most valued inner space: my office.

Although my son has a computer in his room for homework, only my computer has Internet access, so he is always pleading: "Can I check my email?" More recently he has been using the instant messaging service, where the recipient can read the message as you type it.

This means that lately when I sit down at my computer, which is frequently late at night, I am likely to get messages from Mel, or Lee or the Hunted Snow Bunny (whoever that is).

The first time it happened I was reasonably tolerant: "Piss off. I'm working"—signed Mummy". I wrote.

Mel was suitably contrite: "That's cool. Bye" she said. Lee was a little shocked: "That's a bit hard!" she wrote.

My son, who had been called in to help, quickly typed an explanation and told them all to go away, which they did.

The trouble is, when the computer is turned on, they cannot tell whether it is him or me, so lately every time I sit down to work, I'm confronted with Mel, Lee and the Hunted Snow Bunny interrupting my thoughts.

My son was very apologetic and arranged to block them so that they cannot tune in unless he's tuned in first. But one night at about 10 o'clock while I was typing away, a message popped up from Mel.

"Hi Spunky Monkey! Watchya doin'?" she wrote.

"The Spunky Monkey has gone beddy-byes," I wrote back.

Since then, I haven't been bothered too much by late online visitors. Perhaps they realise that the Spunky Monkey has since gone to Queensland with his school's German class.

Without access to email, we have been expecting an old-fashioned communication: a postcard. But so far, we haven't received anything. No doubt it will turn up, as usual, a few days after the Spunky Monkey returns.

Snail mail may be slower, but it doesn't intrude on your work time or your thoughts. With the humble postcard, you can generously write: "Wish you were here", and be secretly glad that they are not. But with instant messaging, they are here, there and everywhere, whether you like it or not.

WHITE LIES, RED FACES

Do you lie to your children? Like most parents you would probably reply with an indignant 'No!" but I can guarantee that you do—big time.

Take a conversation a friend had with her 10-year-old son recently. "The kids at school all say that Santa's not real," he said. "They say it's just the parents."

"Well, what do you think, honey?" she asked, using that tactic well known to media savvy politicians of putting the question back to the inquirer.

"I think he's real," her son replied.

"Well, there you are then!" she said, closing the conversation with a reassuring smile.

Sound familiar? Like me, she'd been lying to her kids for years about Santa, the Tooth Fairy, and the Easter Bunny—not to mention the real reason we don't see Aunt Bertha or Uncle Monty any more.

Parents who don't play this game are considered spoilers, as my friend Rosemary found when she told her children many years ago that there was no Santa. Why should a mythical man get all the credit for Christmas, which is largely organised by women, Rosemary, a staunch feminist, had argued.

But when her children told their friends, Rosemary copped the wrath of angry parents.

Until a few years ago, I would have agreed with those parents. But now, I'm not so sure. What changed my mind, was my daughter's attitude when she discovered about two years ago that fairies were not real.

To encourage her to write, I had started a game writing letters from the fairies. She was enchanted, and wrote back eagerly, and together we created a complex fairy world that culminated in the fairy queen holding a ball in the dolls' house.

At this stage, my husband and teenage son warned me that things had gone too far. But I was enjoying myself too much, reliving the fantasies of my own childhood. How can I go back now, I argued, promising to stop it all straight after the ball?

My daughter and I spent the next few days blowing up tiny water balloons and creating tiny streamers to decorate the dolls' house. We even wrote a tiny note asking the fairies to be sure to clean up.

The next day, with great excitement, we found the dolls' house was littered with fairy dust and party remnants, but as compensation, the fairies had left some little chocolates and gifts and another note of thanks.

Greta didn't tell her friends about the ball. "They wouldn't believe me," she said. But her own faith was absolute—until a few months later when the Tooth Fairy forgot to turn up.

Soon she began asking whether the fairies were real. For a while, like my friend, I neatly avoided a definitive answer, but one day, she cornered me.

"Yes, it's me!" I confessed in the full glare of the kitchen light.

But instead of being relieved, she was devastated. She burst into tears, locked herself in her room and seizing every fairy book on her extensive bookshelf threw them around the room, screaming, "I thought it was real!"

It was days before she would speak to me properly, but gradually we worked out a truce.

"You wanted so much to believe—what was I to do?" I pleaded.

What I should have done was understand that children are much more vulnerable than we sometimes realise. What can be just a game for an adult, can be very real for a child.

Now Greta was faced with the loss of someone who had seemed like a real friend. Her grief and anger were natural.

Teary-eyed, she asked whether the fairies could still visit at Christmas and birthdays—so I agreed, and now we play what we both know is a game, in a wink-wink, nudge-nudge kind of way.

But I am not the only one who has so successfully deceived her child. A friend whose daughter is obsessed with the television show *Charmed*, about three sister witches, told her daughter that witches were real and that she would turn into one when she was 12. Then she would be bestowed with great powers. Meanwhile, anyone who crosses her now is warned that they will cop it later when she's *really* powerful.

Greta scoffed at these claims in the schoolyard but secretly worried about whether this was wise. She knew fairies weren't real, but was not so sure about witches, especially when one of them advertised in the local paper as a purveyor of spells and a fortune-teller.

Of course, this time I told her the truth and hoped that her friend's mother would tell her child the truth, too.

And of course, the Tooth Fairy still visits out house, but these days, she's known as the Truth Fairy.

Another kind of quality time

There are two sorts of quality time. The first is the time you spend with your children as they grow. The second is the time you spend with your parents as they die.

This story is about the second. As I write, my father-in-law, Cec, lies curled up in a hospital bed, as small and frail as a newborn child.

Clear green tubes carrying oxygen circle his head. Morphine, needed to calm him and aid breathing, robs him of his senses. And the hands that once lifted sacks of flour or counted sheep and cattle in sale yards around Victoria, and pounded garden stakes and pruned trees in his much-loved garden, are swollen with fluid that his old heart is too weak to pump through his worn out body.

Day after day, he drifts in and out of consciousness, his eyes fluttering in feeble recognition as family and friends hover over him. We squeeze his swollen hands as he struggles for words, and talk in reverent whispers as we wait for an end to his and our suffering.

Our own lives, like his, are in limbo. Of course work is still done, both paid and unpaid, but our hearts and minds are with Cec as he struggles on the ledge between this world and the next. Whenever possible, we go back to relieve his wife and my mother-in-law Judith of her bedside vigil.

For 42 years she has slept beside him, although now it is on a fold-out bed beside his hospital bed. They have known each other for 50 years, and their two lives have been so tightly wound together that unravelling one is complex, slow and painful.

We talk about their life together, their courtship.

They knew each other for years but it wasn't until she went to stay at his parents' farm for a holiday, at the invitation of his sister, that things got serious. He picked her up from the station and they went to a dance with friends that are still friends.

A year later they were married. "And I've never regretted it," she says. Perhaps it is this bond that holds him here still, we wonder. We talk, hug and cry, missing him already.

When we step out of that world of white sheets and lights, sympathetic friends console us. "There is no quality of life at that stage," they say. And in many ways they are right. Cec, small of stature but strong of spirit and mind, would be hating this.

In the last month at home, bedridden, on oxygen and too weak to even go to the bathroom on his own, he looked at my husband, Rob, and said, "It wasn't meant to be like this."

But in some ways, this long goodbye has its special qualities too. We talk to him and about him. We talk about the way his is, and the way he was. "No one ever had a bad word to say about him," Judith says, and while everyone says this of the dead and dying, in this case it is true.

In the brief intervals at the family home, 10 minutes drive from the hospital, we play the music he likes and tearfully plan his farewell. We talk about the past with him and the future without him. We cannot really plan for it, but we start to see it and accept it.

Sometimes we talk over him, telling our news and accepting him as a presence, but not an active one. We wonder what he hears and understands and hope that his lonely journey will soon be over.

Wherever he is, we are all trying to reach him in our own way. "Hi Pa," we say, holding his hand for a minute or two.

In a moment on their own, Judith tells him: "I love you. Do you love me?" He squeezes her hand in reply. He calls out the names of family and friends as he dreams of the past, but it is her name that he calls the most.

We bring photos and flowers to the room, each wanting to give something of themselves. My daughter, Greta, sings the theme from *Babe* to him. "If I had words to make a day for you, I'd sing you a morning golden and true. I would make this day last for all time. Give you a light deep in moonshine," she sings in her pure clear childish voice.

We all cry and hug again. None of us want this day to last for all time. It is too painful. But if we could, we would all sing him a morning, golden and true, that would last for all time.

WHEN THE PAST HAS A FUTURE

When my mother was raising us, it was common for women to have children who were close in age. My sister and I were only 14 months apart, and despite the fact that she was fair and I was dark, were often mistaken for twins.

But in these days, it is more common for women to have several marriages close together and children who vary widely in age—and I am no exception. With two children eight years apart, I often tell people that I have had two "only" children.

When my son was young, this meant we spent the school holidays going to various holiday happenings together, such as pantomimes, movies and picnics in parks. I cherish these memories, but not enough to be still doing them eight years later—this time with my daughter.

So I couldn't believe my luck when last September holidays, we discovered something that seemed to bridge the gap between her world and mine: *Morning Melodies*.

At first I thought you had to be over 55, as these monthly concerts at the Victorian Arts Centre are sponsored by the Australian Pensioners' Insurance Agency and Magic 693, (the radio station that features ads for funerals, nursing homes, cardigans and holidays where you can stay on the bus).

But when Greta and I fronted for our tickets to the Lux Radio Theatre presentation of *The Mystery of the Hansom Cab*, no one noticed we were underage, and we became the only two dark heads among a sea of grey.

The plot was a little above her head, but she loved the sound effects and the fancy gowns—so much so that we went to the next one, which featured the cast from a local production of *The Sound of Music*.

"She's being so good," said one old lady sympathetically, little knowing that I had brainwashed her from birth and that her knowledge of musicals now rivalled that of TV movie and musical host, Bill Collins.

However, this Christmas holiday, there were no *Morning Melodies*, so I thought I would fuel her interest in art with a visit to the Heidi, the Museum of Modern Art. Modern art, I explained, was not meant to be realistic. It was meant to show how the artist was feeling about things or how he imagined things to be.

But I had not planned on the imagination of artist Albert Tucker.

Greta tolerated the disembodied, angular women, the gaunt explorers in harsh desert landscapes and the self-portraits of a man who was clearly the victim of age and indiscretion. But it was the Images of Evil that got to her. Albert Tucker, she declared was "cuckoo", (a view shared by some of his early critics).

"Let's go and see the other gallery," she said, pulling us towards the women's gallery. But here, it was even more abstract and she was not impressed when she read that a vast canvas of little squares was meant to be somebody's grandmother.

"It's a bit like little kids' art," she said. "They think it's really great, but nobody else understands it."

But things improved when we visited the National Trust property Gulf Station in Yarra Glen. The old homestead, farming and kitchen implements fascinated her and fuelled her interest in history, so I promised to take her to historic Como House in South Yarra the following week.

At Como, we were lucky enough to have a tour guide to ourselves, a gentle man with traces of a lilting Irish brogue, who spared no detail in his encyclopaedic talk.

At first I thought this may be a bit much for Greta, especially when I saw her longingly eyeing the fat, chintz sofas in the morning room. But it was her legs, not her brain that was suffering. As soon as she skipped out into the garden, she declared: "That was fantastic. I want to join the National Trust."

The guide suggested that we visit the Old Melbourne Gaol to get a glimpse of how the other half lived, then we are off to Labassa and Rippon Lea and Barwon Grange and the rest.

In some ways, I am still living in the past. But I am more than happy to live in the past if it is the one that is brought to life so well by the National Trust.

THE ART OF NOT GIVING UP

We had had a busy week and so my seven-year-old daughter had not had much chance to do her piano practice.

"That's okay," I said when she found it difficult to remember some of the notes. "You can do some revision."

She had begun learning at the beginning of the year, and was now on her second book.

"Here you go," I said, flipping through to find an earlier piece, and waiting for her to begin. But instead of playing, her shoulders slumped and her face fell.

"What's wrong?" I asked.

Gradually, it all came out. Revision, it seems, felt like a remedial and menial exercise and her pride was hurt. Worse still, although we never compared her to her brother, who is eight years older and studying eighth grade, night after night of listening to rolling arpeggios had made her feel inferior. "I've been learning for ages and I'm still no good," she sobbed.

I tried hard not to laugh. After all, when you're only seven, I suppose two terms seems like a lifetime. "I don't want to do it anymore," she cried. "It's too hard."

For a moment, I wasn't sure how to tackle this. My husband was not home from work yet and her brother was still at school band practice—so there was no one to turn to for advice. If I insisted that she learn piano, she would probably hate me now. If I let her give up, she would probably hate me later

But then I remembered a similar incident with her brother after he had been learning for about a year.

"I know someone else who felt like this once," I said.

"Who?" she asked, lifting her head from her hands.

"Johannes," I said.

"Johannes!" she repeated in surprise.

"Yes, I remember he said it was boring and he didn't want to do it anymore and when I rang his teacher, she said that he had suddenly found he needed to work hard and he didn't like it."

But she still wasn't convinced. "I still want to give it up," she said tearfully.

"Let's have tea and talk about it later," I suggested. After all, I knew just how she felt. I was feeling very challenged myself at work with all the new technology. So we sat alone in the dining room eating dinner in silence—each feeling overwhelmed in our own way.

After a while, I said. "I think I'll give up work. It's getting really hard and I don't like it anymore."

Greta looked up sharply. "Why?"

"Well, you know this computer course I'm doing? I'm having a lot of trouble with it, so I think I'll give up."

"You can't do that", she said. "You're really good at your work."

"I'm not good at this bit," I said. "I'm really struggling. Of course, I won't have as much money, so things will be a little bit tighter, but that's okay because I'll be happier."

"Don't give up," she pleaded. "You can do it if you try."

"But I'm tired of trying so hard," I said. "I just want to give up."

This argument went on for a while, until she got fed up with me. "Don't be such a wimp," she said finally.

I looked at her and grinned. "That's pretty good advice you're giving me there." And then it dawned on her and she began to laugh uncontrollably.

When she recovered, I said: "Tell you what—let's make a deal? Why don't we both wait until after the holidays and see how we feel? If we still feel the same way, you can give up piano and I'll give up work. Deal?"

"Deal!" she replied.

For the next two weeks she we both practiced diligently each day—me on the computer and her on the piano.

At 8.30am on the first Monday of term, Greta had her piano lesson. Half an hour later, she burst into the kitchen beaming. "I got four stickers for excellent playing!" she cried.

It was a relief for me, because I did not want to see her waste an opportunity—and if I gave up work, we'd all be giving up a lot more than the piano.

Over the top with Mitch and Matt

In our back garden, among the hydrangeas, is a little path. To grown-ups, it leads nowhere. A few short steps into it and you will find an overgrown pond on your left, a fern on your right, then the old grey paling side fence between our place and next door.

But to Greta, this is the pathway to adventure, because over the fence are Jake, Mitch, Matt and Briony.

They are the kids next door—Jake is 10, Mitch is seven like Greta, Matt is five and Briony is three, and together they are an endless source of fun and frustration for Greta.

Fun because she does things with them that she would never think of or dare to try on her own—such a collecting cicada shells, having snail races on the trampoline, and digging up ground yabbies. And frustration, because no matter where she and Mitch go, Matt is sure to follow.

Mitch and Greta are similar in that both like to dominate. "Miiiiiiiiitch!" Greta yells when she can't get her way. "Greddda!" he retorts. When no compromise can be reached, they retreat for a while, then like an old married couple, they forgive and forget—until next time.

Jake, being a little older, is more interested in basketball and books. Briony is irresistible because of her cloud of silky golden curls, her blue eyes and her budding interest in Barbies. But Matt bothers Greta, because while she dips her toe in the water of life, Matt jumps right in—even if he nearly drowns himself and everyone else in the process.

Otherwise known as Mr Love, because of his frequent declarations of amour, Matt mysteriously appears whenever food is offered, and frequently leaves large deposits in our toilet. He trails chook pooh and mud where ever he goes and I never need to ask him to take his shoes off before he comes in because most of the time he isn't wearing any.

"Matt keeps trying to join our club," Greta complained after she and Mitch had spent days holed up in the attic above Mitch's Dad's garage, creating an exclusive clubhouse.

Exclusive meant everyone except Matt, so Matt registered his formal protest by punching Greta in the stomach. This of, course, caused Mitch and Greta to close ranks even more and by that evening, the club had moved to the two-man tent in Mitch's backyard, for their first ever sleepover.

Over the fence Greta went with her kit, determined to spend the night in the backyard outpost with Mitch. With her big brother also away for the night, that just left her father, Rob, and I.

"Let's go out for dinner," Rob said, sniffing freedom.

"I don't know whether she'll last that long," I said, and went out to lurk near the back fence to see how things were going.

Around 10pm, just when we were starting to relax completely, there was a knock on the door, and there stood Mitch's Dad, looking apologetic, with Greta, looking heartbroken. "I missed you and Daddy," she sobbed.

For a week after that, I couldn't get her to leave the lounge room. "What happened to the club?" I inquired.

"It's over," she said. "Mitch is always telling me what to do. He never listens to my ideas."

So for a week we tripped over Barbies and Kelly's while Greta hid in her bunker doing her girlie thing.

Then one day, our Rob came in from mowing the lawn and declared: "The cold war's over." Sure enough, there were Greta and Mitch, trailed by Matt and Briony, playing on the swings.

Now, as usual, there is heavy over-the-fence traffic and I am either left alone while Greta goes wild next door, or scouring the pantry for "treasure" for the five hungry pirates camping under the weeping cherry in our front garden.

When we bought the house two-and-a-half years ago, we were delighted with the big old garden, but it wasn't until we had lived here for a while that we realised the wonderful childhood friendships that would grow there.

2001

SHARING A MESSAGE FROM AN OLD FRIEND

Having your own children provides the perfect opportunity for reliving your own childhood, and no more so than through sharing a favorite book.

So when I came across *A Peep Behind the Scenes* by Mrs O. F. Walton, while fossicking in a rambling second-hand bookshop in Guildford, near Castlemaine, I immediately bought it to read with my eight-year-old daughter, Greta.

My sister and cousin and I had spent one particular wet September holiday together, reading and weeping over this book when were about 10, so seeing it was like greeting an old friend.

The book is about poor little Rosalie, forced to travel from fair to fair in England with her cruel father and dying mother in a travelling theatre.

One day, a visiting preacher hands her a picture of the Good Shepherd holding a lamb, with the text underneath: "Rejoice with me, for I have found my sheep which was lost. There is joy in the presence of the angels of God over one sinner that Repenteth". This picture becomes the symbol for Rosalie's salvation in the Godless world of the theatre.

During that holiday when I was 10, little Rosalie became our heroine. It was only rereading with Greta that I realised that little Rosalie was actually a big pain in the you-know-what.

And so did Greta. By the time Rosalie had converted her fifth sinner and was asking yet another bunch of wayward circus folk, "Has the Good Shepherd found you yet?" she was squirming in her seat and asking. "When we were going to get the fourth Harry Potter book?"

I persevered the next night, but when we came to the sermon about how only the spotlessly white can enter heaven. I was afraid it would scare her, so I said: "The real God isn't this petty. He doesn't expect people to be perfect."

263

"I know," said Greta, then added. "This is a load of bull, isn't?"

"Well it's a bit over-the-top. But it does show the power of words," I said. These days, I said, there were laws to protect child actors, and children in general, and well, the theatre wasn't all that bad and the church wasn't all that good.

It made me wonder who Mrs O.F. Walton was and what sort of credibility she had as an author. To my surprise, a quick search on the Internet showed that her books are part of a rare collection of 19th century Christian books, part of the Lamplighter Rare Collector's Series, according to www.graceandtruthbooks.com. So famous in fact, that the Conference of the Religious Tract Society held late last July in Norwich, England, began its blurb with "A peep behind the scenes of the RTS and Lutterworth Press . . ."

According to Gill Bilski, writing on the Yahoo Bulletin board in response to someone else's query, Mrs Walton was born in 1850 and died in 1939, and wrote about 20 books between 1872 and 1919.

"The books are the short religious type ideal for Victorian Sunday School Prizes," Bilski said. "The one you have and *Christie's Old Organ* are probably her most famous titles and probably the most readable—but unfortunately they are not collected by anyone I know."

I can see why. Compared to Harry Potter, Rosalie Joyce and her piety look very lame. But despite the squirm factor, there is something charming and innocent about the message in *A Peep Behind the Scenes*—a message that holds especially true in a world where drugs are the latest devil.

In its recent review of the book, Lamplighter describes it as: "An excellent book to teach discernment."

At this stage it may only be literary discernment, but perhaps later, like Rosalie, Greta will find the other message, which was also delivered by Shakespeare in *The Merchant of Venice* and Chaucer in his *Canterbury Tales*. And that is that all that glitters is not gold.

DEFINING THE FACTS OF LIFE

My eight-year-old daughter is one of those people who reads for purpose rather than pleasure, so I knew she had a purpose when she shoved her junior Macquarie dictionary in my face during dinner one night.

"I found this in the dictionary today," she declared, pointing to the words "sexual intercourse".

"I'll explain it later," I said, with my fork in mid air. "Just let me finish my dinner."

By later, I meant in another 10 years, but she persisted, so while I was brushing her hair before bed, I dutifully asked: "So what do you want to know?"

She spun around. "Is that true?" she demanded, referring to the very explicit dictionary definition.

She was grinning with embarrassment, so I forced a straight face. "Well, yes," I said, hastening to add that it all started with feeling very loving towards each other.

But she was not convinced. "I'm never doing THAT!" she said. Then added: "Is there any other way to make a baby?" Things were complicated enough, so I said, "Not really."

As I tucked her into bed, she complained: "Why did they put words like that in a school dictionary for innocent little children to read?"

I felt the same way. In my day the facts of life were doled out on a need-to-know rather than a want-to-know basis.

While I wanted to be open, I did not want to scare her with too much detail, so on the advice of a friend, I bought *Where do I come from?*, which explains the basics in simple terms with cartoon pictures.

"Would you like to read this and then we'll discuss it?" I asked, handing the book over the following Sunday.

She grabbed it, ran into her bedroom and slammed the door. Fifteen minutes later she emerged, wearing an even bigger and more embarrassed grin. "That book is amazing," she said.

"Come and sit here, and let's talk about it," I said, patting the seat beside me on the couch.

She sat and then looked at me incredulously. "Why do you *do* that?" she demanded.

"Well . . ." I said, feeling rather shamefaced and lost for words in the face of such accusation. Then seeing the Barbie Family House spread out on the lounge room floor before us, I asked, "Do you think you'll be playing with the Barbie house when you're 20?"

"No," she laughed.

"Well, things change," I said. "The things you liked doing when you were little aren't the same as the one's you like when you're grown up. Besides, you don't do it all the time." I pointed to the page in the book that likened sex to skipping—you couldn't do it all day long.

She turned and looked at me accusingly, then held up two fingers: "There's Hunni (her brother) and me—that's twice!"

What could I say? There was the evidence of my wantonness staring me in the face—literally.

Luckily, she didn't really expect an answer. "I can't imagine you and Daddy doing *that*," she said in disgust.

"Well I'll let you in on a secret," I said. "I can't imagine grandma and grandpa doing it and they couldn't imagine their parents doing it." We agreed it was a rather ridiculous activity, even when glossed over with flowers, chocolates and romantic evenings.

For the next few days she walked around with an embarrassed grin on her face. Then she seemed to forget about it.

But things have changed. I feel embarrassed when our bedroom door is shut—even if its just because I want to wrestle in private with my pantyhose—and even the cuddly bits in G-rated movies make me blush.

I had wanted her maths to improve, but things just don't feel the same now that she knows why one plus one can sometimes make three.

THE REAL PRICE OF FREE-RANGE EGGS

There is something about the ubiquitous quarter-acre suburban block that makes jaded city slickers go all clucky. That's why, when we braved the wilds of the outer suburbs four years ago, we decided to get chooks.

Having grown up with picture books of plump farmers' wives throwing apronsful of grain to fat little red hens, we had assumed that chooks were benign creatures. This was fueled by more modern images of righteous animal liberators rescuing battery hens, which were clearly the victims of cruelty and greed. But by the time we saw *Chicken Run* last Christmas, we knew that Mrs Tweedy was right: the best place for a chicken is in a pie.

It all began with the ad for "abundant layers". Seduced by the prospect of fresh eggs with orange yolks, we bought two red and two black hens and named them Miss Prissy, the Little Red Hen, Clucky Lucky and Henny Penny. We set them up in the abandoned cubby house near the back fence—surely the Windsor Castle of chook runs, and waited.

Six weeks later we discovered that chooks are not only egg machines, they are shit machines. For every egg there is 10 times the amount of pooh, and while it may be great for the garden it is not so great for the carpet, which is where it ended up after the kids had trodden in it.

Our Chihuahua Pepe was enlisted as a chook dog to keep the abundant poohers off the verandah, which was a challenge as the chooks were at least twice as big as he was. "Get the chooks!" we would say and he would leap to the charge.

The Head Chook, by now known simply as Red, exacted her revenge by waiting for Pepe as he came down the back steps each morning and giving him a punitive peck. He, in turn, exacted his revenge by waiting until she was scratching happily in the back yard alone, then running around and around her in ever diminishing circles.

When she was thoroughly bamboozled, he would dash in and bite her on the bum, collecting a mouthful of feathers. The chooks, in turn, would exact further revenge by stalking him every time he tried to get outside and have a quiet gnaw on a bone He would extract further revenge by making sure it was a chicken bone. And so it went on.

Admittedly, the chooks did get rid of the wandering Jew that was choking all other plants, and the snails, and the eggs were delicious, but they got rid of everything else too, which meant that we had to put netting over our vegetable garden.

When Clucky Lucky and Henny Penny died of chook flu the following winter, we abandoned sentiment and tied them up in plastic bags and threw them in the rubbish.

Still clinging to the notion of the suburban farm we decided to replenish with bantams, which we thought would do less damage to the garden and to Pepe. We bought two chicks, a hen and a rooster, and because they were inseparable, we named them Romeo and Juliet.

For a few weeks they were a delightful sight, with their feathered slippers giving them a comical Charlie Chaplin walk. But then came puberty and Romeo turned into Rambo. "The backyard is no longer a feminist enclave," my husband said sadly one day, indicating that Romeo and Juliet were now inseparable at least six times a day.

Within weeks Romeo turned out to be a bully as well as a rapist. For my eight-year-old daughter, collecting the few remaining eggs turned in to a military operation involving a broom, a bucket and some gumboots, as the minute her back was turned Romeo would run at her with his spurs thrust forward.

Then there was the incessant crowing. As soon as some light from yonder window shone, Romeo would go full throttle, not just once but every five seconds of every daylight-saving hour of the day.

Not that he had much to crow about. Juliet had turned into an abundant layabout and stopped producing eggs, let alone chicks, and the constant scratching and lack of rain had turned our backyard into a desert.

Finally, we gave up and started smacking our lips at the prospect of chicken soup rather than omelet—eventually donating our farmyard fascists to a local children's farm where we can also buy free-range eggs. We now realise that the recipe for successful backyard chook farming depends on one vital ingredient: an axe

Trimming Christmas

This year, we've cancelled Christmas—and it was surprisingly easy.

The year had been so frantic and full of stress that the thought of the usual Christmas frenzy was enough to make us want to escape to a desert island. So that's what we're doing.

After spending a day on the phone trying to find a holiday venue that would take four people and one who just thinks he's a person (the dog), we booked a holiday, not quite on a desert island, but an island all the same.

Only one lot of family members was disgruntled, but the need to protect our health and sanity was greater than the need to pacify even family. Others were relieved, as they were facing similar pressures.

The holiday will be our present to ourselves, so we're toning down our usual extravaganza of presents too, which will ease the load on the family car.

My 16-year-old son would rather have money than a present anyway, so the usual sackful of plastic junk has been converted to a slim envelope. My eight-year-old daughter also made it easier to change expectations when she let me know that the Santa game was up by asking: "How are you going to take all the presents?"

But now, having taking the pressure off, a funny thing has happened. I'm actually looking forward to Christmas—so much so that I began looking at my old Christmas cards and thinking about this year's.

Each year, I make my own, drawing the cartoon and writing a little poem. And each year, it seems I have the same feelings of resentment.

Take last year's poem. My first effort was:

A REAL CHRISTMAS WISH

Here's a Christmas card that says
what every body thinks—
that Christmas is a lot of crap
and Santa bloody stinks

It costs a lot of money.
It causes too much stress.
We can't afford the presents,
and we resent the mess.

We don't want a bloody thing!
We don't want any debts!
Forget the family, teachers, friends
the neighbors and the pets.

We'll start a new tradition—
no presents, cheap or dear;
just a chat around the tree
and a glass of wine or beer.

You may think us shocking.
You may think us cheap and hard.
But at least we're bloody honest—
and you got a bloody card!

But after cautions from my husband, who is far wiser than me, I toned it down to:

A REAL CHRISTMAS WISH

Christmas is a time of giving,
prezzies, kisses—and good living

But this year, we'd like to try
to give the thing that you can't buy

Let's spend a little time instead;
Let's drink some wine and share some bread.

No presents, thank you—not this year.
Just join us for some Christmas cheer.

Give us a call, let's make a date;
Make it early or make it late.

We'd like to start a new tradition—
a stress-free Christmas is our mission!

And finally, to an even shorter version:

Just a card to say hello
and wish you Christmas cheer.
We look forward to catching up
when things calm down next year!

That doesn't mean we're cutting down on the essential ingredient of Christmas: peace and goodwill. That's even more necessary in these troubled times. But it seems cutting out the extravagance has left more space for that to blossom.

2002

NOT A UNIFORM RESPONSE

The final year of high school always causes a dilemma. Do you buy more school uniform or endure a year with pants that are just a little too short and shirts that are just a little tattered—or make another big investment in clothes that will only be worn from February to November?

This was the question we faced recently as my son entered Year 12.

When I was in Year 12, way back in the dark ages, we were allowed to wear whatever we liked, in tacit acknowledgement that school dresses looked a bit ridiculous on what were now grown women.

So I was a little surprised when my son reported that not only was school uniform still compulsory in Year 12, but the principal and teachers now patrolled the entrances waiting to catch non-uniform offenders.

Not only that, even when he was just visiting school on his day off to help out with choir practise, he was told he must wear uniform.

When the principal's message reiterated this, amid further warnings about students gathering in public places and ruining the school's public image, I was motivated to reply. Surely gathering in public places was safer and more sensible than going alone, I wrote.

The principal's reply was a little contrite, thoughtful and somewhat surprising. Public perception affects enrolments and enrolments directly affect the school's ability to continue, she wrote. The manager at the nearby shopping centre had complained about students hanging around smoking and swearing, and elderly shoppers found this behavior intimidating.

I don't blame them. It is threatening when the entrances to public shopping centres are dominated by swearing and smoking teenagers.

But it is with some irony that I noted that without school uniform no one would have known that these teenagers came from that particular high school. It seems that uniform only works if the behavior is uniformly good.

I felt sorry for the principal, walking a tightrope between the conflicting demands of parents and the community. It seemed very unfair that the behavior of a few should mar the reputation of the rest—especially as this government school is renowned for its specialist programs and has encouraged my son to thrive.

But all this does not mean I do not like school uniform—I just don't like it when the school's public image is tied to its uniform rather than its achievements.

I have always supported the idea of school uniform, not for it's unifying effects but because it helps mask economic inequality. It is too easy to see who can't afford the latest fashions when there is no school uniform.

But uniform also masks individuality, which can be a mixed blessing. A friend's daughter, who attends a high school where there is no uniform, decided to set her style early in Year 7. "I want to be different, but not weird," she said as she and her mother shopped for clothes.

But it seems anyone different is automatically weird. She soon found her best friend complaining about her fashion choices. "I'm not walking with you if you wear *those* pants," the so-called friend announced on the way to school some mornings.

Even when there is no uniform, uniformity is called for. But it is a further irony that many of us who are no longer at school, still choose to wear uniform, myself included. Mine is the cotton knit top and favorite black skirt and stockings that make me feel slimmer, even if I don't look it.

Recently, though I've added a black leather coat—courtesy of Peter, a Singaporean friend who is a leather wholesaler.

One day my husband was visiting Peter when two friends of Peter's dropped in—both wearing similar leather coats.

By the time my husband left, he was wearing a leather coat, and within a month of that, I was wearing one.

We now realise that Peter is a great salesman and someone who is regarded with uniform affection among his friends.

Lunch-box lessons

Recently, I heard two older women discussing their grandchildren's school lunches. "There's nothing homemade," one lamented. The other shook her head disapprovingly. "It's all packaged stuff," she replied.

It made me think wistfully back to the past—the past two weeks that is, when school holidays gave me a brief reprieve from the daily dilemma of what to pack for school lunches.

Getting the balance between what your child *wants* to eat at school and what he or she *should* eat, is one of life's minor dilemmas. (Minor, because unlike the lunch choices facing many of the world's children, there is too much rather than too little to choose.)

But there is more to this dilemma than the question of nutrition. In these days of pre-packaged bliss, there are school lunches and *cool* lunches.

Cool lunches include fancy potato chips, any sort of chocolate or lollies, and fruit that comes in flat, sticky sweet plastic-like strips.

"It's a status thing," says my friend Karen, a primary teacher, mother of three and a veteran observer and supplier of school lunches. "If you've got cool stuff in your lunch box, you've got power. It's power to trade. Then that leads on to what they play, which leads to being included—or not."

My nine-year-old daughter agrees. "If you have chips in your lunch, and another person has a different kind of chips, you have power to trade with them," she says. "Or if you have four chocolates and somebody else has Skittles, you can trade them for two chocolates for eight skittles or something."

Apart from the chips, the hottest item for trade is chocolate. "A lot of people have a chocolate every day," she says.

Nutritionists may be horrified at this, but then most nutritionists have obviously not been to school for a very long time. Top of the things they recommend in school lunches are bottom of the list when it comes to popularity, particularly tuna, salmon and egg sandwiches. "They stink," my daughter says.

Even if these are your favorite sandwich fillings, it's best not to admit it at school, she says. "You eat some of it, but then you say 'Ooh, yuck!'

and put some of it your bag. But later on, when they're all playing, you might go back and eat it," she confesses.

Often it's not the nutrition or even the taste that determines what gets eaten—it's the time. As lunch must be eaten in the classroom before going out to play, the slower the eater, the less play time.

"You think, what's in my sandwich—peanut butter? I could eat half of that, because I don't want to eat my fruit for playtime, because I don't want to get out later," she explains.

My solution is everything in moderation—even the healthy stuff. So I include some healthy choices as well as a few treats. On the advice of the dentist, I also include a tiny toothbrush kit, so she can clean her teeth after especially sticky or sweet foods. My daughter hates it, but she hates the dentist more.

I am particularly sensitive about school lunches because my own were so uncool. My mother loved gourmet food—except in those days it was known as wog food. Her idea of a good lunch was a spicy potted-meat sandwich or leftover spaghetti sandwich on thick Vienna bread, wrapped in thick waxed paper.

This stuck in my craw when my school chums were delicately nibbling on white-bread sandwiches of hundreds-and-thousands, with the crusts daintily removed.

These days at least, you'd think such gourmet grub would be welcomed in the playground. Not so, reports my friend Karen. "We had this poor little prep this year from India, and his grandparents came and they had this beautiful lunch for him, but it was all Indian food," she said. "He could see everyone else was having a sandwich. He didn't want to eat it in the end."

It highlights what most nutritionists, despite their noble intentions, fail to realise. Just like in the adult world, school food is about culture, not nutrition.

That's why, in our household at least, moves by school canteens to introduce more healthy choices are doomed. "Having fruit in your lunch order is very daggy, because it's the one day you get to have a treat," Greta explains.

How the mighty have fallen! Once, a simple apple was not just a treat but a great temptation.

Letting go—a mother's story

We had always regarding my son's finishing high school as a beginning rather than an ending. Whatever the final result, the VCE would be a passport to a new life somewhere.

But I hadn't expected that passport to take him to the other side of the country. Nor had I expected it to both an ending a beginning for me and the rest of the family.

He had applied to various institutions in our hometown of Melbourne, including the Victorian College of the Arts, as well as the West Australian Academy of Performing Arts (WAAPA) in Perth, never really considering the consequences if he was lucky enough to be accepted there.

So the discovery that he had been accepted everywhere was greeted with a mixture of joy and confusion. Whatever the decision, it had to be made quickly as the offer closed in the first week of January.

At first I was ambivalent. On one hand, I didn't want him to leave home—after all he was only 17, and although he was a brilliant student, the practicalities of life often eluded him.

For example, it was common for him to decide to go to the post office at 6pm on a Thursday, when it was obviously shut, or to declare that he would be going down the street to get a hair cut at 6pm on a Sunday, when no hairdresser would be open. It was also common to come home on a winter's evening to find him sitting in the dark and cold playing the piano, having forgotten the time or his own comfort.

On the other hand, I wanted jump for joy and pride at the opportunities that awaited him and say "Go for it, mate!" After all, this is what all those years of nervous driving on unmade roads up to the piano teacher had been for.

But my role, I decided should be to offer wise counsel and support, for whatever decision he chose to make. So why did I feel like crying every time we discussed it?

"There's no wrong decision," I wisely told him, then unwisely burst into another flood of tears. This only upset him further as he rushed to comfort me.

But the first real issue to confront was financial rather than emotional. The offer was a great honor—but like most honors, it didn't have any money attached, nor was there any government support available.

Funding his accommodation and living expenses for the next three, possibly four years, would be the equivalent of paying another mortgage. It would be difficult, but not impossible, we decided. It was just up to him to decide quickly whether to go.

For the next 10 days, we discussed it with other family members, his teachers, friends and former students of both institutions in question.

As we talked, he waxed and waned. The wistful talk of freedom gave way to even more wistful comments like, "I'm just a baby. I'm not ready for this." But the more he heard about the Perth course, the more interested he became.

In the end, I asked: "Which one excites you the most?"

"Perth," he said."

"Then that's it," I said. Family and friends would always be here, but opportunities like this came once in a lifetime.

So having received permission not to stay for our sake, he made the decision to go and began once again to think of the freedoms—big and small—that awaited him.

One morning at breakfast, he looked up and said in sudden joyful realization, "This means I can have Froot Loops for breakfast any day of the week!" This type of breakfast cereal had been banned in our household except as a holiday treat. But I was relieved that it was Froot Loops and not Ecstasy that he craved.

It was the beginning of his career, I told myself—and, I soon realized, the beginning of the end of mine. Of course, I had a career as a journalist—but my main job, the one that went 24 hours a day for the past 17 years had been as mother.

I had expected to move to part-time mothering as he got older and was prepared for him to leave him at around 22, when he had finished his degree and had a job and was able to support himself. But 17 seemed impossibly early.

Suddenly I found myself recalling the landmarks of his life, and weeping guiltily in the shower for the little boy that had suddenly grown up. Guiltily because compared to the mothers of the lost and homeless, I had no right to grief. And guilty for all the times that I had resented the necessary intrusions that small children make on their mother's lives.

If I had known how soon it as to be all over, would I have been more tolerant? And now with a life less interrupted, would I really do those things I had felt so thwarted from doing, such as write the Great Australian Novel—and did I care about them at all anyway?

I remembered the time when I had had to comfort him when he was four years old as he sat weeping in the bath. I had been sitting on a stool nearby playing my guitar and singing my favorite folk songs. *"He's gone and leave me, he's gone and leave me", He's gone and leave me to sorrow and moan,"* I lamented.

Such songs always had to be sung with one's eyes shut, of course, so I didn't notice him sobbing quietly in the corner of the bath.

"What's wrong?" I said in alarm when I finally stopped.

"Don't—you—know—any—happy—songs?" he had sobbed.

Now just 17 short years later, he would soon be gone and leave me, and I was the one sobbing in the bathroom.

But I wasn't the only one. His step father of 11 years was also grieving. "I'm not ready for this yet," he said gloomily each night when we were alone. "I'm not ready to be a single-child family."

The house, he said, was too big for three. He suggested that we get a web cam so that we could see each other as we talked on the phone. "I don't want him ringing up and just talking to you."

His nine-year-old sister said of course she'd miss him, and then went off to watch TV. At first, I suspected she was looking forward to a shift in the limelight. But a spate of uncharacteristic tummy pains made me realize that she too needed reassurance.

But it was even harder for my son, for he was leaving two families. In the two years since he and his girlfriend, Inneke, had been together, she had become part of our family and he had become part of hers.

So now there were two families to comfort and reassure and miss. There was much trekking between the two households, much sighing and handholding—while we "in-laws" comforted ourselves by celebrating the New Year together and planning a farewell party.

"How are you going?" I asked her sympathetically when we were alone together in the car one day.

"It's so draining," she said. I could only agree.

But for me, at least, grief soon gave way to panic. I felt as if the deadline for an unfinished project had suddenly been moved forward. There was work to do, and quickly.

Within a week I moved from a wailing mess, to military mode. Lists were prepared, but they were no longer lists for me. I headed them "Things I have to do to get ready for Perth" and passed them on to my son. He needed to learn some skills so he could survive in a household of six people.

Despite being a feminist mother, I was ashamed to admit that the most he had cooked was an egg and some noodles and a chop.

As I'd had to cook and cater for his sister, who was eight years younger, it has been easier to cook and cater for him too, rather than encourage his independence.

His musical pursuits, as well as school, had also meant that there wasn't much time for hanging out in the kitchen with Mum.

Now there wasn't any time to lose. I symbolically handed over my recipe books and my grubby floral apron. This had an amazing effect. "When you put that on, you turn into Mum," his sister complained, as flustered and red faced, he shooed her out of the kitchen as he tried to serve up.

At first he was ambitious, wanting to follow recipes rather than take short cuts. As we shopped for chicken thighs to make chicken satay kebabs, I tried to tempt him with the ready-made variety. But he was adamant. He wanted to do it all by himself. So we went out to lunch and left him to it.

When we returned I casually asked him what else he had achieved for his "Things to do for Perth" list.

"Nothing," he said indignantly. "It took me three hours to make the kebabs."

I smiled and raised a "told you so" eyebrow.

His cooking, I'm proud to say, was better than mine, mainly because he took the time to do it properly. But his cleaning up was woeful—also because he took the time to do it properly.

"You'll never be paid by the hour," my husband warned, as with gritted teeth he watched him slowly and laboriously rewash a relatively clean dish that had just come out of the dishwasher. It took him so long that we were queuing up for the next meal before he'd finished cleaning up the last.

"You won't be able to do that in Perth", we chorused, and for the next few weeks, this became our mantra—when he stayed in the shower too long, or forgot to take or pass on vital phone messages or left a dirty pan in the sink.

In the end, he begged for mercy. "I understand what you're trying to do, but I want to remember the last few weeks at home as being pleasant," he pleaded.

"But you're not finished," I said.

"I'll learn when I get there," he wisely said—something that my friends chorused. It was time to let go, they said. I'd done my bit. The deadline was over so it was too late to add anything more.

All I could do now was take comfort in the fact that he was probably far better equipped than I was at the same age, and that throughout history, all mothers and fathers have had to learn to let go.

As the deadline for leaving drew closer, he swung between nostalgia and excitement. "All my friends are doing adult things," he said in wonder one night over dinner. One had a job, another had an apprenticeship and one was studying nursing."

"You're doing adult things, too," I pointed out.

"Yeah, but I don't feel like an adult," he said.

I know the feeling, I replied. When I was his age, I had speculated about turning 43 in the year 2000—never really believing that I could be over 25 let alone the mother of son leaving home.

Delving into the photo file to make a montage for his going away party, he wanted to talk about the past—our past, before his stepfather and sister had come on the scene, when we had lived in various places around Melbourne.

But all this was too much for his sister, who was tired of all the focus on her big brother, even if it was short-lived. "What about me?" she kept interrupting. "What was I like as a baby?" Much the same as now—always interrupting—I thought. But in a few weeks, there would be less competition in the household for her and fewer interruptions for me.

On the positive side, he had set up an email address for her so they could write to each other. And, I must admit, she and I had discussed the possibility of getting a sewing machine and turning his room into a craft room. But, as he quickly reminded us, he'd be back in July for the semester break and he expected his room to be intact, mess and all.

I did a mental calculation. July was only 17 weeks away. Seventeen weeks, I mused. Why that was nothing at all, and here I was thinking that I'd have all the time in the world to do all the things you can't do when you've got teenagers in the house interrupting you with requests like, "What are you doing on Thursday night, because I need a lift to Mt Dandenong and $150 for the school camp on Tuesday and you owe me two week's pocket money and for the formal photos and can you sign this?"

I had no time for grief or indulgent stories like this. Between earning the money to pay for Perth and running my daughter around to her various activities, that only left me a few hours a week to read a book, let alone write one.

But this was a warning—or a heralding—that one day I would have time—one day when the cry of "Mamma!" in the supermarket wouldn't be for me. One day when I would no longer have to rush from one task to the next, fearing the inevitable interruptions of family life.

And when once again, every phone call would be for me or my husband—but none as welcome as the one that began in a growly adult voice, "Hi Mamma! How's it going?"

2004-2007

THAI TALES

From June 2004 to December 2007, we lived in Pakret, Nonthaburi, north of Bangkok, for Rob's work.

Greta attended the International School Bangkok and I continued to work as an online journalism trainer for News Ltd and an occasional freelance writer for *Look East* magazine and the Hong Kong-based industry journal, *Asian Hotels and Catering*, where I was paid to visit hotels and write about their food and decor.

As always, I continued writing a journal.

Various columns I wrote then were later broadcast on the ABC Radio National program *Life Matters* in a series titled *Jane Cafarella's Expat Life*.

Here is a selection.

A CHANGE OF LIFE

When we first announced that we were moving to Bangkok for two years for my husband's work, we were bombarded with questions from family, friends and colleagues. When were we going? Where would we live? What school would my daughter go to? Would I work over there? Would we have servants? How would we cope with the traffic? What about the pollution?

And so it went on—so much so that we became weary with repeating the answers.

But it was my friend Jan who asked the question for which I had no answer—at least not immediately.

"What made you decide to do it—to change your life like that?" she asked.

I began by explaining how it would be good for my husband's career and timely and enriching for my daughter, now in Grade 6.

"No," she persisted, "What made it right for you? What did you want to change and why?"

At first I didn't know. A decision to turn your life upside down implies that it was the wrong way up in the first place. In the film *Under the Tuscan Sun*, the heroine goes to Italy to escape the pain of divorce. But I wasn't escaping anything, at least not consciously.

I wasn't even that enamoured with Asian culture, and the more I read of Thailand, the more I feared I would find it alienating.

In the land of smiles, as Thailand is known, being hot is unavoidable, but being hot-headed is regarded as unacceptable. "Jai yen", or a cool heart, is the cultural expectation.

Coming from an Italian background, where "jai rawn"—or hot heart—is the cultural norm, I feared I would have to change my personality as well as my wardrobe.

Nor am I one of those people who revel in the heat. My feet swell and I go red in the face. Yet, here I am packing up my house and heart and heading for Bangkok.

Was it one of those strange twists of fate, I wondered? It seems like every time I've had an aversion to somewhere, I've ended up there.

Years ago when we lived in Upwey, a tiny town in the Dandenong Ranges in Melbourne's outer east, my husband used to joke about the bogans who got off at Boronia along the Belgrave railway line, on which he travelled for work. He and his professional friends in their business suits dubbed the shifty and lost-looking types, with their nylon jackets and woollen beanies, "Boronia man".

Two years later, we bought a house that we thought was in neighbouring Fern Tree Gully, only to find out that our new address was in, yes, you guessed it—Boronia. Rob gave up commuting after that and bought a car. It was just too embarrassing.

Boronia, picturesque though it is, is one of the suburbs that everyone always says is going to "come on"—but never does. As it's 30 kilometres from Melbourne, it's cheap, so tends to attracted people who couldn't afford to live further down the line, ourselves included.

"How d'ya like B'ronia?" the locals would ask when we moved in.

With its leafy streets and proximity to the hills, we liked it very much. But now I discovered, to my surprise, not well enough to stay there forever.

I was 46 and restless for adventure. My son had grown up and gone to university in Perth the year before. My daughter was still in primary school, so wasn't yet caught up in the pressures of VCE, which would have made uprooting her difficult.

At the same time, having trod that path from Grade 6 to Year 12 before with my son, the thought of treading the same path for the next six years with my daughter made me feel like an explorer who'd been sent back to examine the same territory.

It was time to look at travel guides before I had to start looking at nursing homes.

Not that I really wanted to travel. When friends had raved about their overseas holidays I'd feigned interest and hadn't bothered to contradict them when they'd assumed that I was pea-green with envy.

The idea of queuing up to see the sights never appealed to me. On the other hand, the idea of living in another culture had always appealed. It's just that I'd always imagined it would be French or Italian, in a medieval castle.

"Why couldn't you have a job offer in Rome or Paris?" I asked my husband, Rob.

But Rome and Paris had been explored by multinationals centuries ago, Asia was the new frontier, and Bangkok was central.

My daughter, Greta, aged 11, was like me: lukewarm about the destination.

"Have you told your friends you're moving to Bangkok?" I asked her.

"I've told them I'm moving to Thailand," she said.

"Why not Bangkok?" I asked.

"Muuuummmm!" she said, rolling her eyes in exasperation. "Bang—cock! They'd laugh."

My friends didn't laugh. But they did say things like. "It's a great place to visit, but I could never live there."

The heat was unbearable, the traffic was unbelievable and the pollution made it unliveable, they warned.

At that stage, I had little information to contradict them. What I knew about Thailand came from a Grade Six project back in 1969, the "in brief" pages of Melbourne's daily newspapers, which focused on drug pushers, prostitutes and bird flu, and the Rogers and Hammerstein musical *The King and I*. "Getting to Know You," was one of our favourite songs, but would modern-day Siam really be our "cup of tea"?

I was especially worried about Greta. In Melbourne, she had found her niche by performing in local musicals and training in singing dancing and acting. She was a little star in her own tiny constellation of friends and fans. How would she cope in a different hemisphere?

That's why we insisted on bringing her on the official company-funded "look-see". This was an incomprehensible notion to the person organising the trip, a Singaporean man who thought these matters should be decided by the head of the family. I said that they had. But in their culture, this meant the husband.

"Why does your daughter need to be involved in this decision?" his assistant kept asking in a ping-pong game of emails.

"Because if she's not happy, I'm not happy, and if I'm not happy Rob's not happy, and he'll have to come home, and that will cost you a fortune," I explained. That, they understood.

They also understood the art of seduction. In the limousine that awaited us at the airport, there were orchids and chilled face washers and cold bottled water. Our smiling driver introduced himself as Khun Kunt, and seeing our expressions, explained "It mean trim!"

My husband patted his own expansive girth and said good-naturedly: "I'm the opposite of trim".

"No," replied Khun Kunt, emphatically. "You fat!" and he laughed joyously and uproariously.

It seemed there would be a least one aspect of Thai culture I could relate to—"sanook" or having fun—even if it was at my husband's expense.

After four days of visiting air conditioned schools and houses in charming tropical settings with a charming relocation agent, we were ready to buy the whole adventure. But as my mother often says, everything comes at a price and it's the price that often quells desire

Despite my glowing descriptions on our return, my friend Carolyn, whose idea of a good holiday is staying at home in her pyjamas doing craft work, wasn't convinced.

"I probably wouldn't do it," she said. "Too much trouble."

She was right. The thought of packing up my office, let alone my house, was daunting enough.

But how would I feel if I didn't do it? Perhaps the same way I had felt 20 years ago when

I'd discovered I was pregnant with my son and had had to forgo the trip to Europe that Carolyn and I had planned. She sent me postcards from England and I sent her baby photos from the local park.

I never regretted having children. Raising them has been the most fantastic journey. But it's not the things you *do* that you regret. It's the things you *don't* do. I regret that in the process I missed out on other journeys.

The only other country I've visited is the United States, and it was the sameness with Australian culture, not its differences, that I remember.

This didn't prevent me from becoming a minor travel expert. When my children were small, I wrote briefly for the travel pages of *The Age*— stories that could be researched safely from my home, such as what to do about lost baggage and safe travel tips for women. But the farthest *I* ever went was down to the letter box and back to collect my cheques.

Meanwhile, my office walls became papered with scenes from other people's lives—postcards from friends who travelled and thought of me regularly.

Now, it was my turn. I was pushing 50 and, according to all the biology books, headed for "a change of life". But I wanted more than a change of life. I wanted a change of lifestyle.

My friend Kaye couldn't get over it. "You're the last person I'd ever thought to do something like this. I've travelled heaps and even I wouldn't do it," she said.

Her words thrilled and scared me to the core. For the past 19 years I had done what was expected. Now I wanted to do the unexpected.

VILLAGE PEOPLE

"It's a bit like a retirement village," Rob said one day, as he watched the Samakee mini-bus tootle past our front door on the way to the shops.

"I prefer to liken it to a resort," I replied.

But I had to agree there were many parallels between our new home in Thailand and the retirement village where Rob's mother lived in Melbourne—except that there was no nursing home next door and the list of departures didn't include anyone who had died.

Just like at Nana's place, there is a fleet of minibuses employed to take residents to the various local schools, supermarkets and shopping centres and on other excursions. There is also a manager's office, a clubhouse, a monthly newsletter and a recreation committee that organises regular social functions—except our new home in Samakee Place, is in an "expat compound", one of many around Bangkok and surrounding areas.

The biggest decision you'll make as an expat in Bangkok is where to live. The traffic rules your life, so if you want a life, you need to make sure the distance between home and school or office is as short as possible.

Our decision was based on the premise that it was easier for Rob to travel the distance to work than Greta. That's why we chose Samakee Place in the northern province of Nonthaburi.

Don't worry if you've never heard of it. Most other expats haven't either.

"Where?" the other expat wives say when I meet them over lunch down town.

Most expats live in Bangkok itself, on or off Sukhumvit Rd, the main artery that begins at the eastern end of downtown Bangkok and continues all the way to the Cambodian border.

This is where many of the popular images of Bangkok come from: herds of cars being shepherded by traffic police wearing white cotton masks across roads bordered by towering skyscrapers, huge glitzy department stores, ramshackle street stalls, sleazy bars, beggars and tourists.

However, here in Samakee Rd, there are herds of goats being shepherded by a local goat man. There are also three buffalo, a black and

288

white cow, packs of mangy but amiable dogs milling about or sleeping on the side of the road, and lots of make-shift shops and street vendors selling everything from brooms to strings of cocktail sausages—garnished with street dust and kept warm by the tropical sun.

Nonthaburi was formerly a rural area, known for its durian—the large green spiky fruit that is said to taste like heaven and smell like hell.

But when the International School of Bangkok moved its headquarters from Sukhumvit to a newly created campus in the Nichada Thani compound off Samakee Rd, 12 years ago, the area became home for several thousands of mostly American expats and their families

Here, life mirrors the lives the foreign families left behind. There are (relatively) clear skies, tree-lined streets, beautifully kept tropical gardens and the sorts of houses you see in American movies, along with the sorts of people you see in American movies: well fed and well dressed and with excellent teeth.

Ironically, this means we live exactly the same distance from the city as we did when we lived in Melbourne—32 kilometres. Time wise, the trip is also similar for Rob, but here he doesn't do the driving.

Like most Bangkok expats, we have a driver, as only the bravest or the poorest, attempt to battle the traffic. Khun Manit, our driver, picks Rob up every morning at 6.30 to take him to the office by about 7.30 and then comes back home to take me wherever I want to go, before going back to the office around 4.30 to "stand by" for Rob, who generally doesn't leave until 7pm to avoid the traffic.

The compound is a gated community—by gated, I mean it's comprised of three little streets or "sois" as they are known here, enclosed on each side by high wrought iron and concrete fences, and with a gatehouse and guard at the end of each soi, facing a local road.

The guards, Thais wearing blue Chubb uniforms, monitor people and vehicles as they go in and out, manually opening the gates, while saluting and snapping their heels to attention.

But this doesn't mean that it's a prison, as my mother assumed.

"They lock you in at night in those places," she warned darkly, when we first told her that we would be in a compound.

If anything, the gate is meant to keep the locals—and anyone else who doesn't work here—out, rather than us in.

Not that the locals, who are mostly labourers, street vendors, families and children, pose any obvious threat. But this community, and the nearby bigger one at Nichada Thani, is known as Little America, and in the present political climate, security—or the semblance of it—is paramount.

In reality, the gate serves more as a divide between two lifestyles than a fortress.

In Soi 3, where we live, the houses are large and white, with coconut palms planted either side, white columns framing the porch, marble floors, an in-ground pool, four bedrooms, five bathrooms and maid's quarters outside—yes, that's right, maid's quarters.

When I first sent photos to family and friends they were hugely impressed. "It looks fantastic," they wrote back, and planned their next holiday around a visit to us.

They were less impressed with the second lot of photos, which showed life outside the Samakee gate. Here, between the street vendors and roaming animals, ramshackle houses line the streets.

The more permanent houses are made of wood, and any other bits and pieces that can be mustered, including discarded advertising hoardings.

The temporary houses, erected for itinerant labourers, are made of shiny new corrugated iron, hammered onto bamboo frames—like cake tins lined up in a tropical oven.

In the smaller sois off Samakee Rd, these slum houses straddle dirty khlongs, or canals, where women can be seen squatting over pink plastic bowls, washing clothes and dishes.

Directly opposite our gate in Soi 3 is a small brown lagoon, clogged with water lilies. On the edge of the lagoon, is a tiny tin and wood shack—as fragile as a house of cards.

A washing line with a few clothes flung over it spans one side, and once in a while, a small wizened woman in a traditional Thai straw hat takes a tiny rusty boat into the lagoon.

It's an uncomfortable contrast.

My first reaction was to do what I normally do—take photos and sort out my thoughts and feelings by writing about it.

The other expat wives had a different reaction.

"They want to help them—I want to write about them," I told Rob.

"Somehow I think they'd rather have the powdered milk and the sanitary napkins," I said.

Compared to these houses, Samakee houses are grossly luxurious, but compared to the even bigger houses in neighbouring Nichada Thani, they are almost modest.

It seems the extremes in housing for "farangs", as foreigners are called, knows no bounds, firstly because they can afford them and secondly because they are part of the compensation package for living away from home.

When we came for our "look-see" in January, we were bowled over by the first house we saw in Nichada, with its many cavernous rooms, Roman columns and marble benches and floors.

"It's like a mausoleum," I whispered to Rob.

But Nikki, our relocation agent, a British woman who had been here for five years, said: "You can do much better than this."

Amazingly, she was right. Why have a mausoleum when you can have a small hotel?

That's what some of the city apartments seemed like, with their sweeping *Gone with the Wind* staircases and lobby-like entrance halls.

In stark contrast, the maid's quarters in all these places are pathetically small—a tiny room, usually with a separate entrance, with barely enough room for a bed, a chair and table, plus a small bathroom with a squat toilet and a cold-water shower.

The real estate agents exchanged looks when she saw my shocked face after I asked to see the maid's quarters in each.

In some of the bigger houses, the maid's quarters also include a kitchen. But in many cases, maids prepare their food in the main kitchen of the house and just eat in their rooms. Or, like many people in Thailand, rich and poor, they buy their food from street vendors.

Although most people make a point of providing air conditioning, hot water systems, fridges, television and other comforts for maids, as requested, I am grateful that our maid, Khun Lamai, doesn't live in.

It is hard enough to confront the extremes in income, lifestyle and expectation, without having the people who work for you living such a lesser lifestyle under your own luxurious roof.

Instead, she lives with her husband, Khun Manit, who is also our driver, and their 10-year old son, in their own much more comfortable house nearby, using the maid's room as a lunch and recreation room.

("Khun" means "you" and is the polite honorific, like "Mr" or "Mrs". But unlike English, Thais use their first names, not their surnames.).

Rob had already engaged Khun Manit and Khun Lamai a month before Greta and I arrived, when he first moved into the house.

The night we arrived, excited and exhausted, after our three-month separation and the nine hours on the plane from Melbourne, Khun Manit was waiting for us with Rob at the airport. "Welcome Madam!" he said, shaking my hand, his broad brown face crinkled with smiles.

As we had a lot of luggage, Rob had also engaged the services of his boss Matt's driver, Khun Orr, and their van.

Khun Orr, a tall man who perpetually appears as though he is trying hard not to burst out laughing, looked even more thrilled than Rob to see us.

Grinning and winking in a "nuk nuk" kind of way, he kept repeating, "Khun Rob very happy today!"

Khun Lamai had already gone home as it was after 10pm, but she had left a welcome gift of orchids and roses in every vase in the house and a plate of beautifully cut and arranged tropical fruit.

It was still humid, so despite the fact that I had a cold, we swam in the pool with its underwater lights looking like huge moons, as the real moon swam in the sky overhead.

"It's followed us here from Boronia," I said to Greta.

For me it felt like a ritual baptism, cleansing the past and preparing to be reborn into a new life.

The next morning, Greta and I waited nervously to meet Khun Lamai when she arrived.

"Thank you for making the house so beautiful for us," I said, giving her a shy hug.

Hugging strangers isn't usually my thing, but Rob, a bear-hug kind of bloke himself, had insisted. I guess after someone's been washing your underwear for a month, she doesn't feel like a stranger.

"Thank you, Madam," Khun Lamai said, shyly giving me the traditional Thai greeting of both palms pressed together, known as the "wai".

Then, to our surprise, she stepped forward and pulled up Greta's t-shirt.

"Look Thai!" she said in surprise.

It was something we heard from many people later. With her olive skin from my Italian background, her long straight black hair and Rob's oval face, Greta has a slight Eurasian look.

Later, we wondered whether Khun Lamai was checking to see if Greta was brown all over or just suntanned—or perhaps whether she needed feeding up?

Usually, the Thai people are fascinated with the pale skin, eyes and hair of Western children and like to touch as well as look, but Khun Lamai took the opposite view.

In the next few weeks, she would proudly tell us that when she and Greta went shopping at Carrefour, people would ask "Luk sao?"— meaning "Is she your daughter?"

"Be careful," Rob's mother warned, when I told her. "You don't want her to get to close to Greta: she'll take over."

Yes, I do! I thought. After three months on my own, working and packing up the house and being a single mother, I wanted all the help I could get.

Here the picture postcard not only included the palm trees and the pool, but the people that would allow you to relax and enjoy it.

That's why "Khawp khun ka", or "Thank you", has become my first and favourite word.

Busy Doing Nothing

For years I railed against the fact that while my husband Rob had one job, I had a dozen, if you count the individual duties, such as cook, driver, social manager, medical officer, counsellor etc.

"Sure, he goes to work, but that's *all* he does," I would say to similarly overworked friends. "*I* go to work *and* do everything else."

One of my favourite questions was: "Why are all the famous inventors, painters and sculptors, men?"

To which I would give my favourite answer: "Because all the women are waiting in the queue in Coles, or working in the school canteen or cooking or cleaning!"

If not for all this domestic drudgery, I would have time to *really* write something, I would think, as I banged the pots dramatically down upon the stove each night.

But since arriving in Bangkok two weeks ago, everything I've ever dreamed of has come true.

My shopping is done, my meals are cooked, my dishes are washed, my clothes are washed and ironed daily, my coffee is made, my telephone is answered, my child is delivered to and from school, my plastic bags are even folded into neat little triangles—and I can't think of a damned thing to write other than "This is ridiculous!"

The only other time this happened I was in hospital.

"The only thing missing is the drip," I tell friends from Australia as I make my guilty $1-a-minute phone calls (What else is there to do?)

"This is your life, now," gloats Rob, as he eats the fantastic meal I didn't cook each night. "And I've provided it for you!"

I can't decide whether to thank him or kill him. I am no longer Jane, the overworked journalist, wife and mother, but "Madam", the lady of the house.

"Okay, Madam," our maid, Khun Lamai, smiles whenever I ask for anything: in fact, whenever I say anything.

"You'll get used to it," a new friend, Brigitte, across the street, says. "ISB (the international school where my daughter will start in August), sucks you in," she laughs.

I try not to look horrified. I haven't come all this way and given up so much to spend my new and precious free time hanging around my daughter's school trying to feel useful, particularly as I spurned women who did that back in Australia.

I want to tell Brigitte that I'm a journalist and will be doing loftier things than serving on a school committee, but officially I'm not working, unless you call writing things like this work. I call it cathartic.

But as I'm not sure how whinges like this will go down in the very small community I now live in, it's best not to say anything to anyone, which is pretty easy since most of my day is spent with two people who don't speak much English.

Khun Lamai, our maid, and Khun Manit, our driver, are a married couple with a son, who live nearby. They began work as soon as Rob moved into the house on May 15, so by the time Greta and I arrived on June 1, they had everything down to a fine art.

I have never lived in a place so exquisitely clean. Now, if I drop some food on the floor I just lay a place there and keep eating.

"Half your luck, though—bloody hell!" said my friend Karen in Fern Tree Gully, an outer eastern Melbourne suburb, when I called her a week later.

"Like tonight, I've come home from work, I've had to placate Brendan because he didn't win the stupid damned poetry contest, cook dinner, put two loads of washing on, do the ironing and because our bloody dish washer doesn't work I've had to do them by hand," she lamented.

"Come here for a holiday," I offer. "And I'll go there."

"So you can do the damned dishes?" she asks incredulously.

"So I can do something!" I reply.

The situation is exacerbated by the fact that our shipment of books, TV, DVD, CDs, furniture, pictures and everything else that gives us meaning and purpose in life is not coming for another eight days. All we have in our wonderful big house at present is stuff supplied by the landlord—beds, a dining table, a lounge suite, and some coffee tables—and Khun Lamai and Khun Manit.

Back home in Boronia, I had dreamed about lounging about all day, drinking champagne, stuffing my face with chocolates and watching musicals, instead of having to wait until 9pm each night when I was too tired and grumpy.

Now, when my ship comes in, I can have a 12-hour movie, chocolate and champagne marathon if I want, starting at 8am, when Khun Lamai arrives for work—except the fact that she will be doing my dirty work kind of takes the thrill out of it.

Instead of feeling liberated, I suspect I'll feel like a slob.

"You don't have to feel like that. Just enjoy it," says Rob.

It's all right for him. The two months before he moved into the house were spent in the Conrad Hotel, and the almost-40 previous years were spent in houses where women (his mother and then me) did pretty much everything except the gardening and occasional weekend cooking.

It's not that we set out to be sexist; it's just that his work demands kept him away from the house while mine allowed me to work from home.

Nothing has changed for him except his attitude, which is now one of reverent gratitude. Our daughter, Greta's attitude has changed too. She still leaves her clothes all over the bedroom floor, but now she feels bad about it.

"How come you didn't feel like that when I was picking them up?" I ask.

"I don't know," she shrugs.

I am grateful too—but also guilty. Despite my feminist leanings, I feel as if Khun Lamai is doing *my* work—except I was never paid for it, while she is well paid.

And that's the difference between Rob and me. Like most men he has "helped" around the house, but it has never been his responsibility.

Now, like him, my only responsibility is my paid work—even though both the work and pay are intermittent.

Back in Melbourne, the notion of a maid and a driver had seemed outlandish and almost colonial. Our lefty friends and relatives had regarded us disapprovingly, unconvinced by our claims that in Thailand the notion of master and servant was the cultural norm and unavoidable, even for expats who back home had spouted equality for all.

But once here, faced with the language barrier and the infamous Bangkok traffic and crowded streets and markets, we have found Khun Manit and Khun Lamai indispensable not just as maid and driver, but as interpreters, tour guides and general supporters.

They regard themselves as professionals and pride themselves on providing the best service.

So what am I complaining about? Just the fact that it is one thing to have these privileges but quite another to feel entitled to them.

So that's what I'm working on: feeling entitled. So far so good. I'm feeling very entitled to the cup of coffee that Khun Lamai has kindly placed beside me as write this.

I wonder if I'm entitled to a biscuit too?

KITCHEN TALK BY THE BOOK

For the first few weeks, although we spent most of our day together in the same house, our maid Khun Lamai and I did not exchange more than a few polite greetings.

But gradually as our trust in each other grew, we found common ground—as women do—in complaining about our husbands.

"Oh, Khun Manit—he not know!" she said in exasperation when Khun Manit, our driver, and also her husband, had persuaded me to buy some bargain bananas, which in her opinion were inferior.

Buying the fruit at the local Thai market was her specialty and she prided herself on choosing only the best. It was clear that neither Khun Manit nor I should interfere.

Later I found that mastering the myriad of remote controls was also her specialty. We had just had satellite TV installed and Khun Manit walked into the room as Khun Lamai was showing me how to use the remote.

Picking up one of the other four remotes, Khun Manit smilingly pointed it to the TV and began to press randomly.

Khun Lamai immediately spoke to him in Thai, but he kept smiling and pressing until she snatched it from him, declaring, "I say 'no'!"

As he slunk out, grinning apologetically, she grunted and threw up her hands in exasperation. "Khun Manit! Make Lamai angry. Hrrr!"

She went straight to her battered green dictionary and showed me the word "pretend". "Khun Manit," she said, pointing to the word, and exposing him as a sham.

"He no know. Mister same?!" she inquired, in a clear invitation to bitch about Rob.

What else could I do? It was necessary for female bonding. Even though Rob, in this case is the master of the remotes in our household, there are plenty of other domestic things that he knows nothing about, so I nodded vigorously.

The other thing Khun Lamai and I have in common, apart from the exasperations of married life, is the fact that our children are of similar age.

So one day, when in answer to our usual greeting of "Sabai di mai ka?"(Are you well?) she replied, "Khun Phet mai sabai di ka," (Khun Phet is sick), I immediately suggested she go home to be with him.

"No madam, he outside," she said, pointing to the maid's room outside, which she and Khun Manit use for rest and recreation. "He have fever last night."

"That's too hot," I said, pointing to the small un-air-conditioned room, "Tell him to come inside and he can watch a movie."

"No madam, he okay," she replied. "Lamai give medicine last night."

But I insisted. Sitting in a small hot room with just a fan was no way to recover from a fever.

Still Khun Lamai resisted, "He have fear, Madam," she said, laughing.

"Fear of me?" I asked, smiling. I had already suspected this.

The first time I'd asked her to bring Khun Phet with her one Saturday so we could all meet him, he had insisted of bringing his friend Khun Joe, for backup. And although he played happily with Greta whenever he came, he preferred to play with Khun Joe and his friend Khun Beer at home nearby.

Finally, I persuaded her to persuade him to come inside and lie in the cool on the couch to watch *Spiderman*.

Later, as we unpacked the shopping and shared some spicy fish cakes for lunch, we chatted, as women sharing a kitchen are wont to do— Lamai armed with her battered green Thai-English dictionary, and me with my battered red English-Thai dictionary.

Her story showed that men and women are the same in any one's language.

Like Khun Phet, when she first saw a farang, she was terrified, she told me.

"My friend, she work farang. She say, 'You come, you work too'. But Lamai have fear," she said, hugging herself and crouching with closed eyes to show how she had felt.

In her home province of Ubon Ratchathani, about 10 hours drive away near the Laotian border, there were not many farangs, I guessed.

"Farang, very big Madam. Lamai small!" she said.

So she told her friend that she preferred to work for Thai people as a live-in maid.

"But no good, Madam," she said, showing me the word "oppress" in her dictionary. Visitors to the house had often wanted to touch her, "They say, Lamai beautiful, Madam," she said laughing shyly and miming hands reaching out to touch her. "Lamai no like."

She mimed someone touching her face.

"They hit you?" I asked in horror, miming slapping.

"No, Madam, like this," she said and pretended to kiss.

"When this Madam out—no good", she said and we both exchanged a knowing look.

I showed her the word "exploit" in my dictionary, and she nodded, repeating the Thai word.

"Lamai, no like. Lamai need money. Mama sick, so Lamai think, go work for farang," she said, bracing her shoulders, and with a resolute face, showing the courage she had needed.

"You were brave," I said, showing her the word in my dictionary.

"Lamai work for farang Yemany", she said, (Meaning Germany). "At first, Lamai have fear. Farang very big, Lamai small," she repeated, illustrating how she had barely reached the waist of the tall German farang.

But "Yemany family" turned out to be good. "Oh good, madam," she said. "Lamai very happy."

When she discovered she was pregnant (I assumed she was married to Khun Manit by then), instead of sacking her, as some may have done, they welcomed the child. "Yemany mister and madam, no children," she said. 'They like Khun Phet.'

In fact, they liked him so much they wanted to take him back to Germany to educate him, but she and Khun Manit had refused. Instead, the German mister and madam became like a second father and mother to Phet.

"Oh Lamai very happy," she said.

After the German couple, she worked for an Australian couple, where she was also very happy. A few days earlier, we'd seen a picture of the children, Lachlan and Pamela, in Thai costumes, a parting gift to Khun Lamai.

"Oh beautiful children, Madam," she said, then pointed to her pink t-shirt which had "Adelaide" embroidered on it, along with koalas and kangaroos.

"Madam Karina, she give," she said.

Madam Karina, the Australian Madam, had allowed Khun Phet to come to the house and play while Lamai worked. Phet became like a little brother to Lachlan and Isabella. They still keep in touch every year, she said.

After Karina left, she went to work for another family in Samakee who lived in one of three storey terraces.

"Three children, Madam," she said, holding up three fingers.

"Six o'clock to six o' clock! Oh, work, work, work!" she said, and mimed the children being carried on her back and clinging to her arms and legs as she tried to cook and clean.

By comparison she said that her work for me was "nit noi", meaning only a little bit.

The realisation that she regarded this as a cushy job by comparison made me feel a whole lot better. So did the realisation that she had ambitions beyond being a maid, and even had a little bit of security.

She had a little block of land near the airport, she confided one day, on which she wanted to build a house. Apart from the money she sent to help care for her sick mother up country, she and Khun Manit were both saving to build this house, which is why they snapped up any overtime we offered, encouraging us to go touristing around on Saturday and Sundays.

To help fund the project, they collected any cans we bought for recycling and took all our newspapers, getting 30 baht a kilo (about a dollar) for the great wad of Leader Newspapers that arrived here every week from Melbourne for my perusal at probably 50 times the cost.

Knowing this, I now buy lots of cans and local newspapers and feel no guilt at the accumulating mountains of copies of *The Bangkok Post* and *The Nation*.

And I now understand when she says she doesn't mind if Khun Manit isn't home for her dinner on Sundays because he's working for us.

At first I felt as if our Sunday excursions were at the expense of their family time. But she quickly put that in perspective by pimping on him.

"Madam think Khun Manit stay home with Lamai," she said.

"No stay home. Khun Manit go motorbike visit friend," she said and imitated him tear-arsing around on his bike.

"Work good, madam,' she said.

I could only agree. If he wasn't going to stay home with her, he may as well be tear-arsing around with us and getting paid for it.

Independence Day

My new hero is Burmese pro-democracy leader Aung San Suu Kyi. It's not her politics I admire, though—it's her ability to endure house arrest.

"There may be no place like home," as Dorothy says in the *Wizard of Oz*, but after four days of unpacking and rearranging, I was feeling housebound. So, I made list of things to get—topped by "Get out of house!"

After weeks of being chaperoned either by Khun Manit, Khun Lamai or Rob, I was looking forward to poking around the shops on my own, especially as I also wanted to look at nighties and bras.

The hot weather meant clothes were changed and washed more often and after just a few weeks, my personals were beginning to fall apart.

But as we pulled into the car park, Khun Manit got out of the car with me.

I hesitated. How to escape without committing the social crime of making him lose face? "I go alone?" I ventured gently.

"I come in and help you," he smiled.

"When do you think I could go in by myself?" I asked wistfully.

He reflected: "Maybe next time, Madam" adding kindly "When you know."

There was another pause, as he sensed my disappointment. "Maybe tomorrow?" he suggested.

This was not his fault. As someone who can't find her own front door if someone turns her round three times, I was aware that my previous ventures had not inspired confidence. It was not control that Khun Manit was aiming for, it was protection. I was his responsibility and God forbid that he should have to report to "Mister" that he had lost "Madam."

So we parked and once again I followed him into the shop while he led me down five escalators to the ATM.

But I was clearly dragging my feet and he must have felt sorry for me because he suddenly turned and said: "I think you maybe can go in. I wait for you here. You can come here and call to me."

I was elated. At last I had money and freedom! I headed for the lingerie section.

In Melbourne, I had cursed the lack of service. You could have shot cannon down most big department stories and never hit an assistant, but in Bangkok there would be a massacre,

Not only does each section have its own gaggle of assistants, so does each sub-section and sub-sub-section, all beautifully uniformed and groomed, ready to serve or to talk about you amongst themselves while you browse.

Many of these women are as small and beautiful as children. By comparison, I felt like that famous Thai symbol, the white elephant.

"Sawsadee ka, Madam," the sextuplet of assistants at the nighty section sniggered, as I picked at the dainty items.

"This Size L," one said helpfully, selecting a low-cut sexy number to show me.

Looking at it, I could only assume that the L in Thailand stood for "Little".

But the shop assistant persisted, "This big size, Madam!"

I smiled, thanked her, and moved on. Perhaps, I'd have more hope in the next section, where the material was stretchier?

There, another gaggle of tiny shop assistants awaited me. "This 'free' size madam," one said, as she approached.

I timidly flipped through the rack, feeling like Gulliver in Lilliput. Perhaps I had misheard and she had meant "Size Three", not "Free"?

I stretched the nighty across my chest, which inspired the assistant to run and get a tape measure.

Several heads turned as stretched it across my amble bosom and announced loudly, "Oh! Forty!"

She then measured the front of the nighty, declaring equally loudly, "Seventeen! No fit!"

I slunk off and decided to look at furniture, where it really was one size fits all.

To my pleasure and surprise I found just what I was looking for—a footstool that would take at least four, big tired western feet.

"You can choose fabric, Madam," the shop assistant said helpfully, as her four other assistants looked on from behind a nearby desk.

I flicked through the swatch. "Do you have some samples?" I asked, recalling how in Melbourne I'd been able to take various swatches home to choose the fabric before we had had our couch re-covered.

This request brought surprise and alarm. "Simple?" the assistant asked, then summoned another woman, who frowned and said: "What you want, Madam?"

"Do you have a sample of the material that I could take home," I asked.

"What this 'simple'? she asked, frowning harder, as three other shop assistants came up to see what the problem was. They formed a huddle, talking amongst themselves in Thai. Clearly this crazy farang wanted to take the furniture home to try it

They shook their heads and glowered at me, as if I'd had confessed to intending to shoplift.

"Khawp khun ka," I said, slinking off again, deciding to come back with Rob another time.

In my short time in Bangkok, I'd discovered that Mister had far more power than Madam, especially among Thai women.

So, I decided to get the supermarket items on my list, chief among them hair detangler for Greta, whose hair was starting to resemble string after too many swims in the pool.

The supermarket aisle signs were in English and Thai, so I headed to one that said "conditioners", but although I inspected every bottle on the 20 shelves, I couldn't find any information on them in English.

For all I knew they might be a lubricant of another sort, as the shampoos and conditioners were on the same shelves as other more personal items.

Just then my phone rang. It was Khun Manit.

"We go pick up Greta soon?" he inquired. I looked at my watch.

Bugger, it was almost 2pm. We needed to get back by 2.30 at the latest.

"Just another five minutes?" I pleaded.

"I think five minutes okay," he said and hung up.

Quick! I needed something to show for my two-hour shopping trip, so I grabbed the last item on my list, some air freshener, and headed for the check out.

Khun Manit looked inquiringly at my shopping bag as I plonked myself down in the front seat of the car.

"Air freshener—upstairs toilet smell", I explained sheepishly.

He looked surprised. This was something that Khun Lamai could have bought for me at the local Villa Market five minutes from home.

Still, it was appropriate as even an hour-and-a-half out of the house had been a breath of fresh air.

DIGGING BENEATH THE SURFACE

This is how I pictured myself in Bangkok: after my daughter, Greta, had been delivered to school and my husband, Rob, had been delivered to work, our driver (at that stage a nameless, formless taxi-driver type person) would arrive to take me wherever I wanted to go.

Armed with my notebook and a camera, I would wander the streets and sights of Bangkok, smiling at the locals (who would always smile back), taking photos and interviewing people about their lives for a searingly insightful travel journal or book that I would write when I wasn't writing the Great Australian Novel or Play or Memoir.

Meanwhile, back at the house, our devoted maid would be cleaning, cooking and washing, thus liberating me to achieve what I was born for.

But unlike most other expats, whom I regarded as merely "living on the surface", I would also get to know the Thai people and have Thai friends who would help me learn and understand their culture. I would return home in several years, humbled and enriched—and possibly famous.

Here's how things have panned out so far. The only Thai friends I have a Khun Manit and Khun Lamai, our driver and maid, and most of our conversations are conducted in basic English or through dictionaries about mundane things such as what to eat for dinner or how long it takes to get between Emporium—the favourite farang department store—and Rob's office or when to pick up Greta.

My attempts to wander the streets of Bangkok are thwarted by the fact that I've been sick much of the time and after getting up at 5.30 am to get Greta ready for school, I'm too stuffed. I also have a part-time job, tutoring journalism students on line, so several days a week I am chained to my computer.

Also, in these early days, I like to be home when Greta returns home from school at 2.30 as she likes to "debrief" about her day. This need has become even greater since we have been here, as new experiences at school, and in Thailand generally, need to be unravelled and examined to help her make sense of her new world.

But whereas in Melbourne these conversations took place while I was cooking or cleaning up in the kitchen, they now take place on the couch in the lounge room while Khun Lamai cooks and cleans up.

This is easier in some ways and harder in others, as we both feel thwarted about expressing the intensity of our emotions with somebody in the same room who speaks moderately good English but doesn't have enough understanding of the complexities of our lives to know why we might be feeling this way, and who is likely to broadcast it around Samakee.

So we start on the couch and then retreat upstairs, like fugitives.

The rest of the afternoon for Greta, is generally spent on homework and after-school activities and, for me on getting her to and from school for these activities.

Before we arrived, a Bangkok resident had warned us that if we chose to live out in the suburbs near the school, it would dominate our lives, and he was right.

What we tended to overlook before we came—and what others still overlook—is that while we may be in a foreign country, we aren't on holiday. School and work commitments dominate our lives in the same way that they did when we lived in Australia.

That doesn't leave much time for wandering around Bangkok. In fact, most of the wandering I've done has been into restaurants to meet my two new friends, Susie, formerly of Middle Park, and Margaret, formerly of Hobart, and to do some debriefing of my own.

When I wistfully tell Susie how I had expected to be touristing around more, she smiles knowingly and says, "I remember thinking that when we first went to Korea. By the time we came here, I didn't expect anything."

Like me, her life in Bangkok is spent helping her two boys with school and flitting between a few familiar haunts and, like me, most of her friends are other expats.

Like me, she'd also imagined that she would be able to join her husband on weekend business trips, while her maid (a faceless, nameless but loving, mother figure) cared for her children aged 10 and eight.

The reality is that her maid doesn't speak much English so hasn't formed much of a relationship with her children. After 18 months in Bangkok, she is going on her first weekend trip with her husband next week, and another farang family is looking after the children.

Janneke, another friend who has been here 16 years, says the same, "It is very difficult to make Thai friends," she says in her thick Dutch accent.

"The way you make friends is to share information and find common ground. But if you don't speak the language, there is a limit."

But it's not just the language barrier that you need to scale. As Parul, the cross-cultural trainer hired by Rob's work explained, the way we convey messages differs between cultures.

Asian communication is "high context", she explained. This means the message is indirect. Social setting, class, history, gender, education, gestures, age, social status, appearance and tone all have an influence.

By contrast Western style communication is low context. The message is contained primarily in words—this is a prime example. It's direct, the focus is on task completion and things change rapidly.

My interaction with Khun Manit yesterday is an example.

We were waiting in the car at an intersection, behind a very elderly man with no teeth who was perched on the back of a motorcycle taxi. The man's jaw jutted out like a toothless bulldog and his thin bald head perched on a scrawny neck made him look like an aged turtle.

"No teeth!" I commented.

"Yes," laughed Khun Manit. "He old."

That reminded me of Khun Lamai's mother, who is very ill and is expected to die soon. Every time I inquire about her, Khun Lamai explains, "She old."

Reminded of this, I told Khun Manit, "That reminds me—how is Khun Lamai's mama?"

"She have teef, Madam!" Khun Manit said, smiling reassuringly and gnashing his own in example.

Then there is that famous Thai smile. "Why is she laughing?" Greta asked between her tears, when she fell off her bike recently and came home to my cries of consternation and peals of laughter from Khun Lamai.

Khun Siriluck, another cross-cultural trainer and local teacher, explained that the Thais smile in almost every situation.

"Generally, the smile is to extend friendship and to welcome, but it can also mean "I'm sorry or I don't know, or tough luck," she wrote in our handbook.

"They smile happily, apologetically, hopelessly, nervously, just to name a few. You interpret the smile the same way someone reads a book—its meaning comes from the context."

I was not surprised then when Khun Lamai collapsed laughing when I tried to explain apologetically that Greta's school uniform, which now looked like it would fit a Prep child, should be washed in cold water and dried in the sun, rather than washed in hot water and dried in the drier.

"Lamai not know," she said, giggling so much that she had to lean on the bench for support.

My charades might have had something to do with it. Losing face is taboo in Thai culture which makes it hard to tell someone when they've stuffed up.

Khun Siriluck had explained that most people cannot take direct comments or suggestions from their boss, so you had to skirt around it. She didn't mention charades, but comedy, intentional or not, clearly helped.

Part of the problem was my own cultural misunderstanding. When we first arrived, I couldn't understand why all the maids used electric clothes dryers rather than the local sunshine, which was cheap and plentiful.

Later, I understood why. While sunshine is plentiful, so is heavy rain—for at least five months of the year. So clothes that are happily drying in the sun may soon be wet, which in the humidity can cause mould.

Also, having the clothes dried quickly and efficiently means they can also be put away, so at least one of the many household chores is over and done with.

But it's not just language that makes communication difficult. Janneke, who has lived here for 16 years, says the Thais are also very private. Even those that do speak English, tend not to share too much. The result is that you barely get beyond pleasantries.

Then there is the difference in wealth and lifestyle. Susie says that in Korea, she and her husband occasionally met work colleagues for dinner—but always in a restaurant, never in their homes.

Our cross-cultural trainers explained that the Thais, like the Japanese and Koreans, were unlikely to invite you home because they were embarrassed at the smallness of their houses compared to those of the more wealthy Westerners.

This was proven later when one of the staff at the local hospital (where we are now minor celebrities thanks to my many illnesses) took a shine to Greta and asked to take her out. I agreed tentatively on the basis that I came along too.

"Where you want to go? Your choice? You like Emporium (an expensive department store)?" she said.

But later in the car, Khun Manit warned against accepting such invitations.

"You go, Madam, you pay!" he warned, "No 50-50".

Invitations like this often ended with a request to be sponsored to Australia, he said.

So, despite our best intentions, so far, we remain on the sidelines, observers rather than participants. We live here, but we live so differently from the locals that we may as well be on another planet. And because of the language barrier, the people we tend to share our thoughts and lives with are people like us, expats.

THAI ELVIS

I'd always imagined that when Rob turned 40 we would have a big music party with lots of friends and family.

I'd never imagined we would be in Thailand celebrating with our friends Matt and Sara at a Thai Elvis party.

"Look!" I said to Greta, as we entered the Bangkok hotel where the party was being held.

"There's one of your Bratz dolls!"

She turned to see an ironing-board thin Thai woman strut past wearing a tiny silver lame dress with a big black belt, high-heeled black boots and a black cap over her hair that curled in Medusa-like snakes around her head.

A big red notice board, framed with a white swag and featuring pictures of Elvis, greeted us at the entrance to the ballroom.

Here, many beautifully and some hilariously dressed people, whom we assumed were Thai high-so (high society), stopped and posed strategically for the huddle of press and television camera people that gathered there.

Around the room there were stalls selling the Thai version of American food, Elvis CDs, and CDs from other famous and not-so-famous pop and country and western stars of the 50s, 60s and 70s.

Guests bought coupons and exchanged them for plates of American-style finger food to take into the ball room.

Our table was way at the back near the door, but we could still see all the action on stage from the two huge video screens on the walls either side.

First up was Junior Elvis, who sang "Jailhouse Rock", complete with a white cowboy hat, a white fringed jacket and a Thai accent.

The first drink was free, and judging by how many more Rob and Matt ordered, they must have thought the rest were free too.

After many different Elvises had paraded before us, each one blurrier than the last, we were surprised to see Tom Jones.

"Why oh, why Delilah," he crooned in honeyed and distinctly Elvis-like tones.

Why indeed, we thought.

Tom Jones Elvis was about 55, with a smiley brown face, a cowboy hat, a red-and-white neck scarf and white pants and brown buckle.

As he passed our table on the way back from the stage, Rob reached over and took his hand.

"I really enjoyed you singing Delilah," he said with such dewy, alcohol-induced sincerity that Tom Jones Elvis immediately invited us to his own table, up the front near the stage.

Here we discovered that Tom Jones Elvis owned a button factory in Bangkok and also happened to be associate judge in property law, as well as part-time Elvis impersonator.

"How did you get to be doing this?" I asked, incredulous.

"My parents, they make me learn piano and sing," Tom Jones Elvis said.

"How many buttons do you make in one day," asked Rob, yelling above another Elvis singing "Teddy Bear".

Tom Jones Elvis threw back his head and laughed as he held up his fingers to count.

"I have nineteen machines, all making 90 per minute," he said.

That's about 820,000 buttons, he informed us proudly.

We had no idea there was such demand for buttons—or Elvises.

Tom Jones introduced us to his friend, a tall elegant Thai woman in her 60s, wearing a brown cowboy hat, a black Western style shirt and sucking on a cigarette through a long black holder.

Khun Pap, as she was introduced, owned a Thai newspaper and was the mother of three handsome sons, one of whom was a Thai movie star— and from her handbag she flipped out a wad of photographs to prove it.

Before I'd even had a chance to introduce Greta as my daughter, she cast an eagle eye over here and leaned forward and caressed her face.

"She is so cute," she said, then taking her arm and stroking it.

"So long," she said admiringly and then added, "You speak Thai?"

Greta shook her head and laughed.

"No," I explained, "We have only been in Thailand two months. We're from Australia."

"When she speak Thai, you call me," Khun Pap said.

"She can be on TV doing the ads and in the soap opera. She very cute. You call me when she speak Thai," she repeated, and handed me her card with her telephone number.

After a while, Khun Pap went to circulate and another beautiful Thai woman with a girlish figure and pretty wavy dark hair, wearing a red and white floral dress sat down beside us.

"This is Kun Vicki, she in soap opera star on Thai TV," Tom Jones Elvis explained.

Khun Vicki smiled as we introduced ourselves.

"This is my daughter, Greta," I said, "She is 11."

"I have a granddaughter the same age," said Khun Vicki, causing me to fall off my chair.

As for the rest of the night, it is a blur. But I do have some recollection of all the other locals leaving our table in disgust, and Rob doing a cartwheel across the room.

Greta never did become a Thai TV star, for the good reason that she never mastered Thai.

She did learn study it at ISB for a term, but someone the lessons never progressed beyond the basics.

"We've done this test before," Greta and her classmates would complain to the amiable Thai teacher.

"Do again," the Thai teacher would say encouragingly.

"But I got 20 out of 20 last time," Greta said.

"Do again! Get 20 again, na ka?" the teacher would reply triumphantly.

I guess that's why Greta eventually took up French.

As for Rob and Matt, they are planning a Thai Elvis reunion for Rob's 50th.

BAD HEART

Everyone warned us not to get too close. "They'll take advantage of you," said one expat friend, when we confessed that not only had our driver, Khun Manit been to restaurants with us, he'd come to the movies with us too.

Nikki, our relocation agent, had warned during our look-see last January, "They don't' want to be your friends."

But this attitude had offended Rob's natural sense of egalitarianism. As a lefty Labor man from way back, he was not the type to sit in the back of the car giving orders. His approach was humanitarian.

"They're not slaves," he had said when we first arrived. "We must be able to be ourselves.

At a family conference shortly after Greta and I arrived, he had said, "The bottom line is that we must treat all the people that help us with respect and courtesy."

A few days later, Greta was accompanying Khun Manit to the nearby Carrefour supermarket. During the trip, he taught Greta to count to 10 in Thai and the names of the roads, while she helped him with some English pronunciation.

But before they returned home he asked her whether "Mister" and "Madam" had "jai di" or "good heart". Greta assured them that we did, and he said he and Khun Lamai did too. The Lonely Planet Thai phrase book says there are hundreds of expressions relating to "heart", and that these denote "feeling", so perhaps he was asking whether we were happy, as much as whether we were contented and good people?

Either way, Rob's egalitarian approach seemed to please them because shortly afterwards, Khun Manit declared; "I think maybe you stay 10 years!"

Later I found out that this was not just flattery. The longer a driver or maid is in someone's employment, the bigger the bonus when they leave. Encouraging us to stay was also an investment in their security.

This sort of encouragement became a bit of a mantra for Khun Manit, who often declared that Greta should finish school in Thailand

and go to university here and that when our son finished university in Australia, he should come to Thailand and marry a Thai girl.

Khun Manit also liked to tell us how lucky we were: "Other maid and driver fight," he said. "He no want to take her shopping. You lucky."

And we felt lucky. Very lucky. We seemed to have a very different relationship with our staff than other expats, who began to look disapprovingly when I mentioned that Khun Manit had come to the restaurant at Hua Hin with us, or had a beer with us while we worked in the garden, or when they noticed that I sat up the front, instead of in the back.

"I used to do that in Seoul," said my friend Susie, a veteran expat. "But I soon learned." Sitting up front, she said, encouraged them to think that you were a soft touch. Her driver had eventually started stealing from them and not turning up for work.

Rob's boss, Matt, and his wife, Sarah, also our good friends, reported a similar experience with their first driver, who continually left them stranded. "And we even bought him a motor bike so he could get to work on time," Sara said.

Nikki said that her driver had got drunk and had crashed her husband's brand new BMW.

We listened to these stories with polite disbelief. This may be the case with other expats, but our situation was different, we told each other. Our driver and maid were married. They not only liked each other, they loved each other.

The fact that they chatted in the car and laughed and joked together, seemed proof, as did their morning breakfast ritual.

Each day at about 10.30am Khun Manit would buy some breakfast for Khun Lamai at a street stall and come smiling and knocking at the kitchen door to urge her to come and eat.

They would retreat to the maid's room, where they were spread their breakfast of rice and spicy soup or barbecued chicken on a mat on the floor and eat together.

Khun Lamai began to complain that this ritual was making her fat. "Friend say Lamai ewan mak! (very fat)," she said.

When we went shopping together, I bought lunch for us to share as we unpacked the bags. I wanted them to feel welcome and to be part of the family– although I struggled every day with my lack of privacy.

Everything I did was now so public, not only at home but everywhere I went.

"Good shopping?" Khun Manit would say, smiling as he peered into each shopping bag before putting it the car.

"He shouldn't be doing that," frowned Sara when I complained.

He also shouldn't have been just popping in and out of the front door uninvited, nor should he have been inquiring into our private financial affairs.

"Khun Manit asked me how much canteen money I got," Greta reported one day.

"Khun Manit asked me about how much it cost for Johannes at university," I told Rob another day.

"Tell him nothing!" Rob said.

"It's a bit hard, he caught me unawares," I said. Besides, I thought that telling the truth—that to keep Johannes at University for one year cost the equivalent to of two years' wages for a driver—would stop him asking for more money as he regularly did, despite the fact that we topped the company wage up out of our own pocket each month.

We were grateful for his support—perhaps too grateful. The difference in our lifestyles embarrassed me, so I tried to over compensate by being generous of spirit and treating them a part of the family.

The fact that Matt and Sara's maid, Khun Jib, was also best friends with Lamai and Manit, made it all feel like one big happy family—which is why Sara warned in the beginning that there was to be no gossip between households.

But gossip, we found, was like rice to the Thais: a staple. We soon learned intimate details of Matt and Sara's lives—which dishes they preferred to eat, what washing powder they used and how much they spent on electricity—and we presume they learned about ours.

But one day the hotline of gossip froze over.

It seemed that Khun Jib had asked Khun Manit to help her brother-in-law in his new job, but Khun Manit had not been that helpful. It was about this time that Khun Jib began to tell Sara that Manit was a bad man and a drunk.

Both households regarded this as vengeful talk and dismissed it. But then Khun Roong, a friend of Lamai who also worked a few houses down from us for Rob's colleague, Helena, began to tell us that Manit was drinking and Lamai wasn't happy about it. We had never smelled alcohol on him and he had always been reliable and cooperative, so we put this down to gossip, too.

"Don't get involved," Rob said.

But the day after the tsunami, we were forced to.

We had been staying at Hua Hin, on the opposite coast line about three hours south of Bangkok, when the Tsunami hit. The first news reports we saw in our hotel room that night gave no indication of the real impact.

It wasn't until we got home the next day that we began to realise what had really happened. Our first concern was for friends from Samakee and school—and to allay the fears of the many friends and family who were calling and emailing to find out whether we were safe.

At that stage we didn't know of anyone directly who had been affected, and we went to bed around 10 o'clock that night, grateful that we hadn't been able to afford a holiday in Pukhet.

But about 10 minutes after I'd gone to bed, the phone rang.

Rob picked it up. "It's for you," he said. "It's Roong. She says she must speak to Madam."

I was puzzled. Roong was Lamai's friend. What was she doing ringing me at this hour?

"Madam, come quickly," she pleaded, obviously upset. "Khun Manit, he try to kill Lamai!"

"What?!" I said.

"Khun Manit, he try to kill Lamai," she repeated. "Lamai she call me. She very scared. She cry, 'Roong help me!' I think he kill her. She say she try to get away and come here. Madam, come quickly!"

For one moment I thought this must be a joke. But the fear in Roong's voice made Rob and I scramble into our clothes and run down to her house, about five houses away. She was shaking and crying as she explained that Manit regularly beat Lamai.

"But she no talk. He say, 'You no talk or no have job!', so Lamai she no talk to no one," Roong said, portraying Lamai with sad face and eyes downcast.

About 20 minutes later, Lamai arrived with her 10-year-old son, Phet, on motorcycle taxi. She was still wearing her nighty, her hair was dishevelled and her face was red from crying and from the large welts across one side of her face.

I hugged her as she got of the bike and she clung to me, weeping, as we went into the house.

"What happened?" I asked, as we sat on the couch together.

"Oh, Khun Manit, he boom!" she said imitating an open handed slap in the face.

"Why?" I asked.

"Lamai not know," she said, crying. "Khun Manit bad heart," she said, touching her own heart.

"He angry, Madam. "Lamai work, work, work—very tired. Lamai sleeping, Khun Manit say 'No sleeping!' and take," and she imitated him pulling her by the hair, then slapping her and kicking her.

She touched her left ear. "Cannot," she said, shaking her head, indicating that she was deaf.

"We have to get a doctor," I said to Rob. "She might have a brain haemorrhage. I'll get Brian."

I soon returned with Dr Brian Smith, a doctor with the US Embassy who lived in our soi (street).

He examined Lamia and declared that there would be no permanent damage, but if she wanted to go to the police and the hospital to make a report, he'd recommend it.

"Police know Khun Manit," Lamai said. "Have report already."

We were even more shocked. Apparently this had been going on for years and Manit had had warnings before. For a while, everything would be okay, but then he would start drinking and the beatings would start again.

As Helena, Roong's Madam, was away on home leave in Denmark, it was decided that Lamai and Phet would spend the night with Roong, while we worked out what to do next.

"We'll have to sack him," Rob said when we returned to our house. "He's obviously lied to us and we can't have a wife-beater working for us."

I was still reeling. Was this the same person who bought us plants for our birthday, who built a fence in the garden to stop our little dog escaping, who taught Greta to count in Thai, and who, unlike some other drivers, had never let us down? I couldn't believe it.

But nor could I have someone in my house who had done such a thing. Nor could I have someone with a drinking problem driving our family.

But, more importantly, I did not want my daughter to think that this was acceptable and normal behaviour from men.

I felt that our trust in him had been broken. We had been betrayed. He had been hurting Lamai, lying to us and forcing her to lie to us too. He had a police record and had been in jail before. I no longer felt safe with him.

But at the same time, I didn't want to take away his livelihood. And what about Lamai? How could or should we help her?

Brian, who had lived in Thailand longer than us and was more familiar with the welfare system, or the lack of it, explained that there was no refuge or service for battered wives and there was little that could be done.

It was up to Lamai whether to stay or go, but where she went depended largely on her private means or friends.

"We'll speak to Khun Samniang, about it tomorrow," Rob said.

This turned out to be the best decision. The next day, Khun Samniang, the Samakee manager, who spoke English well and could translate for us, listened patiently, hardly raising an eyebrow when we reported what had happened.

"This is normal for Thai people," she explained. "Believe me, this is not finish. She will go back. I know. I see many times before. This is why is no good when maid and driver they married. If they have problem, you lose both."

"But it's not normal for us," I said. "How can we have him driving for us when he's drinking every night and beating his wife? Lamai wants a divorce."

"She want a divorce now, but when he come around talk good to her, believe me she will go back," she laughed. But she agreed to speak to them on our behalf.

But Khun Manit wanted to plead his case personally, so we met at our house later that morning. He didn't look at me or Khun Samniang, but appealed directly to Rob. "I want to have sex with her but she fight me," he said, displaying a scratched arm.

"That is your problem, not the problem of your boss," Khun Samniang explained.

"This is not the farang (foreign) way. They don't like someone who drink and beat their wife to work for them. They didn't come to Thailand to have this problem."

"I no have wife, I no have job, I die," Khun Manit pleaded.

But Samniang was not convinced "You are good-looking man, Manit. You find another woman and maybe you learn from this and you don't beat her. You are good driver. The boss will write you a good reference and you will get another job."

It distressed Rob and me to see Khun Manit so humiliated, but we felt we had no choice. "I am very sad, Khun Manit," Rob tried to explain, placing his hand over his heart.

"You have been a big help to me and my family. But if you and Lamai are fighting like this, I cannot have you working here."

Finally, Khun Manit seemed to accept that we could no longer employ him.

"You are good man," he told Rob as he shook his hand. "I no bother your family again."

But he did. As Lamai and her son were now living in our maid's room, it infuriated him that he had lost his job but she had kept hers.

But it was not just the loss of his job and his wife that made him so bitter: it was the loss of face.

So, despite the fact that Lamai miraculously applied for and obtained a divorce a week later—proudly showing us an elaborate certificate singed by the police—and despite having been paid his dues and given a good reference, he began a campaign of harassment that lasted the next four weeks—even putting his threats in writing.

In a letter to Khun Samniang he said he wanted to hurt Lamai and that he didn't care if he went to jail again.

"Again!" I said to Kung Roong, who was visiting. "What's he been in for before?"

"I think he kill someone," Kung Rung said obligingly, her eyes wide.

In the next few weeks, he rang our home and Rob's work at all hours, rang Lamai and threatened to slit her throat and make her child motherless, and attempted to bribe our new driver, Khun Pong.

We began to have to lock our doors, and look over our shoulders. "Am I safe?" asked Greta one night when she went to bed.

Finally, when Manit rang Rob at work yet again, breathing heavily into the phone but not speaking, Matt, Rob's boss, advised us that enough was enough—it was time to get rid of Lamai.

"But it's not her fault!" I begged.

But in the end, as Rob was due to start travelling again all over Asia again, it was clearly unacceptable to have someone living at our house who was being threatened with murder.

So regretfully, we had to sack Khun Lamai too. We gave her a big payout and a letter of recommendation and arranged for her to escape under cover of dark one night to her mother's place in Ubon Rachatani, near the Laos border.

She said she would stay there for a month then return to stay with a friend nearby, so her son, Phet could still go to school. Instead of going on the public bus, a teacher would take him in a private car, just until everything calmed down.

She left the following Friday night, amid tears and hugs. I gave her a lucky Buddha pendant and ornament and hoped that she would be able to come back to us some day.

But that day came sooner than I expected, as just a few days later, she came back to collect her things—and to go back to Khun Manit.

Khun Roong was furious. "I say 'Lamai, why you go back? Why you not safe for your son? Everybody try to help you, but you no help yourself. I like you very much Lamai, but I finish with you,'" she told me, re-enacting her speech.

And she advised me to finish with her, too.

"You good heart. You 100 per cent nice," she said "I think this not good for your family. I think you need be 10 per cent bad," she said.

But I didn't' feel good heart. I felt 100 per cent bad heart. I felt shocked, stupid, naïve and betrayed.

Now, with the house—and all its mess—to myself, I tried to reclaim my territory and come to terms with what had happened.

I had come full circle. This was no longer the charming land of smiles, but a land of wife-beaters and rip-off merchants, whose smiles hid a seething mess of envy and hatred and ignorance.

I felt sad, too. These people had helped us so much in our first six months here, yet obviously it had all been a charade.

Looking back, I now realised that there had been many little hints in my conversations with K. Lamai, but I had been too naïve and blind to realise it.

Our expat friends were more sanguine about it. "Domestic violence cuts across cultures and class," one said.

"It's almost like a rite of passage, something like this happening," said another. "Everyone has to go through it."

But I was also feeling betrayed and abandoned in a strange land. I wanted to go home.

"I feel like I've been through a divorce. I'm emotionally drained and broke," I told Rob. This was not possible in the short term at least, so I did what I always do when I need to heal myself emotionally. I took out my guitar and the wine bottle and played and sang myself better. I also played all my favourite musical DVDs, including *Phantom of the Opera*, summoning my own Angel of Music to heal my cynicism.

In between, I had to go out to the laundry, which was outside near the pool, and do some washing. This caused great consternation to our new driver, Khun Pong, who did not like to see his new madam working like a maid.

"Why you not have new maid?" he pleaded. "Why you do for yourself, Madam?"

"I will later—part time," I said.

I wasn't ready yet. I had to reassess how I felt about having help in the home. If I did so again, it would need to be on my terms. I would be fair, but not too grateful and would not encourage conversation.

"I've got just the person for you," Sara said shortly afterwards. She's only available two days a week though."

"Is she deaf, dumb and mute?" I asked.

"Almost—she doesn't speak English," Sara replied.

"Perfect," I said.

I would do the cooking for half the week, though, I decided, and we'd eat out more.

"It's all part of the adventure," Rob said, as a few days later we found ourselves gazing at each other over plates of chops and broccoli rather than Khun Lamai's Pad Thai.

"More like a series of unfortunate events," I said, thinking of the Lemony Snicket book Greta was reading.

It had been more than a year since we had been seduced by orchids and chilled washers on our look-see. Now the romance was officially over.

The new adventure would be finding out whether there was enough to sustain the relationship.

Post script: *Lamai eventually did leave Manit.*

Months later, she came to visit me bearing a gift of some beautiful teal blue silk that she said her sister had woven.

She said she had been to the temple for a month, as a nun, that she and Manit were now no longer together and that she had another job and that she and Phet were happy.

We hugged each other as we said our goodbyes and vowed to stay in touch, knowing that neither of us would, as she didn't read or write English well and I didn't read Thai at all. She had moved on and so had we.

I think of her often: her gentle face, her incredible cooking and house skills and her strength.

When people discover that we lived in Thailand for two-and-a-half years, they imagine the beaches at Phuket and Ko Samoi and the shopping and hotels.

They don't imagine the complex relationships that are borne out of the inequities in Thai society or the challenges and the joys we faced.

The joys were the relationships we formed with our good friends Khun Chai, Greta's accompanist, and Tangkwa, his girlfriend, and the many expats from Australia and the US who remain friends.

We didn't go to many tourist places in Thailand—we were too consumed with school and work during the term and had obligations back in Australia during the holiday breaks, and we also had our share of drama with illness. However, we did take part in the birth of an opera company; the Metropolitan Opera of Bangkok, established by Greta's singing teacher, Sophie Tanapura.

But that's another story.

2011

THE REAL FUTURE FOR MOST OF US

August 19, 2011

It always amuses me to see how writers and scientists envisage the future. It's almost always apocalyptic.

They imagine the world coming to an end in a catastrophic way, either at the hand of nature or through the wrath and destruction of monsters, aliens, or the latest—*Transformers*.

They don't realise that their world will come to an end through a series of much smaller catastrophes.

These may start in a way that is barely noticeable—that first grey hair, that first twinge of arthritis, or the first age spot on an otherwise youthful complexion.

But these days, unless you meet an untimely end through accidents or other misfortune, your world is likely to end slowly, painfully and possibly alone in a nursing home.

I know, because my mother is in a nursing home.

As nursing homes go, this one isn't bad. The staff do their best and are as attentive as they can be, even painting my mother's nails when she is expecting visitors and being patient when she asks for painkillers five minutes after she has just taken them.

Being "high care", most of the residents are "ga ga", as my mother puts it.

"I don't want to be in there with all those cuckoo people," she said before her place came up.

My mother has short-term memory problems caused by stroke, but her long-term memory is pretty good. This means unlike most of the other residents, she knows where she is, but not always why she is there.

The reason is that three years ago she had her leg amputated due to vascular disease. This and the fact that she has congestive heart failure, has left her frail and weak and unable to care for herself.

Until recently, Spencer, my 88-year-old stepfather cared for her at home, with the help of a house cleaner who comes twice a week and a nurse who came each day to shower mum and change dressings on the many ulcers that plague her.

But poor Spencer has problems of his own and it was becoming increasingly difficult for him to cope with the transfers from wheelchair to toilet and bed.

For the previous six months, my mother was shunted between various hospitals and hospital wards, rehab and acute wards, a square peg in a round hole on every occasion.

"This is the worst hospital in the world," she said every time she was moved, trying the patience of everyone who was trying to help her.

We had hoped that with the move to the nursing home, we could make the room more homely, but she has refused all offers to decorate it with things from home. Instead, she says she is waiting to "go to the cloud".

"It might take a while," I say wishing she could try to enjoy the little time she had left. But she is steadfast in her view that this is a waiting room, not a home.

As the nursing home is in the country and I am in the city, I get there when I can and ring every few days.

"How are you?" I ask, lamely when I call.

"Awful, just awful," she invariably replies.

Her only consolation is the champagne and cake I take when I visit. I buy too much, in the hope that she will eat a little, and we sit in her over-heated room watching opera and getting quietly sozzled together.

Occasionally, we go for a "walk", which involves me pushing the wheelchair around the corridors, past rooms with cheerful nametags in the form of a laminated A4 poster bearing a photo of the person they once were, or cutesy photos of puppies or kittens or flowers.

There's Richard, standing in a river, wearing a hat and smile almost as big as the fish he is holding. The other Richard, the person he has been reduced to, is sitting in an arm-chair facing the door, his chin on his chest, his eyes closed; a smaller withered version of the Richard in the photos.

There's Jean, whose name tag has a floral theme rather than a personal photo. Jean lies on a mattress on the floor, a sheet pulled up to her chin, shroud-like. Her skin is white and papery, and her head is tilted slightly back. Her eyes are closed and her mouth is open, forming an o, like the entrance to a small cave. Her room, like her, feels lifeless.

I feel like closing the door, so that Jean does not suffer the further indignity of being observed by strangers like an animal in the zoo. But closing the door would shut her off completely. Perhaps that is why it is open—so the life that goes past can filter in rather than hurry by?

Then there's Dot, who spends her day doing laps of the centre on her walking frame, her brow furrowed. "Nurse!" "Nurse!" she cries, when she sees me.

"I'm a visitor, but I'll get the nurse for you," I reply, knowing that even if I do, Dot may not really need her. It's an automatic response.

"How are you, Lorraine?" a nurse cheerfully asks my mother, as she passes us in the corridor.

"Awful, thanks," my mother replies matter-of-factly.

I don't blame her, but it makes it difficult to further the conversation.

We turn left into another corridor and find a section that I haven't seen before. It's newer and smells of paint. There's a lovely wood heater fire with warm orange and blue flames dancing. There's a piano and some chairs.

"Oh, look!" I exclaim, my voice high with relief at such cosy normality.

"I don't want to go in here. It's lonely," my mother says.

As we approach, I see two white heads and a crocheted rug and realise that the two-seater couch is occupied. The two women staring at the fire sit together but alone, neither able to communicate with the other. The TV chatters on about things that no longer matter.

As we turn around the corner, where there is another cosy nook, with bookshelves, games and a couch, we see another resident stuck in mid-air—suspended between her walking frame and the couch, her buttocks sticking out.

"Oh, what can I do? What can I do?" she cries helplessly.

I rush to help her, taking her arm to guide her awkwardly into the couch, where he sits heavily, rubbing her arm and crying, "Oh, look what you've done! Look what you've done!"

I realise that helping her was a mistake. I am not qualified to help bodies that are stiff and old and dead-weights. I peer in to the corridor where there is a nurse with a trolley. "I think this lady needs help," I say, hoping that I have not caused any further harm to someone obviously distressed.

Back in her room, Mum fusses as I try to position the wheelchair in the right spot. The room is stuffy so I offer to open a window, but she refuses.

At first I think she is being difficult, but then I realise that without a buzzer to call the nurse, she worries that she will not be able to have the window closed later. As she kept pressing it every five minutes, the buzzer was reluctantly taken away from her.

For the umpteenth time, she asks, "How's Greta?" and for the umpteenth time I reply that she is studying for exams and will come and see her soon.

I am relieved and guilty when it is time for me to go.

"It was lovely to see you," she says, as I turn the telly on for her—her only window to the outside world.

Spencer comes to pick me up, bringing her washing and her vitamin D tablets, before driving me to the station.

The air outside is cool and fresh as we climb the hill together to the car park, his tall frame bent into a question mark as he lurches forward.

"Don't go so fast!" I say, struggling myself. But I know he needs to go fast to maintain his momentum so that he can keep his balance.

We debrief in the car on the way home, seeking solutions where there are none.

"See you next time," he says, and I wonder if, like me, he hopes that for all our sakes there won't be a next time.

My mother passed away peacefully on July 22. This was written earlier, but was not published on my blog until later. I have done so now in memory of my mother and all others who are spending their last days in similar nursing homes.

A New Life Journal 2

December 2011

2012 is going to be a big year for me. I am leaving the country, and my children.

The reason? My husband has a new job in Singapore and we are moving there.

I have been an active participant in this decision. I was excited and proud when he got the job and looking forward to another adventure together. After all, hadn't we cut our expat teeth in Bangkok from 2004 to 2007?

Singapore, where everyone speaks English and it is illegal to litter and to chew gum, would be balm after the chaos of Bangkok.

So why have I spent the past few months feeling as if I am being deported?

Perhaps it is because it's all happened so fast. One minute I was complaining about being overworked and underpaid—holed up in my office for three months at a time with my computer, a bottle of vitamin D tablets and an aging Chihuahua—and the next I was the proud holder of a Dependant Spouse Visa and a new suitcase.

Perhaps it was also because it felt like an ending rather than a beginning. 2011 was also a big year. My mother died, my daughter left school and went to university, and I spent the final months closing my business, my home and my life in Melbourne.

Perhaps it's also because this move has coincided with the need for a hysterectomy. "That's what happened to me," my friend Marg said when I told her. "Just as my kids left home, I had my womb ripped out."

But in my case, my kids are staying and I am leaving.

Perhaps this is why I can't stop crying—even when my daughter calls me a "nong" again for not being able to work out the remote control—again.

"I'll miss being nonged," I weep, to which she replies, "You nong!"

"I feel like a guillotine has come down on my life," I tell my husband. I find myself empathising with convict girls—torn from their families and shipped to a foreign land against their will.

Walking through the Fitzroy Gardens and seeing rainbow lorikeets squabbling for pollen and nectar makes my dewy-eyed, as does Melbourne's changeable weather. "I'll really miss this," I say, as I grab a coat, an umbrella and my sunscreen before leaving the house.

Even watching groups of young men swaying down the narrow streets of Richmond, stubbies in hand, as they make their way back from the MCG, makes me go "AWWW!" instead of "ARGGGHHHH!"

But then, like all good journalists, I begin to do some research, starting with the Lonely Planet Guide *Singapore Encounter*. We are going to live somewhere near Orchard Rd, so I flick to page 38, which begins, "A veritable canyon of concrete, glass and steel, Orchard Road is a monument to the Singaporean obsession with shopping, though it's really a chicken-and-egg proposition: did the obsession spawn the malls, or did the malls spawn the obsession?

"Either way, Singaporeans love these monoliths, spending vast amounts of leisure time bathing in icy air-conditioning, shopping, eating, drinking and movie-going."

Hang on. This is what I like doing. In fact, shopping, eating, drinking and movie-going are my next favourite activities after writing. Maybe Singapore won't be so bad after all? I start to salivate instead of commiserate.

While I can work later if I want, there's no hurry, my husband explains. I can spend my days writing (or shopping or eating or drinking or movie-going) and finally have some time to get fit by taking advantage of the pool and gym that are standard features of every apartment.

Gulp. Now there will be no excuses. 2012 will be the year I metamorphosise from fat journalist to skinny author. I will have a new life.

This is ironic since it was almost 19 years ago that the then-editor of the Melbourne *Age*, Alan Kohler, asked me to write a column about my daughter's first year of life.

This is why I've decided to call this new blog A *New Life Journal 2*. I plan to write about my new life in Singapore and what it feels like to leave the nest yourself, instead of waiting for your children to leave it.

Until now, I've been teetering on the edge, staring fearfully below without daring to flap my wings. A new life in Singapore may be just the nudge I need.

2012

When Parents Leave the Nest

January 2012

It was when I saw all her personal possessions—pillows, linen, clothes, cosmetics, shoes, computer and books—lined up near the door ready to be carried out, that it hit me. My daughter was leaving home just one month shy of her 19th birthday—and it was my fault.

These days all the talk is about the full nests and being packed to the rafters, but my husband and I are bucking the trend. We are not only leaving the nest, we are leaving the country, and in the process forcing my daughter to spread her fledging wings and well . . . . we hope she will fly.

My husband, Rob, has a new job in Singapore and as a result, we all have a new life.

We wouldn't have even considered it if our daughter, Greta, hadn't been nudging her way to the edge of the nest already. When we broached the subject cautiously of us moving and her staying and living at the university college, I saw the tiny dimple in the right side of her cheek flicker as she tried to suppress a smile. Perhaps there was even a hint of glee, I told my husband indignantly later.

But now that the weeks are galloping by and our leaving date looms, we are all a little scared. Between shopping for the things she will need in her new room she speaks about her fears of being cut adrift, along with her delight in her new independence.

"Do you want a cup of tea?" she asks, when we come home laden with bags and thoughts of our new lives, and I know that this is code for "Do you want to talk?"

We sit on her bed, her long thin fingers circling her cup of milky tea. She doesn't drink tea in the way that our generation and the one before us did: sweet and dark tan-coloured. Her tea contains the comfort of childhood with a splash of adulthood.

She worries that the only people who truly know her will be far away in another country. I know what she means. To be truly known and accepted is to be loved. That's how it is with families: warts and all.

I reassure her that we are only seven hours away by plane, and seven seconds away via Skype. I type up a list of my friends and their phone numbers and head it "Mum's committee".

I listen to her talk, the words like waves, alternatively whispering and crashing, washing rhythmically over me: the rhythm of our life.

Now, bleary and baggy-eyed, clutching my recent hysterectomy, and with bones that feel as if they have been replaced with sand, I need to go to bed. Badly.

But I cling to these moments like a drowning woman to a raft, knowing they are finite. When she leaves, when we leave, we will still see each other, but by appointment. Her life will take off, as will mine, and these spontaneous moments will become elusive and precious, like a memory, or perhaps a dream.

I tell her not to worry, to forgive herself and others for self-perceived imperfections and to be confident and enjoy her life. It takes a long time to learn to be a good friend I say, knowing how long it took me.

It's okay to say no, I say, having just learned to say it myself. You don't have to be with a boy you don't enjoy being with, even if he is a nice person, I say, having been with plenty myself out of kindness rather than love.

You don't have to let dogmatic people stamp over you with their ideas, I tell her. Ask them how they can be so sure, I say—knowing that the only thing I am sure of these days is that I don't know enough.

I see my daughter's taut little body uncoil, relieved of emotional pain. She stands and stretches, lighter, like a bird that has been freed . . . until next time when life cages her. "Thanks Mamma," she says and sprints up the stairs.

I heave my way up the stairs too, clutching the railing cautiously. I feel like an organ donor. I have given, she has taken, and I go to bed too, with a hole where worry creeps in.

In the morning, she is like the sun, bright and glowing. "See!" I say, "This is why no decision should be made late at night, when demons take over our minds." She rolls her eyes and sighs. "Mamma!"

We decide to watch the rest of the movie that was interrupted by our talk, a chick flick, of course. Words from every movie we have shared have entered our lexicon, giving us a secret language that we have to refrain from using when friends are around.

"And that why that no work!" she declares—a line from *My Big Fat Greek Wedding*—as I fumble with the remotes.

She grabs them from me, impatient as always "Ya nong!" she says, wielding them like wands. I would have got there in the end, given a chance—just as she will.

She insists on chopping her own fruit for breakfast, but her hands are tiny and bony and her stick-figure arms have no strength, so now it is my turn as I sigh and snatch the knife from her. "I can't stand it," I say as I produce fruit salad like magic.

"Mamma, I have to learn to do this myself," she complains.

I wonder if I have done the right thing by her. She can sing, but she can't cook, or drive and she has seldom had to do her own washing or cleaning. Her schedule just did not permit it.

But in the weeks that follow, when my husband has left to go back to work in Singapore, our roles are reversed.

I can't lift or carry anything until I am healed, so to my relief and delight, she does what all the women in our family have done for generations: she rolls up her sleeves and sets to work, emptying the dishwasher as she talks, chopping the fruit, cooking eggs on toast, making tea and coffee, wiping the bench, in-between putting on a load of washing and complaining that the place is a mess and needs a good clean.

The next day, she gives it a good clean, pulling up rugs, moving furniture, and throwing out things she doesn't like, including my spice rack. "I've always hated that," she says.

"And you have to get rid of these," she says, pointing to my tea and coffee canisters. "They're disgusting."

Rob's knick-knacks are also in the gun, disappearing into drawers while she dusts the remaining few that accord with her excellent taste.

"You don't have to do all this," I say, half wishing she would leave well enough alone.

"Yes, I do," she replies. "I can't move into college and leave you in a mess."

In between, she goes for runs in the gardens, meets friends for coffee or dinner, enrols herself in uni again, cleans out her room, donates her clothes to charity, organises folders with color-coded tabs ready for the new academic year, and sings for practice and for fun—filling the building and my soul with the richness of her voice.

I stand back and am amazed and touched. I feel like an artist who comes back wearily but lovingly to a long-laboured over canvas, only to step back and find it is finished after all.

Moving day comes and all the things that were upstairs come down stairs. I stand helplessly as I watch Greta and Kaye, my friend of 27 years, dismantle our old life and construct a new one, putting my daughter's familiar things in an unfamiliar room.

I go home later alone to a house that is like a lizard that has shed a skin. Just me and the dog and my husband, Rob, now reduced to a giant, often pixelated, head on Skype.

He checks in morning and night, and hands out assignments, like Charlie from *Charlie's Angels*, and shows me around our new apartment with his webcam.

It feels strange to be peeling away our life without him. I prefer real-life sharing, rather than virtual reporting, and I worry that he is lonely and working too hard. We both stay up too late, finding no purpose in going to bed alone, and then spend the next Skype appointment yawning at each other.

I remember my mother saying that there is nothing like the silence in a house when your children leave home, so I turn on the telly loudly and watch all the junk that my mother disapproved of.

I tell myself that I am good at being alone. I learned how to do it between husbands. Instead of feeling sorry for yourself, you have to indulge yourself. You do all the things that you couldn't do before—and then some.

Day five and I begin to revel in my freedom, and so does Greta. When we meet for lunch in town a few days later she tells me that the morning sun comes into her room, and that she went for an early morning run, and that she and a friend sat in her room and drank tea from her favorite frog cups.

I tell her how instead of watching the news, as we have always done, I watched *The Help* and ate walnuts. No one else in this house likes walnuts. Instead of making dinner, I go out for lunch and have cheese on toast for dinner and watch musicals. No one in our house likes musicals as much as much as I do.

"Ring me anytime," I say, looking earnestly into her young face, and she does.

It's 1am a few days later and she feels sick and wants my advice. "It feels scary to be sick and alone," she says and my heart sinks. How can I leave her?

"Is there a doctor on site?" I ask.

"Yes," she says, "And lots of med students." But she doesn't need a doctor, she needs a hug.

We talk for 20 minutes until she feels better, and then I lay awake for the next few hours worrying. I know she will be fine during the day . . . but the nights?

"Do you want to come home and stay a night here while you can?" I text.

"Yes," she replies. "That would be nice."

But in the morning, she texts to say there are information classes about her subjects that she should go to, and she needs to practice for her singing lesson the following day.

"It's okay," I say. "As long as you're okay."

And it is okay. My days are busy organising documents for our move to Singapore and catching up with friends, while recovering from my operation and thinking about my own new life.

It is 19 years since I first began writing *A New Life Journal,* the story of our family life.

Now, it is my new life that I am writing about, and not for any purpose other than my own enjoyment.

And for the first time, (this post notwithstanding)I will not be identified foremost as a mother, but as a person.

But as my own mother often said, everything has a price. The price for my freedom and my daughter's is our physical separation.

In a few weeks, I will be there, and Greta will be here.

"Ring me anytime," I remind her again. "I don't care if its 2am (11pm Singapore time in summer)," I say, telling myself not to panic if she does.

In a few weeks, I won't be able to meet her in Carlton for breakfast, as I am doing tomorrow, or in town for lunch, or hear her step in the hallway or exchange thoughts over an impromptu cup of milky Earl Grey tea.

In a few weeks, we will turn the page and close a chapter of our lives forever.

There will be new pages, and new chapters for all of us, but I know that I will always go fondly back to the old ones, reliving the years that began with story books and songs, Barbies and Bratz, singing and dancing lessons, and ended with bras and boyfriends—when my children and I grew up together.

WHERE ARE THEY NOW?

March 10, 2014

Johannes Luebbers, 29, is now a jazz composer and musician, based in Perth, and Greta Williams, 21, has just finished a semester in Paris, studying politics, French and philosophy at the Paris Institute of Political Science, otherwise known as Sciences Po.

Next semester she will finish her Arts degree at the University of Melbourne and the following semester she will finish her Diploma of Music (classical voice) at the Melbourne Conservatorium of Music under the tutelage of mezzo-soprano Suzanne Johnston.

Before leaving for Paris, she spent the previous two years as a soprano with Trinity College Choir at Melbourne University, and last year she toured Germany, Russia and the Eastern bloc with the choir, performing in some of Europe's most famous churches.

In 2010, her VCE year, she was a soloist in the Victorian Youth Opera production of *The Little Sweep*, playing the role of the children's nurse, Rowan, and was also a featured soloist in the Victorian State School Spectacular *Shine On*.

Singing has taken a back seat this year, as she has pursued her Arts degree in Paris, but the many wonderful performances she saw there have ignited her passion again.

This year Johannes has also returned to being a student. He received a scholarship to complete his PhD on "Exploring collaborative frameworks in new music creation" at the Western Australian Academy of Performing Arts, where he completed his honours degree in jazz composition in 2006 and where he also teaches.

As a freelance composer, arranger, pianist and Australia Council Music Board member, he is involved in many different aspects of music. He is head of the Perth Jazz Society, a founder of the Listen/Hear Collective, a new record label promoting new music, and he composes and conducts for two of his own bands, the JLD—Johannes Luebbers Dectet—and a new septet, yet to be named, which debuted at the Art Gallery of Western Australia last month.

In the past few years, he has also collaborated with librettist Nicholas Christo on a new musical on the life of Dame Nellie Melba. Simply called *Melba*, the musical focuses on the star's career and the little known struggle that she faced to keep custody of her son, George.

A workshop production was held at Chapel Off Chapel in February this year, featuring soprano Dimity Shepherd and mezzo-soprano Maria Mercedes.

In the past few years, he has also produced his second album of compositions *The Exquisite Corpse of Beethoven*, for which he was awarded the 'Young Australian Jazz Artist of the Year' (Australian Jazz 'Bell' Awards) in May 2011 and the 2011 'Jazz Work of the Year' (APRA/AMC Art Music Awards).

http://www.johannesluebbers.com/
http://listenhearcollective.com/.

However, by the time you read this, everything will probably have changed. As my mother used to say, "Nothing stays the same". But what ever happens, it is their story now.

As for Rob and me, we are enjoying life in Singapore, where he is working for a bank and I am working on developing my skills as a playwright.

Most of our parenting is done by phone, text and Skype these days.

My days of family journal writing are finally over, although I do occasionally write a blog about life in Singapore.

However, I am careful to remember Greta's plea when I first told her about the blog: "Can you not write anything about me?"